Quality Concerns in Distance Teacher Education

Quality Concerns
in
Distance Teacher Education

Edited by

Dr. M.T.V. NAGARAJU

Assistant Professor & I/c Head

Department of Education

Dr. B.R. Ambedkar Open University,

Hyderabad (A.P.), India

Commonwealth

Quality Concerns in Distance Teacher Education

Edition : 2027

ISBN 978-81-311-0426-2

Published by :
COMMONWEALTH PUBLISHERS (P) LTD.
4831/24, Govind Lane,
Ansari Road, Darya Ganj,
New Delhi - 110002
Ph. : 23242541, 23272541
e-mail : commonwealthpublishers2016@gmail.com

Distributed by :
ARJUN PUBLISHING HOUSE
4831/24, Govind Lane,
Ansari Road, Darya Ganj,
New Delhi - 110002
Ph. : 23242541, 23272541
e-mail : arjunbooks2001@gmail.com
arjunpubhouse@gmail.com

Laser Typesetting by :
Dimple Computers
Delhi

Printed at :
Balaji Digital
Delhi

PREFACE

Education is a process of human enlightenment and empowerment for the achievement of a better and higher quality of life. A sound and effective system of education facilitates in the unfoldment of educant's potentialities and capabilities besides enlarging their competencies and transforms their interests, attitudes and values.

Recognizing such an enormous potential of education all progressive societies across the globe incorporated in their respective constitutions their commitment to the universalization of primary education with an explicit aim of providing "quality education for all". Some societies even gone to the extent of providing secondary education for all, with this commitment to school education for all, all governments strived to achieve accessibility of schooling to all. In the process, quality in school education has become a concern. Particularly during the last quarter of 20th century, quality concerns in school education attracted the attention of all those who aimed at quality life and thereby quality society. Many Committees and Commissions were appointed across the world to look into the quality concerns in school education, while delineating the different aspects, which matter for quality education universally, recognized the significant role that the teacher is expected to play.

Once the role of the teacher is recognized in the process of achieving the quality, the empowerment of the teacher attains prime importance. In the context of knowledge explosion, rapid changes that are taking in view of the integration of technology teacher's further or continuing education becomes the need of the hour. Otherwise, those teachers who fail to professionally update themselves will be ejected out and they may be suitable only to impart compulsory mis-education.

Therefore, every teacher requires recurrent education both in the content and as well in pedagogy. In a context like ours, where a million teachers are working in the schools, it is humanly impossible to cover all of them in a regular interval with face-to-face mode. To cover such a huge number of teachers, the only alternative strategy is distance mode in teacher education. Many intellectual groups suggested several models to be followed through distance education to empower the working teachers.

Therefore, it is needless to state that the distance education plays a vital role in empowering the teachers and thereby the quality in education can be a reality. Recently NCTE has developed a National Curriculum Framework for Teacher Education Programmes (NCFTE-2009) and given certain quality parameters how to maintain the quality in the Regular as well as ODL system of Teacher Education Programmes. Even IGNOU has also looking into seriously about the quality parameters in the Teacher Education Programmes.

With these parameters, the Department of Education has identified the most relevant theme **"QUALITY CONCERNS IN OPEN AND DISTANCE LEARNING TEACHER EDUCATION PROGRAMMES"** and conducted a Two-Day National Seminar with financial assistance of Andhra Pradesh State Council of Higher Education (APSCHE) on 7-8 September, 2010 in BRAOU campus.

The seminars invites well researched papers from all sectors of the intellectuals based on primary research, field investigations and case studies on the theme and are the following **sub-themes**:

1. Barriers of ODL Teacher Education Institutions
2. Changing roles of the Teachers and Teacher Educators.
3. Curriculum Design and Instruction for ODL Teacher Education Programmes.

4. In-Service Training to Teacher Educators in ODL System.
5. Regular and ODL Teacher Education Programmes.
7. Quality Parameters of ODL Teacher Education Programmes
8. ODL Teacher Education Programmes and Other ODL Programmes

In the Inauguration, Dr. M.T.V. Nagaraju, Seminar Secretary and I/c Head, Department of Education, Dr. BRAOU give the importance of the seminar for facilitate to the delegates to present their research papers. Four Technical sessions are arranged and Four Panel discussions are also arranged with the Deans, Heads of the Department of Education from the different conventional and open Universities in A.P. and other States to discuss elaborate on the Seminar Theme.

Prof. Ghata Ramesh, Principal, University College of Education, Kakatiya University, Warangal in his Key-Note Address has spoke on the certain issues and concerns in maintain the qualities parameters in the ODL programmes especially in the regular and ODL mode of Teacher Education programme. He also pointed that the NCTE is come out with the NCFTE-2009 document to enhance the quality of Teacher education in regular and ODL mode.

The Hon'ble Vice-Chancellor Prof. O.R. Reddy and Chief Guest of the Inauguration function also speaks on this occasion and given important qualities in all the level of regular teacher education programmes as well as the ODL teacher education programme. He also quoted any ODL programme is to sustain when ICT tools are effectively used.

Prof. S.V. Rajasekhar Reddy, I/c Director (Academic) and Dr. C. Venkataiah, Registrar, Dr. BRAOU are the Guest of Honour of the inauguration and speaks on this occasion. Nearly 70 research papers are presented in the seminar. The deliberations and discussions are gone fruitful.

In the valedictory, Dr. M.T.V. Nagaraju, Seminar Secretary and I/c Head, Department of Education, Dr. BRAOU presented the two days proceedings of seminar.

Prof. B. Ramachandra Reddy, Dean of Education (Rtd.), S.V. University, Tirupati in his Valedictory Address has spoke on the certain important measures take by the universities those offering the Teacher Education programme through Open and Distance mode. He said that though the apex bodies suggested certain quality measures to the universities and institutions, it is the responsibility of the concern university to maintain the standards to compete to the present trend.

Prof. G. Srinivasacharyulu, Head (Rtd.), Department of Education, Dr. BRAOU and the Guest of Honour of the occasion also raised some of the issues especially in the Teaching Practice and Internship Programme to the student teachers of the ODL mode. He suggested thinking over that the ODL student teachers are in-service teachers and keeping on their past experiences, the curriculum should be designed.

The Hon'ble Vice-Chancellor Prof. O.R. Reddy and Chief Guest of the Valedictory function, Prof. S.V. Rajasekhar Reddy I/c Director (Academic), the President of the function also spokes on the occasion.

Dr. M.T.V. Nagaraju, Seminar Secretary is proposed vote of thanks and highly appreciates to the Authorities of the APSCHE and Dr. BRAOU to extend the financial support to organize the seminar. He also thanks to all the delegates who presented their views and discussed and deliberated upon the issues from different perspectives and also thanks to who directly and indirectly involve with the seminar. The function was close with the National Anthem.

I am thank to the contributors namely Dr. S. Fiayaz Ahamed and Dr. D. R. Sharma, G. Nagarani and T. Siva Prasad Reddy, Dr. D. Balaramulu and V. Gurunadha Rao, T.S. Shrivalli and Dr. Srinivas Rao Vaddanam, Dr. E. Suresh Babu and Dr. N. Venkateswarlu, A.J. Praveen Kumar, T. Gladis Grace and B.J. Sujani, Dr. D. Ashalatha and N. Jayaprada, A. Vijayalakshmi and Dr. S. Vijaya Vardhini, D. Vishwa Prasad, J. Komaleswari and A. Gayatri, Shaik Subhan and M.P. Dayal, V. Hema Kameswari, Chandrakala and Dr. G. Paul Ratnakar, Dr. G. Suneetha Bai and Dr. T. G. Amuthavalli, Dr.

R. Ramudu and K. Adilakshmi, Dr. P. Lakshminarayana and Dr. V. Govinda Reddy, Dr. Najma Unnisa, Ch. Sandhya and Dr. L.V.K. Reddy, Prof. G. Vijayalakshmi, Dr. K. Krishna Reddy and Dr. G. Dayakar, Dr. D. Hassan and Dr. A. Amruthavalli, P. Renuka and Dr. P. S. Pragathi, Dr. T. J. M. S. Raju, Dr. S. N. Rao and Dr. T. Sharon Raju, Shakera Parveen and Shamim Ahmad, Najma Begum, Dr. M.T.V. Nagaraju, L. Chinna Reddeppa and Dr. K. S. Prabhakaram, Shamshaad Begum, A. Lakshmi Devi and Dr. K.C. Shankaraiah, Ghazala Ansari, Dr. G. Laxma Reddy, Dr. K. Sumalatha and A. Nagamani, N. Ch. Shekhar, K. Anitha Raj and Kiran Singh, Dr. D. Ugandhar Raju and Prof. G. Ramachandraiah for contributing the valuable papers.

Hyderabad **M.T.V. Nagaraju**

Contents

Theme–III
Curriculum Design and Instruction for ODL Teacher Education Programmes

Theme–IV
In-service Training to Teacher Educators in ODL System

Theme–I

Barriers of ODL Teachers Education Institutions

1

Barriers of ODL Teachers Education Institutions : A Case Study of Teacher Education Programmes in A.P.

Dr. S. Fiayaz Ahamed
Deputy Director, IGNOU Regional Centre, Hyderabad
Dr. D. R. Sharma
Deputy Director, IGNOU Regional Centre, Hyderabad

ABSTRACT

Teacher Education Programmes in India, which prepares teachers for both Primary and Secondary education have of late been criticized on a number of counts and the primary concern of all those who are associated with teacher education programmes is the quality of teacher education programmes imparted in teacher training institutions. If the conventional teacher education programmes which are offered on-campus and face-to-face mode are under severe criticism for want of quality teacher educators and such other issues in the teacher training institutions in majority of the cases, the quality of teacher education programmes offered through Open and Distance Learning Institutions are bound to have criticism on a number of other counts as well.

This paper attempts to trace the need of teacher education programmes through ODL and also discusses the barriers in offering these programmes through ODL system.

"Those who educate children well are more honoured than parents, for these only gave life, those the art of living well"

—Aristotle

Introdution

The teacher education programmes offered in the Indian context for the preparation of school teachers have always been under the focus of various education commission and committees appointed by Government of India from time to time. Different Education Commission (Ministry of Education (1953 and 1966) and various Committees (Ministry of Education,1963; NCERT, 1966; NCTE,1978) have also enlisted their concern for the qualitative aspects of teacher education programmes and have also enumerated the goals of teachers education in different set of circumstances.

Research in teacher education does not have a long past. It is only about last three and half decades that research in this education surveyed the progress and problems of teacher education in India outlining the inadequacies of pre-service education (Sharma, 1982).

The surveys of teacher education conducted from time by institutions as well as individuals provide information relating to several variables like the size of the institution and facilities in terms of staff, equipment and materials obtaining in teacher training institution (Pandey,1998).

The All India Education Surveys, right from the first all India Education Survey to the Seventh All India Education Survey have also pointed a number of studies have mentioned, is about the untrained teachers in the schools.

Quality Aspects of Teacher Education

The quality of education hinges on the quality of teachers and in turn the quality of teachers is dependent on the quality of teacher education programmes offered in the teacher training institution. The New Education Poilcy (1986) observed that 'the status of teacher reflects the socio-cultural ethos of society and no people can rise above the level of its teacher,' The Post-Independent era in the Indian context witnessed the spurt of education institutions at levels: Schools, Colleges and Universities. This expansion of education facilities resulted in lack of trained teachers being recruited in the majority of schools. Though a number of teacher training institutions were established to cater to the demand for trained teachers their number was not sufficient to train all the untrained teachers. Even today as per the latest information available 1.2 million trained people are needed to fill teaching vacancies (Times of India, September 5, 2010).This speaks the magnitude of untrained teachers.

Teacher education institution must shoulder the great responsibility of providing educational leadership from primary and secondary education through the provision of quality education for teacher because improvement in school education is essentially related to good and effective performance in a teacher education system. (Singh and Sharma, (1998). As the number of teacher training institutions was not accessible and sufficient in number to train the untrained teachers, there was a felt need for an alternative mode of training. It is during this, that some of the universities launched teacher training programmes through correspondence courses.

The development of teacher education in India can be examined in two distinct periods. The first period is one where the teacher education programmes through face-to-face mode in training colleges were offered to those who wanted to join the profession of teaching and with the spurt in a number of schools, a number of training colleges were established to cater to the per-service teacher training programmes and the second period being the programmes offered through correspondences courses launched by many universities in the late seventies and eighties so as to cater to the huge demand of unemployed youth seeking employment in education sector.

Concern for Quality Education Programmes

The quality aspects of teacher education programmes offered through regular face-to-face mode were/are under sharp criticism for lack of adequate infrastructural facilities and it is observed that teacher education programmes in India suffered from adhocism, politicization, militancy and groupings from teacher educators, half-hearted efforts at developing teacher competencies among student teachers.(Pandey,1998).

As this was the case with formal teacher training programmes offered in the face-to-face mode, the teacher education programmes offered through the correspondence education model to cater to the huge demand also cane in sharp focus as they lack quality for the sample reason that universities admitted a record number of student and the major outcome of such a policy would be the quantity versus quality dilemma. The teacher education programmes offered through this model for over two decades no resulted in the increase of a number of trained teachers without being any improvement in the quality of school education. The programmes offered through correspondence model of education did not follow the rigorously the input-process-output model thereby the quality of teacher education programmes touched the lowest ebb. The quality of teacher education was not monitored properly and there was no mechanism to check the quality aspects of these programmes offers. It is opined that most of the universities which offered teachers education programmes through this model were earning revenues for the universities which resource crunched.

With the establishment of National Council of Teacher Education (NCTE) in 1993, teacher education in India was put on the road to qualitative improvement. NCTE was established with a view to achieving planned and coordinated development of teacher education, the regulation and proper maintenance of norms and standards in teacher education system and for matters connected therewith (NCTE Act,1993).

As a first step towards the qualitative improvement in teacher education programmes, the teacher education programmes offered through correspondence model were scrapped throughout the country. It was a major milestone in the history of teacher education in India.

Need for Alternative Model to Teachers

Nevertheless, the demand for trained teachers as mentioned in the beginning of this paper has increased considerably and keeping in view the large expansion of school education system in the country, we need to have alternative modes of the teachers for school education. The open and distance learning model of education undertook this challenge and the launch of teacher education programmes by Indira Gandhi National Open University marked a watershed in the history of contemporary teacher education. The earlier correspondence model of teacher education programmes had the barriers of the following order: historical barriers, socio-cultural-barriers, structural and perceptual barriers, and economic barriers and technological barriers.

IGNOU and other ODL institutions have overcome most of these barriers with the new model of open and distance learning which has been practice.

The misconceptions that the teacher training programmes cannot be offered through this model of open and distance learning have been proved wrong and IGNOU has been successfully offering B.Ed. programme.

Barriers in IGNOU's Teacher Education Programmes in A.P.

1. *The Barriers of Language :* IGNOU offers its academic programmes through the media of English and Hindi. A majority of learners from AP, particularly from rural background have experienced the barrier of language. The barrier of language is now being resolved with other ODL institution offering B.Ed. programme in regional medium.
2. *Structural and Perceptual Barriers:* The other aspect which has become a barrier for IGNOU's B.Ed. programme is the curriculum. The curriculum of B.Ed. developed and Education. At present there are 6 methodologies being offered in IGNOU for its B.Ed. programme. Out of the six methodologies learners have to opt for two methodologies. One of the methodologies on offer is "Teaching of Science" which includes both Physical Science and Biological Science. When it comes to promotion and recruitment Policies in Government

of Andhra Pradesh, it recruits teachers for Physical Science and Biological Science separately. Prior to this practice, teachers who had studied Mathematic and Physical Science as methodology subjects at B.Ed. level were given the task of teaching Physical Science. Since IGNOU does not have separate methodologies for teaching of physical and biological science like the regular face-to-face teacher training colleges in AP, student teachers who have complete B.Ed. programme with teaching of science as methodology are facing hardships. A Government order has also been issued on promotion of teachers, which has further aggravated the problems of IGNOU learners. We have made an appeal to the Government of AP to resolve this barrier so that learners who complete IGNOU B.Ed. programmes are not put to such problems. Teaching of Science is a comprehensive methodology and learners from both biological and physical science have been give ample scope within the question paper to attempt questions pertaining to their area of specialization. Therefore, the teachers can be promoted/recruited as school assistants based on their subject of study at graduation level. This appears to be perceptual barrier, which needs to be removed at once and on a priority basis as hundreds of learners who have completed their B.Ed. from IGNOU are facing many hardship without promotions.

REFERENCES

1. Ashustosh Biswas, Jaishree Das (2001), Quality norms for teacher education: Needs of the Hour, University News 39(21), pp. 7-11.
2. Delors, J. (1996), Learning: The Treasure Within, Report of the UNESCO of International Commission on Education for the Twenty-first Century, Peris, 146.
3. Fiayaz Ahmed, S. (1992), Revamping Teachers Education, News Time, Campus Notes (27-2-1992), p. 5.
4. Fiayaz Ahmed, S. (1996), Toning up the quality of teaching, News Time, Campus Notes (15-5-1996), p. 5.

5. Kumarswamy, K. (2000),Teacher Education in the Twenty-first Century, University News, 38(48), pp. 11-13.
6. Pandey, Nityanand (1998), Researches in Teacher Education in India: Some Emerging Issues, University News, 39(3), pp. 8-12.
7. Poonam Chauahan (2002), Restructuring of Teacher education for quality improvement, University News, 39(53), pp.14-16.
8. Singh, S.D. and Sharma, V.P. (1998), Management of teacher education at institutional level, University News, 36(20), pp. 4-6/10.

2

Barriers of ODL Teacher Education Institution

G. Nagarani
School Assistant (SS), ZP High School, Bomalaramaram, Nalgonda Dt. AP

T. Siva Prasad Reddy
Principal, Vivekananda College of Edn., Shadnagar, M. Nagar (Dt.)

ABSTRACT

Distance learning is an excellent method of reaching the adult learner. Because of the competing priorities of work, home and school, adult learners desire a high degree of flexibility. The structure of distance learning gives adults the greatest possible control over the time, place and pace of education; however, it is not without problems. Loss of student motivation due to the lack of face-to-face contact with teachers and peers, potentially prohibitive startup costs, and lack of faculty support are all barriers to successful open and distance learning. This literature review explores open and distance learning and its barriers.

Open learning is any organized educational approach or activity which takes as its starting point an analysis of the needs of the intended group(s) of learners and then seeks in its policies and practices to design the programme in ways that minimize any barriers to learning in terms of either access, or of time and place, pace, method of study, curriculum content or any combination of these. Open learning, therefore, is not so much a particular type of education but rather a set of open qualities, which may exist to a greater or lesser extent in any form of education or training.

Distance education is an organized educational programme, often accredited, where the learners at a geographical and/or time distance from the learning provider- the educational institution and tutors - and where all or much of the communication between teachers and learners is conducted through electronic or print mediums. To overcome the physical distance and build in interaction, the provider may try to use the two-way potential of, for example, mailed assignment marking, e-mails, telephone, tele - and video-conferencing, call-in radio or TV, as well as prerecorded video or audio materials. It may also build in face-to-face components such as bringing dispersed students in for occasional tutored group meetings at a study centre or summer school.

Conversely, the central provider can send travelling tutors to the learners or enter into agreements for locally-provided support (e.g. by a formal or community school, or university). An example would be a programme, offered by a national open university, providing initial teacher training at a distance to unqualified school-based teachers. The programme allows the teacher to remain in situ, and the chance to experiment with new practices in their immediate classrooms.

The term *Open and Distance Learning (ODL)* is frequently used as an umbrella term to cover educational approaches that reach learners in places that are convenient or accessible to them, provide learning resources for them, or enable them to qualify without attending school or college in person, or open up new opportunities for keeping up to date no matter where or when they want to study. While understandable, the conflation of the terms can be confusing and in this report we will substitute open learning as the umbrella term, with distance education as one type of open learning.

BARRIERS OF ODL TEACHER EDUCATION INSTITUTIONS

1. Barriers of Student Demographics

Changes in technology have accelerated the growth of distance learning. The improved access and availability of electronic technology has enabled more adult students to participate in the learning process. Students who enroll in distance learning courses do so for convenience. They are either time-bound due to work or travel schedules or location-bound due to geographic or family responsibilities.

Distance learning is student-centered learning; thus knowing the characteristics and demographics of the distance learners helps us understand the potential barriers to learning. Although students' characteristics and needs may not guarantee success in a distance education course or program, it is easy to defend these factors as contributing to success. Additionally, knowledge about student characteristics and motivators help us understand who is likely to participate in distance education and, conversely, why others choose not to participate.

Student motivation has a powerful affect on attrition and completion rates, regardless of institutional setting. Motivators for adult distance students are often different from those of traditional students. Knowles (1980), in explaining the advantages of knowing the learner, believes that learner behaviour is influenced by a combination of the learner's needs plus the learner's situation and personal characteristics. Knowing these personal characteristics is an important aspect of planning distance learning courseware and strategies. More importantly, knowing the participants can help drive program planning and policy formation, factors that are important to participation and success in distance learning.

2. Student Barriers to Open and Distance Learning

Problems and barriers encountered by the student fall into several distinct categories; costs and motivators, feedback and teacher contact, student support and services, alienation and isolation, lack of experience, and training.

More so than traditional students, distance learners are more likely to have insecurities about learning (Knapper, 1988). These insecurities are founded in personal and school related issues such as financial costs of study, disruption of family life, perceived irrelevance of their studies and lack of support from employers. These pressures often result in higher dropout rates than among traditional students (Sweet, 1986).

A second area of concern for the distance student is the perceived lack of feedback or contact with the teacher. Because there is not daily or weekly face to face contact with teachers, students may have trouble in self-evaluation. Keegan (1986) believes that the separation of student and teacher imposed by distance removes a vital "link" of communication between these two parties. The link must be restored through overt institutional efforts so that the teaching-learning transaction may be "reintegrated" (Keegan, 1986, p. 120). Citing Tinto (1975), Keegan hypothesized that students who did not receive adequate reintegration measures such as electronic or telephone communication, would be less likely to experience complete academic and social integration into institutional life. Consequently, such students would be more likely to drop out (Sheets, 1992).

These barriers can be mitigated through technological methods such as e-mail. Computer conferencing and electronic mail can be integrated into the delivery of the course to provide the missing interactivity. Because both are essentially asynchronous, they continue to leave the student in charge of setting his or her own work times—a critical success factor for the distance student. It is important that the student receive prompt feedback in any institutional setting, particularly in distance learning where the learner is impaired by the lack of casual contact with the teacher and other students. This is especially important for those students who live outside metropolitan areas. They may not have access to reliable telecommunications, computers, and postal mail. The frustrations resulting from problems with communication between student and academic institution are factors of which distance education planners should be well aware (Wood, 1996).

3. Faculty Barriers in Open and Distance

Learning Faculty experience problems such as lack of staff training in course development and technology, lack of support for distance learning in general, and inadequate faculty selection for distance learning courses, sometimes the coursework for traditional and distance students is the same. Often it is not. There can be a lot of up front effort in designing distance learning material. This can impose a burden on teachers who already have material for traditional classrooms. Computers, video equipment, communications software, and the like, present challenges and frustrations, faculty must know-how to the use these technologies if they are to teach distance courses. Training students and staff, particularly in troubleshooting problems, is imperative to success in technical distance learning.

Perhaps the biggest problem for distance programs is the lack of support by the faculty. The endorsement by department faculty is viewed as a critical instructional element in any distance education program. More than any other participant, faculty roles must change the most in administering distance learning programs. This can be difficult adjustment for some teachers. They must change teaching styles to that of a mentor, tutor and facilitator. They must meet the needs of distance students without face-to-face contact. Since the majority of distance learners are adults, teachers may need to change their teaching style. This may be challenging for teachers who are used to teaching with 18 to 22-year-olds. Faculty is responsible for changing their course content to accommodate diverse student needs and expectations. So long as college faculty feels there is a burden associated the distance education program currently in place, there will be little support for expanding distance education opportunities. There are a number of reasons for this lack of support.

4. Organizational Barriers in Open Distance Learning

Student and teacher concerns represent the human aspects of distance programs. Organizational problems, especially infrastructure and technology problems, also present challenges. Faculties who teach distance education courses need organizational and administrative support from the institution. Funding should be provided to create an administrative unit that is to be responsible for managing the program. Institutional leaders must be committed to distance programs. Marrs (1995) agrees when he says, "Without this support, distance education is at risk of becoming a peripheral activity, without commitment from or significance to the institution." (p. 21)

Technology considerations are self-evident but are the most easily solved. Technology problems include; financing new technology, telecommunications, hardware issues, course production and technology, and Internet problems.

A primary concern for both learning institutions and students is availability of funds. When technology is used, the costs increase substantially for both the student and the institution. Universities must consider the initial costs as well as the continuing costs of installing, maintaining, using, and upgrading technology to support distance services. Telecommunications and connectivity costs such as those needed to use the Internet, are ongoing costs. Washington State University (WSU) did not anticipate connectivity costs and subsequent barriers in planning their distance program. This led to additional investments in toll-free lines and computers (Oaks, 1996). Institutions must also plan to have competent computer staff to support Internet use. These staff must then be kept up-to-date on the newest, fastest, cheapest technology available; therefore, ongoing staff training costs must be considered. The student must also incur technology costs. If the Internet is used, then the student must have access to a computer, modem, and associated software. Additionally, telephone charges to the Internet service provider will be incurred. For many institutions; however, technology pays for itself in terms of allowing more students to participate, thus increasing tuition funding. This sounds good on paper but technology must not be abused to save money. Regardless of cost issues, distance education should be instituted to advance the cause of education for the institution, not as a sole effort to save money. Kinnaman (1995) cautioned that "It's about a collaboration between teachers and technology that overcomes the restrictions of time and space, enabling students to learn more in less time, and with far less overhead." (p. 58).

(a) Personal Barriers

Most of the respondents indicated to have fewer skills in studying in distance learning. This might be attributed by the previous learning experiences. Most of the learners joining ODL come from traditional learning and thus when joining are enthusiastic to learn and later develop a negative experience toward learning. Especially when most of the learning materials are to be found electronically and where printed books are unavailable for the given course. As one of the respondent noted I do not know how to use computers as such I cannot search materials in the internet and getting access to internet is a problem as I stay in remote areas there are power problems. In alleviating such barriers for the case of OUT there are short courses for training both staff and students. However, such courses are available in centres where there are permanent buildings. Thus, still there are problems for students to meet the cost of travel and living when in town centres. There is also lack of time to concentrate in studies as some students noted: In my case I am employee thus concentration to studies sometimes is minimal as I do not get enough time to study. ...1 am an able to pay for my studies.

(b) Institutional Barriers

In this part most of the respondents indicated issues concerning management and administration of higher distance education in developing countries. According to a survey of 170 university students contacted by Adewale and Inegbedion (2008) it was observed that most of open and distance education students withdraw from studies because of problems caused by institutional procedures, pattern of facilitation schedules, availability of course materials, poor academic and administrative support, and poor tutorial support. Other studies like Iran (2001), Galusha (1997), Carr (2000) also reported on drop-out rates in distance learning. In this qualitative study on OUT students, students had the following to say: The cost of studies is low, it is easy to get admission, study materials and supplementary readings are provided in both print and electronic media and sometimes they are handwritten, it has centres in every regions and some regions have more than one centre, offers practical experiences in collaboration with other universities.... According to Mbwette (2005) OUT contributes 25% of the enrolments in higher education in Tanzania. With current efforts of implementing ICT and other regulatory procedures it is likely to contribute much higher percentage in the future. This was also supported by the staff on the availability of electronic resources. Some of the staff said .. ..now it is easy to assist students as one can just access the information needed via internet. The problem with internet is that sometimes it is not accessible.....

(c) Infrastructure Barriers

Participants in this study noted barriers attributed by infrastructures. Some participants said it is difficult for them to travel especially during rainy seasons, I did not attend face-to-face because of transport as it was raining and that I got Information on face-to-face session late..... Thus the how, when and where (Ellington, 1997) to study is hindered by infrastructural barriers of which OUT is addressing through its plan to use cellular phones in delivering contents and other information that might be necessary for students. In this effect already OUT has contacted Up Code Company based in Finland and there is another programme which is under pilot study using phone technology. Rationally for phone usage in Tanzania is due to the increasing number of phone users which comparatively high (Jabiri, et ai, 2004) and the increased use of ICT (Mbwette and Mboma, 2000). However, there are cost implication to both students and the institution.

Summary and Conclusion

Although distance learning is not new, it has not received respect in the academic community because of the number and seriousness of problems presented here. The dramatic growth of the adult learner population is making distance learning an increasingly popular choice of learning techniques. Further study of student demographics and motivators will help target the adult learner population and will help institutions develop course materials and techniques appropriately. Close scrutiny of the intrinsic problems in distance education will help overcome problems encountered by students and faculty. Understanding and mitigating technology problems are important, especially with the rapid expansion of technology. Further research into course development techniques will help learning institutions understand which methods work best in the distance learning classroom.

REFERENCES

1. Bullen, M. (1996), Distance Education and Technology, Continuing Studies.
2. Coldeway, D. (1986), Learner Characteristics and Success, Distance Education in Canada, pp, 81-87.
3. Cookson, P. (1989), Research on Learners and Learning in Distance Education: A Review, American Journal of Distance Education, 3(2), 22-34.
4. Creating the Virtual Community (1996, Nov/Dec), Syllabus magazine, 10(4), p. 38.
5. Harden, T., Barnard, L. and Donnan, P. (1994), Success with science at a distance, OLAA Occasional Papers, Number 1, pp.15-19.
6. Harry, K. (1992), Distance education today and tomorrow: A personal perspective, Educational Media International, 29(3), 189-192.
7. Hartshuh, T. (1991), Technology in the classroom of the future, New Horizons in Adult Education, 5(2), p. 4.
8. Jackman, D. and Swan, M. (1994), Alternative instructional models for IVN delivery (Vol. 1). Fargo: North Dakota State University, Central Duplicating.

9. Keegan, D. (1986), The Foundations of Distance Education, London: Croom Helm.
10. Past, Present and Future. Englewood, Colorado: Libraries Unlimited Inc.
11. Suisun, California: Learning Resources Association.
12. http://www.cstudies.ubc.ca/disted Chou, P. (1994), Guide to managing a telecourse/distance learning program.

Theme–II

Changing Roles of the Teachers and Teacher Educators

3

ICT and the Changing Role of Teacher in the 21st Century

Dr. D. Bala Ramulu
Associate Professor, IASE, Osmania University, Hyderabad
V. Gurunadha Rao
Research Scholar, Rayalaseema University, Kurnool

ABSTRACT

In the fast changing world of the early 21st Century public education is also changing. As part of the changes the role of education will also be different both in the educational system and in the society. Together with them the role of teachers will also change. The change in teachers' roles in light of society's new demands is an issue of the utmost importance nowadays. Teaching in distance learning environment, overall, sets the teacher in a new position and emphasises some of the roles of teacher over the other roles. The education of teachers in new technologies allows each teacher to understand, through his own reality, interests and expectations, how technologies can be useful, the effective use of technology by the student first undergoing assimilation by the teachers. The paper will discuss the changing role of teacher while adapting ICT. The new learning environments demand new teaching and learning skills. What is the impact of ICT on teachers and teaching? How is the role of the teacher changing? ICT is one of many factors stimulating change in classrooms everywhere. It is distinctive in its universal prominence and in its dual role as both a reason for change and a means for achieving it. This paper examines the impact of information and communications technology on two key aspects of education, communication and learning, and goes on to consider how it affects teaching and learning. Change is the only constant in this world.

Introduction

> **"Education is the process of the individual mind getting to its full possible development....It is a long school which lasts a life time."**
> **–Dr. Zakir Hussain**

Education plays a very significant and crucial role in the development of human resources in any given society. The general definition of education is that it is a preparation for life. This entails that education is the preparation for every aspect of living; that is, for the satisfaction of people's material needs, the growth of their personal talents as well as their personal character. It is, above all, the vehicle to national development and prosperity. The advent of the information society has called into question many of our assumptions about education. New Information and Communications Technologies (ICT) are changing the world we live in, and the way we learn to live. ICT changes teaching and learning through its potential as a source of knowledge, a medium to transmit content, a means of interaction and dialogue. Thus, ICT is both a cause of change and a means of achieving it. Information and Communication Technology (ICT) is universally acknowledged as an important catalyst for social transformation and national progress. However, disparities in the levels of ICT readiness and use could translate into disparities in level of productivities which would influence a country's rate of economic growth. Understanding and leveraging ICT is therefore critical for countries striving for continued social and economic progress.

Teaching for Tomorrow

ICT, communication and learning has highlighted some significant changes in the teacher's role:

- Change in relationship with pupils;
- Change in role to facilitators and managers who support learning;
- Change in the content and scope of teaching;
- Changing locus of control, from teacher to learner.

The emergence of a globalize world underscoring a framework of competition coupled with the pressures of an exploding knowledge base has given birth to new challenges for schools as social institutions all over the world. New demands are placed on the school, in addition to the existing ones, to be equipped with current knowledge and modern methods of acquiring new knowledge. This has become particularly complex with the far-reaching impact of ICT on almost every sphere of human life. It is clear that the school continues to hold its supremacy, more through the invincible mechanisms of the centralized curriculum and examination than by virtue of what transpires in the school. It is within this context that one has to understand the changing face of the school and the role of the teacher in its management.

National Mission for Education Through ICT

The recent developments in technology have changed the world outside the classroom; it is more eye-catching and interesting for a student then the classroom setting. As a result, students find classroom instructions as dull and devoid of life and do not interest them for learning. The information technology has made learner WWW-afflicted. This is because technological developments have brought developments in two ways: First, by enhancing human capabilities by helping people to participate actively in social, economic, and political life in a society at large. Secondly, by giving advantage to technological innovation as a means for human development due to economic progress and increased productivity. The power of information is such that almost all decisions made in different sectors like science, technology, economics, and business development will be based on information that has been generated electronically. Information has become a key asset of the organization for its progress. Therefore, access to information is a key factor in the generation of wealth and there is a strong link between a nation's level of development and its level of technological development. Educators and policymakers believe that information and communication technologies are of supreme importance to the future of education and, in turn, for the country at large.

Distance Education and the New Roles of the Teacher

Distance education has a long history. For a long time, distance education institutions offer courses through postal mail, for pupils and students who cannot attend a school. But ICT suddenly increases the possibilities, resources and tools for distance education. In a knowledge society, distance education is no longer only a replacement for those who cannot attend school, because they are ill, or far away. It has become a core component of education. A knowledge society needs competences linked to distance education, such as being able to learn at a distance, to learn through distant resources, to learn through digitized systems, to learn through collaborative distant tools such as learning environments and learning platforms.

Distance education is not only technology. Designing a distance course needs a specific pedagogical approach. It is not just transferring traditional courses to CDs or web pages. It needs to reconsider the pedagogy, the relationship between the student and the knowledge, the interaction between the student and the teacher, and the collaboration between students. It needs to reconsider the content of the course, and to organize it in a specific scenario. Distance education is not only courses available on digital supports or on the web, it also includes services. It may be access to diverse resources, it may be evaluation, but it is mainly tutoring. The development of distance education and e-Learning has involved a huge development of tutoring, under diverse forms: e-mail, chat, etc. More interesting is not the technical aspect, but the changes it brings in the relationship between the student and the teacher.

Distance education can also be a tool for educational systems for improving equity among pupils, making them able to access high quality courses in any subject, independently of their local conditions. More and more, distance education is used by schools for specific subjects which are not necessarily available in a presentable way, or for complementing their regular programme and for supporting pupils having specific difficulties. At the world level, distance education can bring some help for making learning accessible for every child, but this needs strong policies at different levels.

Teaching and Learning Effectively with ICT

As Laurillard points out, most e-learning which incorporates some form of ICTs in higher education continues to promote the traditional forms of university teaching such as delivery of lectures and digital resources promoting the acquisition of knowledge metaphor and passive learning. However, recent research on teaching and learning successfully with ICTs emphasises the importance of building engaging learning environments which enable students to have personally meaningful learning experiences from various forms of learning relationships which generate interaction between the learners and content, learners and learners, and learners and teacher (Anderson, 2003; Godwin and Kaplan, 2008; McConnell, 2005). According to Coomey and Stephenson's (2001) comprehensive study of successful online learning and teaching, students' active participation in the learning process results from *intentionally structuring* learning activities and designing learning materials "... to promote dialogue, secure active involvement of the learner, provide personal or other support and feedback and enable the learner to exercise the degree of control expected" Deakin University from the kinds of learning relationships which can be fostered using ICTs.

The changing roles of teachers and students have been aptly summed up in the quip that teachers change from being "sages on the stage" to becoming "guides on the side".

Along with changed student and teacher roles, ICT is contributing to changing the whole structure of distance education system.

ICT in Education : "Make it Work"

In July 2005, the participants of the IFIP 8th World Conference on Computers in Education (WCCE), held in Stellenbosch, South Africa, designed the "Stellenbosch Declaration": "ICT in Education: Make it work". The

Table 1
Changes in Student and Teacher Roles in Teacher-centred and Learner-centred Learning Environments Resulting from ICT Integration

Learning Environments

Teacher-centred	*Learner-centred*
Student role	*Student role*
• Passive recipient of information	• Active participant in the learning process
• Reproduces knowledge	• Produces and shares knowledge, participates at times as expert
• Learns as a solitary activity	• Learns collaboratively with others
Teacher role	*Teacher role*
• Knowledge transmitter, primary source of information, content expert, and source of all answers	• Learning facilitator, collaborator, coach, mentor, knowledge navigator and co-learner
• Controls and directs all aspects of learning	• Gives students more options and responsibilities for their own learning

declaration was written for all stakeholders in ICT in Education (teachers, practitioners, researchers, academics, managers, decision-makers and policy-makers), in order to improve the integration of ICT in Education as a resource for better teaching and learning and as a preparation of citizens for a knowledge society. This Declaration has been produced from the ideas provided by speakers and participants in the WCCE 2005. We can say that it represents the state of the art, in 2005, of the main trends, concerns, domains of interest, challenges of the educational community. The declaration has been widely disseminated all around the World.

The declaration addresses the challenges of a knowledge society. As educators, the contributors want not only an information society, but a knowledge society, enabling all children and all people to access and acquire knowledge and to benefit from being educated. Education is a key issue in the knowledge society, and educators have a major mission. Particularly, it is the responsibility of all educators and decision-makers around the world to help developing countries take part in the developments of ICT in Education.

Teacher plays a pivotal role in the process of teaching learning. Hence, knowledge of ICT and skills to use ICT in teaching/learning has gained enormous importance for today's teachers. Teachers are expected to know to successfully integrate ICT into his/her subject areas to make learning more meaningful. This knowledge development during pre-service training has gained much importance with the notion that exposure to ICT during this time is helpful in increasing student teachers' willingness to integrate technology with classroom teaching. Finally, the role of the teacher is central. ICT does not reduce the role of the teacher. It increases the range of tasks for a teacher, it increases the set of competences a teacher must have, it makes the human interaction more central and visible in education. In a knowledge society, the teaching profession should be a high-status profession. Technology makes the teacher focus on his/her core pedagogical mission. Being a teacher in the knowledge society requires new specific competencies: a teacher has to deal with new knowledge, new ways for accessing knowledge; with a networked world and with new types of co-operation and collaboration; with a society in which knowledge plays a crucial role; with lifelong learning. Teachers are the key agents in the education system. It is our common responsibility to help all countries to train and recruit teachers, and to involve all teachers in international networks. ICT changes teaching and learning, but technology is not the main issue. "Technology matters, but good teachers and good teaching, matter more".

Final Considerations

There are difficulties, through conventional means, to prepare teachers to adequately use new technologies, for its necessary to educate to correspond to the created expectations.

- Knowledge of new technologies and the ways to apply them;
- Ability to allow the student to justify and discuss his essays;
- Stimulate research as a basis for constructing knowledge through the computer.

New technologies may have a significant impact on the role of teachers, through the constant recycling received via the network, in terms of content, methods and usage of technology, supporting a general model of learning that faces students as active participants in the process of learning and not as passive receptors of information or knowledge, the teachers being persuaded to use networks and start reformulating classes and encouraging students to participate in new experiences.

By having access to information technologies, with its application to knowledge, students will later be agents for change in the productive sector by natural influencing in its use. The adequate use of these technologies stimulates the capacity to develop research strategies; selection criteria and information processing abilities, applicable not only to the programming of activities. On the other hand, it stimulates the development of social abilities, the capacity to communicate coherently, the quality of written presentation of ideas, allowing for autonomy and creativity.

Thus, students and teachers have numerous resources that facilitate the task of preparing classes and doing research work, with the possibility of students accessing information networks worldwide during the course of the school year, regardless of their geographical positioning, amplifying their vision of the world and their capacity to communicate with people of other cultures, interests and idioms.

It is expected that in this century, it falls to the teacher to help sow both individual and collective development and that he knows how to work the instruments that culture is indicating as representative of civilized means of living and thinking, specific to a new age. For that end, much research into information technology is still needed, as well as cognitive models, interaction among peers and cooperative learning adequate to models based upon technology that orients the teacher's training in its development. The galloping evolution of the need for knowledge imprints the need to train teachers to assume themselves as proactive agents in the management of knowledge. The technologies offer vast opportunities for the development of contacts and exchanges with the rest of the world. Incorporating the technologies successful into schools requires careful advanced planning and preparation. Significant financially and human resources are required, with training as an essential component of the process. Redundant and robust systems must be put in place. Innovators have to be prepared to confront bureaucracy and conservative attitudes, including resistance by teachers and other educational staff. The following points must be kept in mind while designing the content as well as the process of education: The following points must be kept in mind while designing the content as well as the process of education:

- ICT will have a deep impact on the way formal education is carried out;
- The rate at which we have to respond to changes affecting education is much faster than ever before;
- It is urgent to realign the curriculum framework to provide outcome-based, flexible learning paths leading to mastery learning;

- Training and orientation of teachers, administrators and students to the new learning technologies is an immediate requirement;
- Teachers already in the profession should have the right to adequate time and resources for continual professional development to acquire and maintain ICT skills;
- Teachers should have adequate time to plan the introduction of ICT into their pedagogical practices to ensure high quality and appropriate learning;
- To ensure that teachers, educational authorities and other stakeholders enjoy the maximum benefits from the use of these technologies, all should be involved in information sharing, consultation and negotiations, according to the issue involved;
- Building appropriate information systems, including channels for sharing and communication. Also identifying means for accessing/developing knowledge and ensuring their use in taking critical decisions;
- Redefining some of the processes and procedures, with an in-built emphasis on answerability towards people. In other words, "people sing" the processes. The focus should also be on transparency and the use of information/ objective criteria;
- Reorienting administrative/academic personnel with a focus on (i) sectoral goals and objectives, and the role/ responsibility of administration in achieving the same, (ii) functioning with a sense of accountability towards people, and (iii) use of information and knowledge for making decisions;
- In-depth review of mechanisms and modes that exist presently in different states/ programmes for ensuring horizontal linkages, in different states in the area of education, as well as in other social sectors; identification, analysis and development of the most suitable state-specific means to facilitate faster, co-ordinated and improved administration for the elementary education sector.

CONCLUSION

Academics, build a body of knowledge on how we could make best use of technology in learning. Online learning is offering us the opportunity to evaluate critically our pedagogies and our role as educator. Tutors globally are still exploring the best way forward. The paper highlights some aspects of the changing role of the teacher. It is important that academics share their experiences in order to build an account of practice in the growing debate on online learning and teaching and the role of the teacher. The focus of this short presentation has been on the importance of building appropriate teaching and learning relationships first before ICTs technologies can be employed effectively to create rich learning environments.

REFERENCES

1. Anjali Khirwadkar (2005), Integration of ICT in Education: Pedagogical Issues, Center for Advanced Study in Education, Faculty of Education, M.S. University, Baroda, India.
2. Bernard Cornu Cned-eifad (2007), New media and open and distance learning: new Challenges for education in a knowledge society.
3. Felipa Lopes dos Reis and António Eduardo (2008), The specifics of the Teacher's Education adapted towards New Technologies, Martins Open University, Portugal.
4. Heikki Kynäslahti and Petra Wager (1999), Changing Roles of the Teacher in Inter-Institutional Networks of Schools, University of Helsinki.
5. Hennessy, Harrison and Wamakote (2010), Teacher Factors Influencing Classroom Use of ICT in Sub-Saharan Africa.
6. Kamlesh Mittal (2006), ICT Integration in Teacher Education, India Report, NCERT, New Delhi (India).
7. Janet, M. Jenkins (1999), Open classroom conference – Teaching for tomorrow - The changing role of teachers in the connected classroom.
8. Mary Low O'Sullivan and Gayani Samarawickrema (2008), Changing learning and teaching relationships in the educational technology, Deakin University.
9. Michael Connolly, Cath Jones and Norah Jones (2007), New approaches, new vision: capturing Teacher experiences in a brave new Online World, Open learning, Vol. 22, No.1, The Open University of Glamorgan, UK.

10. Nilay Ranjan and Naimur Rahman (2002), Role of Teacher in enhancing learning achievement of child and emphasis on Teacher Skill Development, Knowledge Building and ICT.
11. Serdal Terzi, Abdurrahman Celik (2005), Teacher-student interactions in distance learning, Suleyman Demirel University, Computer Sciences Research and Application Center, Turkey.
12. *www.ifip.or.at/home/TheStellenboschDeclaration.pdf.*

4

The Next Generation of Training and Learning : Pockets of Potential

T. S. Shrivalli
Ph.D. Research Scholar, Osmania University, Hyderabad
Dr. Srinivas Rao Vaddanam
Asst. Professor of History, Dr. BRAOU, Hyderabad

ABSTRACT

This paper reflects on the role of mobile training and learning in teachers' professional training. It argues that effective professional training and learning requires reflection and collaboration and that mobile training and learning is ideally suited to allow reflection-in-action and to capture the spontaneity of learning moments. It suggests that authentic artifacts and anecdotes, captured through mobile technologies, can enable the sharing, analysis and synthesis of classroom experiences by teacher educators and teacher trainees. Such analysis and synthesis helps to encourage collaborative reflective practice and is likely to improve training as a result.

Keywords : Distance Learning, Mobile Training and Learning.

Introduction

This education process has been going on since time immemorial. It is the central process in the conservation and development of human culture. It began at the dawn of time and has continued to today. Conventional education and training has three fundamental characteristics:

- The educator and the training group come together at a fixed time in a fixed place for the purposes of learning.
- The trainee/learner forms part of the training and learning group.
- Interpersonal communication is the means by which the process of education and training takes place.

Today there are two forms of education and training: conventional education and training and distance education and training :

The wondrous developments of technology during the Industrial Revolution brought about, for the first time in history, the possibility of distance education. The first distance educators

- separated the teacher and the learner
- separated the learner from the learning group
- used a form of communication mediated by technology and still claimed that the essence of the education and training process was maintained intact.

Distance training and learning systems used technology to separate the learner from the teacher, and the learner from the learning group, while maintaining the integrity of the education process.

These systems attempted to replace interpersonal communication, and the inter subjectivity between the teacher and the taught, which is the essence of the educational transaction, by an a personal form of communication mediated by technology.

In Instructor-Led-Training/face-to-face (ILT) systems in training centres or lecture halls, this interactivity is automatically set up.

In distance training and learning it has to be artificially achieved by what is known as the re-integration of the teaching acts: that is, the development of excellent distance training and learning materials for teacher trainees studying at a distance, and the creation of excellent trainee support services for trainees in their homes, or workplaces, or some other place not normally geared to education and training.

Benefits of Distance Training and Learning to Teacher Trainees

Distance training and learning brought great benefits to teacher trainees. It freed them up so that they could study at any time and in any place and in structures suited to their personal and professional commitments.

Most of the goals that today characterise just-in-time training and learning, or life-long learning, were anticipated by distance training and learning:

- Training when it is needed
- Training at any time
- Training at any place
- Trainee-centered content

The logistics of any educational system mean that cohorts of trainees are grouped together either by age or by study goals or by level of previous examination results and are then taught in classes, seminars, lectures or research cohorts. The individual characteristics of these trainees, their disabilities or their brilliance, are brushed aside and they are placed in groups with their teacher educator, mentor, facilitator, or professor.

The damage to the slow learner, the weak learner, the dyslexic learner, the learner with native language problems, the foreign language learner is often great. The damage to the brilliant learner, the high achiever, the future intellectual leaders, held back by the training and learning group, and held back by teachers educators teaching at their conception of an average ability level of the training and learning group vaguely decided upon, can also be great. Streaming holds back and damages the training and learning of the best teacher trainees.

Streaming and the bypassing of the individual abilities of teacher trainees in group-based training and learning situations is best regarded as an inherent characteristic of conventional education.

Distance education is different and broke the structure of the training and learning group and treated its teacher trainees as individuals. A creative one-to-one relationship was set up in the best distance teaching systems which had great benefits for training and learning.

The advent of third generation phones and the prospect of increased speed in data transfer have developed further opportunities for both trainees and teacher educators to meet together, access and exchange information in virtual spaces whilst on the move. Therefore here we develop understanding of professional practice in light of mobile training and learning opportunities and consider the theoretical perspectives.

Mobile Training and Learning

The four elements of flexible training and learning according to are accessibility, choice and control, responsibility and support. But for this the utilization of technology is must, which is no more a trainee's choice and acceptance of the same is a challenge for some. To survive in the digital world these 'immigrants' into the digital world have to adapt to the new digital environment.

On this background mobile technologies are a familiar part of the lives of most educators and trainees today. We take it for granted that we can talk to other people at any time, from wherever we may be; we are beginning to see it as normal that we can access information, take photographs, record our thoughts with one device, and that we can share these with our friends, colleagues or the wider world. Newer developments in mobile phone technology are also beginning to offer the potential for rich multimedia experiences and for location-specific resources. The challenge for educators and designers, however, is one of understanding and exploring how best we might use these resources to support training and learning. The whole world is going mobile. Phones, computers and media devices now fit in our pockets and can connect us to a variety of information sources and enable communication nearly everywhere we go. There is considerable interest in exploiting the almost universal appeal and abundance of these technologies for their educational use.

There are several exciting projects underway around the globe at the moment, focusing on different perspectives of m-learning. They cover a broad range of technologies and learners and are starting to show some exciting results.

Here are some scenarios for m-learning:

- I am bored and waiting for a bus. I am taking my methodology test in next week and am a bit nervous about it, so I load a classroom situation onto my phone to practice 'quiz'-style questions while I wait.
- I am studying a foreign language. To practice listening, I call up a phone number that simulates various dialogues with me (e.g. buying a bus ticket) and gives me feedback on my understanding or even on my pronunciation!

Mobile training and learning is defined as the provision of education and training on mobile devices: Personal Digital Assistants (PDAs), smart phones and mobile phones. One of the characteristics of mobile training and learning is that it uses devices which people are used to carrying everywhere with them, which they regard as friendly and personal devices, which are cheap and easy to use, which they use constantly in all walks of life and in a variety of different settings, except education.

Why Mobile Training and Learning?

According to Attewell (2005) as quoted by Yousuf (2007) and Becking et. al. (2008) there is several advantages inherent in mobile training and learning over Internet:

- helps trainees to recognize their existing abilities
- can be used for independent and collaborative training and learning experiences
- helps trainees to identify where they need assistance and support
- helps to overcome the digital divide
- helps to make training and learning informal
- helps trainees to be more focused for longer periods
- helps to raise self-esteem and self-confidence
- it is portable form one place to another
- more wide spread and popular than Internet
- not much technological pre-requisites
- cost is pretty affordable as comparatively less recurring cost and one-time investment
- provides real time and location independency.

The common problems of distance trainees can be summarized as follows:

- Lack of personal contact and immediate instructor feedback that some learners
- Sense of isolation
- Requirement of pre-course orientation to help manage
- Requirement of the tutor and educator support counseling sessions during course of study
- Improved information and formative advices.

M-training and Learning Applications

M-training and learning can complement other teaching and learning methods or replace them, and can be modeled in the same ways as other methods. It can also enhance non-academic and academic support, such as:

- Pastoral care, feedback and remediation
- Motivation and guidance
- Supporting teacher trainees across the institution
- Course administration and management
- Institutional quality assurance
- Some negative aspects of m-training and learning include the possibility trainees may feel
- Pressure to learn or train anywhere, at any time
- That location-aware technology is monitoring their movements
- That devices which hold appointments, tasks and contacts may jeopardize their privacy
- That encapsulating their professional knowledge on a computer de-skills them.

Transmitting Content

Use lectures, seminars, books and handouts, Web pages and computer-assisted learning packages from teacher educator to teacher trainee, as a guide. M-training and learning offers a range of content transmittal choices, but delivered in smaller packages, such as:

- Daily or weekly study tips, reminders and alerts

- Multiple-choice quizzes with immediate feedback
- Browsing and searching of short texts
- Following links to selected websites
- Glossary and reference information
- Concepts or definitions for revision.

Shared Discussion

Use trainees' discussion during seminars, discussions and tutorials, perhaps facilitated by a teacher educator, as a guide.

(a) Independent Study Skills and Information Management

M-training and learning supports this through:

- Quick communication amongst trainees and teacher educators
- Data collection for projects and innovative approaches to educational research
- Graphical tools that support mind-mapping
- Tools to help trainees link together the different elements of a course

(b) Workplace Education

Students of education discipline need to gain practical experience and m-training and learning can provide:

- Continued access to course and reference material in the workplace.
- Continued access to other trainees within their online community.
- Data-collection capability for completing assignments.
- Support with personal information management in a new environment.

Discussion

Mobile technology can effectively support a wide range of activities for trainees of all ages. Mobile technologies provide for each teacher trainee to have a personal interaction with the technology in an authentic and appropriate context of use. This does not mean, however, that the use of mobile devices is a panacea.

CONCLUSION

According to P. Seppala and H.Alamaki (2003), "Mobile technology is beginning to take its first steps in academic teaching and learning. The opportunities it creates have been recognized and the idea of a wire-less campus is spreading in universities. The integration of the Internet and mobile solutions will transform the use of ICT in teaching and training and take it in the direction of open teaching, provided that mobile technology is seen as a choice for academic development. The core characteristic of mobile training and learning is that it enables trainees to be in right place at the right time, that is, to be where they are able to experience the authentic joy of learning."

Each innovation is going to bring a number of challenges for us, but making the system user-friendly, keen monitoring and research in this regard are certainly going to help.

REFERENCES

1. Becking. D. et al (2008), How to Match Mobile Learning Resources with Learners Current Needs: The Didactic Profiling. http://pi1.fernuni-hagen.de/publikationen/pub2005.html
2. Commonwealth of Learning (COL) Knowledge Finder: Online ODL resource base. www.colfinder.org
3. M-learning Project, European Commission's Information Society Technologies (IST): Basic m-learning skills. www.m-learning.org
4. Mobile Learning in Developing Countries http://www.col.org/resources/publications/trainingresources/knowledge/Pages/mobileLearning.aspx
5. Seppala. P. and Alamaki. H. and Oy Radiolinja Ab (2003), Mobile learning in teacher training, Journal of Computer Assisted Learning, 19, 330-335.
6. Yousuf, M. (2006), Effectiveness of mobile learning in distance education, Turkish Online Journal of Distance Education-TOJDE, Volume: 8 Number: 4 http://www.google.co.in/search?hl=en&q=%22EFFECTIVENESS+OF+MOBILE+LEARNING+IN+DISTANCE+EDUCATION%22&meta

5

Changing Roles of the Teacher in the Technological World

Dr. E. Suresh Babu
Head Master, MPUP School, Apparachervu (Vil), B. Palli (Md), Anantapur
Dr. N. Venkateswarlu
Principal, GRD College of Education, Poddur, Tiruvallur Dt. TN

ABSTRACT

Teaching as well as teacher has a great significance in the process of education. To enhance in students achievement teacher has to play a number of roles over the years almost every teacher comes to develop some kind of philosophy and technique about the job in which he/she is engaged, whether he/she is aware of it or not, he/she has a defined notion in his mind with regard to the purpose and mode of teaching.

A teacher is no longer viewed as the transmitter of knowledge, or dispenser of wisdom, but as a diagnostician guide, assistant whenever appropriate encourager, stimulator, promoter and an interactive participant in the education process. A teacher walks on a tight rope between the reality of today and the anticipation of tomorrow and the distant future.

National policy on Education (1986) emphasizes the teacher and his/her important role in bringing about desirable changes in education. It says, "The government and community should endeavour to create conditions which will help motivate and inspire teachers on constructive and creative lines. Teachers should have the freedom to innovate, to devise appropriate methods of communication and activities relevant to the needs and capabilities of and the concerns of the community".

Information Technology

Networking of computers gave birth to Information Technology (IT). UNESCO considered Information Technology as "Scientific, technological and engineering disciplines and management techniques used in information handling and processing, their application, computers and their interaction with men and machines, and associated social, economical and cultural matters". According to Smith and Cambell (1982), a mosaic of technologies, products and techniques have combined to provide new electronic dimensions to information management. This mosaic is known by the name of Information Technology. OECD (1987) treated Information Technology as "a term – used to cover technologies used in the collection, processing and transmission of information. It includes micro-electronic and info-electronic based technologies incorporated in many products and production processes and increasingly affecting the service sector. It covers inter alias computers, electronic office equipment, telecommunication, industrial robot and computer controlled machine, electronic components and software products." Sansanwal (2000) defined IT as the use of hardware and software for efficient management of information, i.e., storage, retrieval, processing, communication, diffusion and sharing of information for social, economical and cultural upliftment.

The Information Technology leads to development of Websites. Government, Corporate sector, educational institutions, etc. started uploading the information on their websites. It provides facilities for Chat, e-mail, surfing, etc. It opens up a new source of information which increased the limitation of access to information. Prior to IT, people were using only the print material for searching the information. It limited the search. This limitation has been overcome by the IT.

Information and Communication Technology

IT was limited only to the textual mode of transmission of information with ease and fast. But the information not only in textual form but in audio, video or any other media is also to be transmitted to the users. Thus, the ICT = IT + Other media. It has opened new avenues, like, Online learning, e-learning, Virtual University, e-coaching, e-education, e-journal, etc. Third Generation Mobiles are also part of ICT. Mobile is being used in imparting information fast and cost effective. It provides e-mail facility also. One can access it anywhere. It will be cost effective. The ICT brings more rich material in the classrooms and libraries for the teachers and students. It has provided opportunity for the learner to use maximum senses to get the information. It has broken the monotony and provided variety in the teaching-learning situation. The ICT being latest, it can be used both at school and higher education levels in the following areas:

- Teaching
- Diagnostic Testing
- Remedial Teaching
- Evaluation
- Psychological Testing
- Development of Virtual Laboratory
- Online Tutoring
- Development of Reasoning and Thinking
- Instructional Material Development

THE NEW ROLES OF THE TEACHER

1. The Teacher as Facilitator and Guide

As facilitators, teachers must in many ways know more than they would as directive givers of information. Facilitators must be aware of a variety of materials available for improving students' skill, not just one or two texts. The textbook is no longer the sole source of information. Multimedia programmes offer sound and vision, showing how native speakers interact; electronic dictionaries and encyclopedias are available for instant reference; online newspapers provide up-to-date information on current affairs in the countries of the target; (official) websites offer background information on policy, tourism, political views. Teachers need to know how to teach learners to use all this material effectively. As facilitators, teachers have to be flexible, responding to the needs that students have, not just what has been set up ahead of time based on a curriculum developer's idea of who will be in the classroom. Teacher training is a key element to success in this more flexible classroom, so that teachers can use multimedia and other resources effectively.

2. The Teacher as Integrator (of Media)

Teachers must not only know and understand the functions of different media available in a media-rich environment, they should also know when best to deploy them. In the joint construction of projects with their learners, they need to guide learners in the use of word-processing, graphics and presentation programs. Integration of audio-visual elements will bring home to learners the fact that the foreign subject environment of the target subject is as vibrant and multi-faceted as the society in which they live.

3. The Teacher as Researcher

To keep abreast of developments in the countries of the target language in an increasingly complex world, teachers need to know how and where they can access information for their own and for their learners' use. Knowledge and competent use of search engines and reliable information sources are essential. For those concerned with mainstream education, the propriety and reliability of information sources must figure as one of the main criteria for the selection of background material. Familiarity with the use of electronic tools for subject analysis (e.g. concordances) will enable teachers to further develop their own professional competence and increase their confidence in the use of the subject.

4. The Teacher as Designer of (Complex) Learning Scenarios

In order to orchestrate successful learning scenarios, teachers need to learn how to put together tasks and materials to guide their learners to successful execution and conclusion of their projects. Unlike work with conventional teaching materials (textbook, workbook, audio and video materials), which have been graded, pre-assembled and collated in a chronological order, the design of learning scenarios is much more complex, requiring higher order skills involving researching and evaluating source materials, setting overall aims and objectives and breaking down tasks into meaningful and manageable sequences. For the teacher tackling this for the first time, the task is very daunting indeed. Encouragement, help and advice is needed in terms of examples of good practice which may be emulated or serve as sources of inspiration for similar undertakings. If this new role of teachers is accepted and encouraged by educational authorities, the implications in terms of duties and responsibilities need to be considered. Lesson preparation time increases as these tasks are taken on and this fact must be honoured in teaching contracts, if teachers are to adopt and accept the approach.

5. The Teacher as Collaborator (with other Teachers)

The investment in time and effort in 1.4 above implies a sharing of responsibilities and tasks among teaching staff, if there is not to be a general rejection of new technology because it confronts them with an impossible workload. Collaboration with colleagues will lighten the burden and make the efforts more fruitful and rewarding. Obviously, co-operation within a specific teaching institution will prove more efficient, producing tailor-made responses to the local situation, but the new media provide possibilities for exchange between institutions and beyond (national) borders. Teachers of the less widely taught and used languages could well profit from such internet exchanges, helping them to overcome the sense of isolation many experience in their teaching situation. New management patterns must emerge to ensure fair distribution of workloads, and revised job descriptions will be necessary to share and co-ordinate the tasks in hand.

6. The Teacher as Orchestrator (Technology, Learners, Curriculum)

Teachers will need to develop fairly sophisticated management skills in order to be able to provide a healthy balance between the different elements which make-up the new learning environments. Mastery and confidence in the use of technology needs to be applied to the learning inclinations and abilities of individual learners whilst covering the prescribed syllabus or curriculum which is often set by outside authorities. Because of the immediacy of ICT, many decisions have to be made on an ad hoc basis and time budgets need to be constantly reviewed if optimal results are to be attained. Present indications are that traditional time frameworks of 45–60-minute lessons drastically needrevising, if the potential of the new media is to be exploited to the full.

7. The Teacher as Learner

For many teachers, opening up the classroom to the outside world presents as much a threat as an opportunity. Their authority is challenged in a world of constantly changing patterns, when it is often difficult to establish, for example, the difference between "correct" and "incorrect" language use. In the protected environment of the textbook they have recourse to the authority of the author(s) and publisher. In the wild mangroves of the real world they must constantly be searching for new patterns confirmed by reliable data from trusted sources. A further challenge is often presented to them by learners who possess more advanced computer skills than they do. However, if they are prepared to enter into the adventure of ongoing learning together with their pupils, they will find it a rewarding and fruitful experience. A prerequisite is that they are prepared toact as the experienced guide for their learners and not as the all-knowing guru who controlled and dominated the classroom of yesteryear.

8. The Teacher as Evaluator

If task-based, project oriented work in the foreign language classroom using the new media is to become the norm, or at least form an important part of activities, then models of evaluation need to be revised radically. Standard multiple-choice examinations are, for example, hardly likely to test the learners' newly acquired skills in (foreign language) Web literacy. A portfolio-based approach to assessing language competence and skills acquired would seem to be a more appropriate way of recording progress in the target language. As the skills to be acquired by learners are largely identical to those to be mastered by teachers-in-training, this form of evaluation should be practiced in initial and INSET training courses, providing teachers with first hand experience of the system and with direct relevance to their own situation.

THE NEW SKILLS

In order to function adequately in the world of the new media, teachers need to acquire and master a whole range of new skills that are often taken for granted in today's usiness life. The listing of roles above overlaps to a great extent with the following inventory, yet by recording the new skills required here, we wish to emphasize their importance and would warn against assuming that they are part and parcel of everyone's repertoire. In addition, in the context of education and training, they take on a different perspective and dimension.

1. Technical Skills

Teachers need to become completely computer-literate and have the confidence to use the available technology adequately. They should be able to cope with the most common problems arising from the use of computers very much in the way that average car drivers can cope with commonly occurring problems with their motor vehicles, i.e. no specialist knowledge of the machine, but knowing what to do when routine breakdowns occur. It is impossible to list here what this entails, as advances in technology mean that problems of the past are often eliminated in later generations of equipment.

2. Organizational Skills

New organizational and pedagogic models are called for, including ICT for teacher education (using a learning by doing and reflecting approach), and dissemination / up scaling of successful models. The innovative potential of languages going online must be fully grasped, where teachers can:

- build and sustain communities;

- dismantle them when they have exhausted their function;
- link minds and hearts in order to negotiate everyday concerns or complex vocational issues.

On the other hand, true success with the new media will be attained when tried and trusted routines and materials are combined and integrated successfully.

3. Conceptual Skills

There is a quantum leap for teachers moving from well-tried, controllable media like the textbook with its accompanying supplementary materials to the more open, inquiring approach required when exploiting the new media to the full. Teachers must move to a role in which they are designing learning experiences and planning encounters for their learners with the target environment, often in situations where complete control of the means at their disposal has to be abdicated to the learner. Good, practical examples with convincing theoretical underpinning giving a rationale for choices made are needed when introducing this "change of paradigm".

4. The New Literacy (Scientific, Digital, Critical, Linguistic, Cultural) Skills

The skills, competencies and attitudes required to participate in all spheres of life have changed. One aspect of the quality of lifelong learning is the extent to which an education and training system is successful in equipping people to negotiate the shifting demands placed upon them. Teachers in particular should be given the opportunity to update, extend and acquire new skills so that they are better equipped to meet changes in the workplace and in society at large as well as putting them in the situation where they can pass on such skills to their learners. Teachers need to understand and master the new illiteracies (scientific, digital, linguistic, cultural) which are emerging and the demands they place on both learners and teachers. In addition, an awareness of new types of forms and genres, and to what extent acquisition must be complemented by socialization, is essential.

4.1. *Scientific literacy* relates to the ability to think scientifically in a world which is increasingly shaped by science and technology. This kind of literacy requires an understanding of scientific concepts as well as an ability to apply a scientific perspective. PISA defines scientific literacy as the capacity to use scientific knowledge, to identify questions, and to draw evidence-based conclusions in order to understand and help make decisions about the natural world and the changes made to it through human activity.

4.2. *Digital literacy* relates to the ability to use ICT adequately and apply them in a principled way to the subject matter at hand. For the language teacher, it refers in particular to Web literacy, i.e. the ability to make use of the World Wide Web for language research, to the use of linguistic tools and standard programs for exercises and testing.

4.3. *Critical literacy* implies the ability to evaluate the credibility, usefulness and reliability of any given sources of information. It also encompasses skills in sifting and identifying the relevant and important in the flood of information which threatens to engulf the unprepared.

4.4. *Linguistic literacy* in this context refers to the ability to recognize different genres as they develop, to track developments in use and usage and to adapt teaching materials and approach to the changing situations.

4.5. *Cultural literacy* relates to observing and recording changes in the society or societies of the target subject together with implications for subject teaching. Such changes may be of a general nature leading to convergence between own, native culture and the target culture or to changes particular to the target culture. The new media provide a greater sense of immediacy than was possible in the past as trends can be followed as they develop.

4.6. *Mediation Skills*: The role of mediator is not new for subject teachers as it has always been their task to act as intermediary between two cultures as they introduce learners to new cultural concepts. However, again, the immediacy offered by the new media forefronts this role and gives it a new weight. Within the relatively safe confines of traditional textbooks, teachers could introduce relevant aspects of the target language and culture in small, manageable chunks. Access to the "real world" of the target culture and, at times, confrontation with it, requires new strategies and approaches that need to be learnt and practiced.

CONCLUSION

Inspite of rapid developments in the field of science and technology and various communication media, the International report has said that teachers have always been valued in the society as major agents in individual and social development. There fore in the 21st century teacher's role is likely to be more critical and significant. The traditional role of the teacher as a figure of authority and repository of knowledge and value has under gone change. The teachers are to be provided with the various facilities for improving their roles effectively. They have to be more democratic, open and responsive to the needs and aspirations of the society.

Hence, a teacher today is required to play a multidimensional role in order to meet the challenges of education (NPE-1986,Yadav, 1988,POA-1992, Kohli,1992) nevertheless, the effective performance of these roles are associated with the competency of a teacher.

REFERENCES

1. Allie Hodges (2008), E-learning and its Effectiveness in Corporate Training Programs, The University of Alabama, July 28, 2008.
2. Anjali Khirwadkar, R.L. Madhav (2006), ICT in education, An integrated approach, Edutracks, pp. 14-17, July, 2006.
3. Jasmeen Kaur (2009), ICT and changing roles of teacher education, New Horizons, Vol. 6, No. 22, Jan-March, 2009.

4. Paily M.U. (2006), Integration of ICT in Teacher Education, Edutracks, Vol. 5, No. 6, pp. 5-11, Feb., 2006.
5. National Policy on Education 1986.
6. National Policy on ICT in School Education, Ministry of Human Resource Development, Government of India.
7. Thakur. S.K.(2008), X-PDITTE Towards Excellence in Education, Intel Teach Program.

6

Changing Roles and Professional Ethics of the Teacher

A. J. Praveen Kumar
Asst. Professor, Gulam Ahmed College of Education, Hyderabad

ABSTRACT

Among the greatest of all services that can be rendered by men to Almighty God, is the education and training of children, so that they can foster by grace in the way of salvation, growing like pearls of divine bounty in the shell of education and will be one day the jewel in the crown of abiding glory.

The teacher is the yardstick that measures the achievements and aspirations of the nation. The worth and potentialities of a country get evaluated in and through the work of the teacher. The people of a country are the enlarged replica of their teacher. They are the real nation builders.

It needs no description that the teacher is the pivot of any educational system of the younger students. On him rests the failure or the success of the system. If the teachers are well educated and if they are intellectually alive and take keen interest in their job, then only, success is ensured. But, if on the other hand, they lack training in education and if they cannot give their heart to their profession, the system is destined to fail. Hence, the teacher is another vital component of the school.

The teacher is a dynamic force of the school. A school without teacher is just like a body without the soul, a skeleton without flesh and blood, a shadow without substance. There is no greater need for the cause of education today than the need for strong manly men and motherly women as teachers for the young. As social engineers, the teachers can socialize and humanize the young by their man-like qualities.

Introduction

Many teachers today, however, are encouraged to adapt and adopt new practices that acknowledge both the art and science of learning. They understand that the essence of education is a close relationship between a knowledgeable, caring adult and a secure, motivated child. They grasp that their most important role is to get to know each student as an individual in order to comprehend his or her unique needs, learning style, social and cultural background, interests, and abilities.

Definitions

The teacher is a Brahma, the creator, he is God Vishnu, he is God Maheshwar. He is entire universe, salutations to him.

— *Indian Prayer*

The true teacher is he who can immediately come down to the level of the student, transfer his soul to the students soul and see through and understand through his mind. Such a teacher can really teach and none else.

—*Swami Vivekanand*

The teachers place in society is of vital importance. He acts as the pivot for the transmission of intellectual traditions and technical skills from generation to generation and helps to keep the lamp of civilization burning.

— *Dr. S. Radhakrishnan*

A teacher can never truly teach unless he is still learning himself. A lamp can never light another lamp unless it continues to burn its own flame. The teacher who has come to the end of his subject, who has no living traffic with his knowledge, but merely repeats his lessons to his students, can only load their minds. He cannot quicken them.

—*Tagore*

Every teacher and educationist of experience knows that even the best curriculum and the most perfect syllabus remains dead unless quickened in to life by the right method of teaching and the right kind of teachers.

—*Secondary Education Commission*

Changing Roles of the Teacher

(i) *Teacher as a Role Model:* Role Models are people who set good examples by the words they speak and by the actions they take. Students tend to copy the behaviour and mannerism of the teachers. The teachers' entire personality is a reflection on the minds of the students. If the teacher is honest, leads a balanced and disciplined life, the children adopt these virtues as a ideal conduct unconsciously. The ideal teacher s one who through his thoughts, words and deeds, gives and an impression of an honest upright life which can serve as a model for the students to copy, follow and emulate.

(ii) *Teacher's Character:* A flower in bloom is loved by all and in this lays its glory. Similarly, man may be viewed as having achieved everything in life when he becomes perfect in character. If the best flowers among mankind take to teaching, society is abundantly enriched; their fragrance and beauty are then made the best use of. If the teacher becomes an embodiment of right conduct in thought, word and deed, the students by their association will learn virtue and develop manly qualities. They can be humanized and can live and act like normal human beings. They can become thoughtful, concerned and courageous.

(iii) *Teacher's Personality:* Every teacher must have a good personality. Radiant, pleasing and impressive personal appearance, refinement, pleasant manners, industry, enthusiasm, drive, initiative, open mindedness etc., are some of the essential traits of an ideal teacher. External appearance has a psychological effect upon the students. By attractive appearance, he/she can win the love and affection of his students and can command respect. He/she should be frank, tolerant, kind, fair and straight-forward so that he/she can stimulate learning.

(iv) *Teacher's Mental Health:* We speak of education as a lamp lighting another lamp, one life making another life and a spirit speaking to another spirit. We can achieve this objective, if the teachers have good mental health. Students develop interest in those subjects, which are taught by pleasing and genial teachers. The teacher makes the emotional atmosphere in the classroom. If he has a good mental health, he can create love, interest and enthusiasm for learning and a taste in the subject he teaches.

(v) *Teacher's Physical Health:* A teacher should possess a sound body along with a sound mind. He should have a sound physical health, physical energy, vitality and he should be free from physical defects. This will make him alert, cheerful, happy, dynamic and enthusiastic. He can maintain emotional stability.

(vi) *Teacher's Social Adjustment:* Sociability is another important quality of a teacher. He should have a sound social philosophy and he should make his best contribution to the society. He should know how to adjust himself to the social surroundings in which he lives. He should not be quiet, retreating and introverted. He should be free from worry, anxiety and thinking and feeling about himself. He should mix well in society to have a large body of friends and to take a helpful interest in his neighbours. Normal social life outside the school will go a long way to give him happy social adjustments.

(vii) *Teacher's Professional Efficiency:* The teacher must possess a strong sense of vocation and true devotion towards teaching. He should have a genuine love for his calling. For his professional efficiency, he should have knowledge of psychology, educational philosophy, aims, contents, methods and materials of instruction, skill and interest in teaching. He must possess a fair knowledge of current affairs about his own country and other countries of the world.

(viii) *Teacher's Professional Training:* The teacher must have the required professional training; without which he will commit serious pedagogical blunders. Prof. Monteque in his book Education and Human Relations asserts that, no one should ever be permitted to become a teacher of the young unless by temperament, attitudes and training, he is fitted to do so.

(ix) *Teacher's Accountability:* Lessinger advocates that each child has a right to be educated in order to become a productive citizen of a country. The parents and the citizen have a right to know the progress of education of their children. Teachers, being the educational or human engineers are accountable for the progress of the children they teach. Because of this, the National Policy on Education 1986, in India, has made this concept very popular.

Professional Ethics of Teachers

Teachers, who consider their job as a profession, work only for pay cheque. Their work is considered useful for their own sake. Since perchance they have occupied a professional chair they try for their own good, at the cost of others. But our cultural heritage proves that true teachers are those who consider their job as honourable. Such teachers work with a sense of self-fulfilment and self-realization. Prof. George Herbet Palmer once rightly said, If Harvard does not pay me to teach, I would gladly pay Harvard for the privilege of teaching. This should be the professional value of an Indian teacher. An ideal teacher should not work with pecuniary motives, but with a sense of education and for the cause of education.

(a) *Towards Students:* It shall be our primary duty to understand them, to be just, courteous, to promote a spirit of enquiry, fellowship and joy in them, not to do or say anything that would undermine their personality, not to exploit them for personal interests and to set before them a high standard of character, discipline and personality.

(b) *Towards Profession:* It shall be our primary duty to be sincere and honest to our work and to go thoroughly prepared to the class, to endeavour to maintain our efficiency by study and other means; not to do or say anything which may lower our prestige in the eyes of our students; not to write or encourage the use of help books; not to exert any pressure upon our students or their parents to engage private tuition, not to act as an agent or accept commission and other compensation for recommending books.

(c) *Towards Society:* It shall be our primary duty to set an example in citizenship, to endeavour to promote the public good, to uphold the dignity of our calling on all occasions, to size up the demands and aspirations of the society, to be dynamic leaders when required and to be ideal followers when desired.

Their job is to counsel students as they grow and mature—helping them integrate their social, emotional, and intellectual growth—so the union of these sometimes separate dimensions yields the abilities to seek, understand, and use knowledge; to make better decisions in their personal lives; and to value contributing to society. Students work harder when teachers give them a role in determining the form and content of their schooling—helping them create their own learning plans and deciding the ways in which they will demonstrate that they have, in fact, learned what they agreed to learn.

The day-to-day job of a teacher, rather than broadcasting content, is becoming one of designing and guiding students through engaging learning opportunities. An educator's most important responsibility is to search out and construct meaningful educational experiences that allow students to solve real-world problems and show they have learned the big ideas, powerful skills, and habits of mind and heart that meet agreed-on educational standards. The result is that the abstract, inert knowledge that students used to memorize from dusty textbooks comes alive as they participate in the creation and extension of new knowledge.

But today's world is awash in information from a multitude of print and electronic sources. The fundamental job of teaching is no longer to distribute facts but to help children learn how to use them by developing their abilities to think critically, solve problems, make informed judgments, and create knowledge that benefits both the students and society. Freed from the responsibility of being primary information providers, teachers have more time to spend working one-on-one or with small groups of students.

To truly professionalize teaching, in fact, we need to further differentiate the roles a teacher might fill. Just as a good law firm has a mix of associates, junior partners, and senior partners, schools should have a greater mix of teachers who have appropriate levels of responsibility based on their abilities and experience levels. Also, just as much of a lawyer's work occurs outside the courtroom, so, too, should we recognize that much of a teacher's work is done outside the classroom?

CONCLUSION

Mass education in India appears to be in a degrading condition. Education imparted by some teachers is far from satisfactory. Majority of the students lack fundamental knowledge in different areas of education. Such teachers do not feel it to be their responsibility. They are involved in private tuition and coaching centres to get some remuneration. Many parents cannot educate their children in costly public schools. Commitment on the part of the teachers has been reduced to a great extent. Therefore, there is a need to make the teachers aware of their accountability to their profession. Reinventing the role of teachers inside and outside the classroom can result in significantly better schools and better-educated students. The rest of us—politicians and parents, superintendents and school board members, employers and education school faculty—must also be willing to rethink our roles in education to give teachers the support, freedom, and trust they need to do the essential job of educating our children.

7

Changing Roles of the Teacher and Teacher Educators

T. Gladis Grace
Research Scholar, Dept. of Education, Osmania University, Hyderabad
B. J. Sujani
Research Scholar, Dept. of Education, Osmania University, Hyderabad

ABSTRACT

The role of teacher and teacher educator in the present day has changed from knowledge transmitter to that of a facilitator. Teachers and teacher educators are messiahs of educational improvement should understand the importance of working to fulfil personal goals and mission of the changing scenario. Teacher education is seen today not merely as a spreader of traditions and customs but also a transforming agent who helps teachers and schools to discover, familiarize, and operate fresh and improved ways of performing teaching and related tasks. Teacher training institutions which are part of the system should seek and utilize fitting ways of addressing the challenges confronting the education sector. Teacher trainers must bring awareness in imparting and utilizing their skills to play different roles by developing creative approaches in training, design ingenious materials, understanding pedagogy and a thorough indulgence of theory and practice, propagate current research techniques and amalgamate substance and facts with teaching technology; detect individual student needs and wisely run the resources by integrating ICT in teacher education, constructivism approach on par with the orientation to the curriculum and develop positive attitude in student teachers which is the first rung on the ladder of professional success. Mentoring by experienced colleagues to all the greenhorns is critical to the success. They should experience orientation programmes to provide them with opportunities to learn from the best practices of their knowledgeable contemporaries to enhance their competencies and produce better results for students. Teachers should involve parents into the school which can always produce successful students. The above listed roles of a teacher and the teacher educators can obviously bring about the expected change in the educational scenario for a better pillaring of the future generations.

Introduction

Teaching is always a dynamic activity which unfolds a world of knowledge and information, skill and style. It indicates how far a teacher is justified to the profession and how pupils respond to learning in the best possible manner. Education enriches a society, but teacher education enriches it more in the sense that the qualitative development of a society depends primarily on qualitative teachers and teaching.

The role of teacher and teacher educator in the present day has changed from knowledge transmitter to a facilitator. Teachers and teacher educators, are messiahs of educational improvement, should understand the importance of working to fulfil personal goals and mission of the changing scenario.

Every society in the making is in utter confusion in the elusive rush for so-called modernity in education with the application of newer and more attractive gadgets in the areas of education which in turn has affected the teacher education severely. Teacher educators are, therefore, related to teacher efficiency and as such, the avenues of effective teaching and the strategies adopted for that purpose necessitate orientation and reorientation with changing needs and priorities in teacher education. Teacher education is seen today not merely as a spreader of traditions, and customs but a transforming agent which helps teachers and schools to discover, publicize, and maneuver fresh and improved ways of performing instruction and correlated tasks.

Duty of the Teacher Training Institutions

Teacher training institutions which play a crucial role in bringing the change should seek and utilize fitting ways of addressing the challenges confronting the education sector. It is not in making candidates worthy after their entry but a scrupulous check should be done before they enter the teaching profession. There is a lot of teaching and training but very little learning and understanding. To improve the education or the education system first we ought to focus our attention on where or why our education has failed.

Causes for the Failure

1. *Attitude of the Trainees:* An individual who enters a teacher training institution these days is a teacher not by choice but by chance. The discarded ones from the Medicine or Engineering find the doors to the teacher-training course always open. This mind-set lacks pledge in doing justice to the profession and the system.
2. *Status of the Teachers:* Teaching is a noble profession was the then relevant jingle but in the present scenario it is an underprivileged profession. The West is aped in all aspects except the status of the teachers. In the West, the teacher is better respected than most other professions as they believe that teachers make lives of the future generations.
3. *Eligibility Test:* The criterion of the eligibility test should be a valid one with clarity. It should test the individual's knowledge rather than making him toss a coin for the answer. Such multiple choice questions should be replaced with the questions that would be descriptive, relevant and skill based. Only a worthy candidate with commitment would get through.
4. *Applicability in the Course:* The teacher training course does not expose trainees to the necessary life skills which enriches and enables teachers to understand the attributes of modernity and development. Proper educational audit has to be developed for the whole course where the clarity should reflect in the course.

Need of the Hour

1. Teachers need to develop sensitivity to develop the individuals to build a better society and become better individuals.

2. Trainees should be active participants in learning through their own problem solving methods rather than systematic methods of teaching.
3. Teacher education should co-ordinate with the practicality of the problems in the real life situations in the field of education. Activity based projects should be implemented in the teacher education.
4. Teacher education should encourage the student teachers to examine the textbooks critically rather than blindly following the given curriculum.
5. The focus of the teacher education activities should not be tailor made but make the teacher trainees utilize their latent talents in handling the situations according to the rising need of the problems.
6. The teacher education programme should inculcate the awareness to produce a finer human with inclusion of traditions, cultural practices, community knowledge, and perception of the society, harmony within oneself and also with the environment to promote peace and thoughtful values.
7. Teacher education should uplift its standard to upgrade the trainees to handle any target group. (Government, Private or Corporate schools).
8. *Course Materials and Learning*: Teacher training institutions and Teacher trainers must bring awareness in imparting and utilizing their skills to play different roles by developing creative approaches in training, design ingenious materials, understanding pedagogy and a thorough indulgence of theory and practice, propagate current research techniques and amalgamate substance and facts with teaching technology; detect individual student needs and wisely run the resources accordingly.
9. *Target programme to be implemented immediately*: Teacher Education Curriculum needs to incorporate *Information and Communication Technologies* (ICTs) in its programmes have the potential to equip the

students with the necessary skills required in the 21st century. They can play a vital role to enhance access, quality, and effectiveness in education in general and to enable the development of better teachers in modem times. As computer hardware becomes available to an increasing number of schools, more attention needs to be given to the capacity building of the key transformers in this process, namely, teachers.

Applications of ICT in Teacher Education

(a) ICT has the potential to support several and diverse learning activities. ICT acts as a motivating factor to use internet and multimedia technologies as educational tools and serve as a facilitator of the learning process.

(b) It acts as the gateway to the world of information and enables teachers to update themselves with innovative trends in instructional methodologies, evaluation mechanism etc.

(c) ICT acts as a tool for effective implementation of certain student centric methodologies such as project-based learning.

10. *Constructivism in Education*: Constructivism has created a major paradigm shift in education. It emerged after the behaviourist movement as a refreshing view of learning that centers on the active learner within the teaching-learning process. Constructivism describes how learning takes place. The theories in it state that knowledge is constructed out of the learner's experiences rather than received from an intentional world or peripheral actuality.

The emergence and application of constructivism in education has changed the role of teacher to a facilitator who helps the learner to get his or her own understanding of the content. Constructivism offers teachers/teacher educators instructional approaches that are congruent with current research on learning. By viewing learning as an active process, taking students prior knowledge into consideration, building on preconceptions, and eliciting cognitive conflict, teachers can design instruction that goes beyond rote learning to meaningful learning. Constructivism applications are commonly found in schools through the widespread use of cooperative and collaborative teaching strategies such as: Discovery learning, Problem-solving, Group work, Interaction among peers, Teams-Games-Tournaments, Student Teams Achievement Division etc. In each of these, the emphasis is on having students working together while sharing ideas and challenging each others perspectives. The trainees should imbibe into the system where the output would be reflected in the outcome of the student they would produce.

Though measures are being taken to implement the above in the teacher education, the seriousness in the rigour should be implemented.

Lastly, experienced colleagues, green horns in the field and parents should join hands for better results for the pillaring of the future generations.

CONCLUSION

Teachers and Teacher education is going through an unprecedented period of change where quality of teachers is the main concern and also the growing number. So the teacher with quality should emerge from the grass roots of the system that he/she is imbibed in and should adapt the scale of demand and meet the challenges in the complicated system of education with ease and grandeur. In spite of the constraints of the crises in education, teacher trainees would show patriotism and continue to play their role for the nation's development without hesitation, selflessness and zeal.

8

The Prominence of ICTs in the Changing Roles of Teachers and Teacher Educators

Dr. D. Ashalatha
Professor and Head, Dept. of Humanities and Sciences,
Sri Venkateswara College of Engineering and Technology (SVCET),
Chittoor, A.P.
N. Jayaprada
Asst. Professor, Dept. of Humanities and Sciences,
SVCET, Chittoor, A.P.

ABSTRACT

Improving the quality of education through the diversification of contents, pioneering methods, promoting experimentation, innovation, diffusion, sharing of information and best practices are the strategic objectives of education. The radical implications ICTs (information and communication technologies) have for conventional teaching and learning predict the transformation of the teaching-learning process and the way teachers and learners gain access to knowledge and information. With the emerging new technologies, the teaching profession is evolving an emphasis on student-centered, interactive learning environments. Designing and implementing successful ICT-enabled teacher education programmes is the key to fundamental, wide-ranging educational reforms. The concept of quality is complex. But in the ODL system, quality means the attainment of the expected knowledge levels necessary for managing the learner's personal and social transaction in day-to-day life. This quality is to be attained by all distance learners, in a given time frame. For education to reap the full benefits of ICTs in learning, it is essential that pre and in-service teachers are able to effectively use these new tools for learning. Teacher education institutions and programmes must provide the leadership and model the new pedagogies as well as paraphernalia for learning. Technology is a part of our daily life. To confront the fast paced-globalization it is crucial that students of today are equipped with pertinent knowledge and skills. Learning is undoubtedly, the essence of human identity. Teacher education institutions may either assume a trendsetting role in the transformation of education or be left behind in the swirl of rapid technological change.

Introduction

The need for learning arises from the point of view of its adaptability, productivity, utility, universality and teachability. The importance and meaning of learning pertains to the fact that receivers and senders of messages are connected through space and time. In the present day world ICTs, challenge conventional theories, ideas and concepts of interpersonal as well as mass communication. They enables us to use diverse forms of communication like mass communication via world wide web, group discussions in the internet chat forums, person-to-person communication by e-mail, the use of multi-media and interactivity through one way and text only messages. Internet enhances group communication in collaborative work. Computer mediated communication influences the way collaboration is formed, advanced and maintained. The internet enables varied configurations of communication exchange like e-mail, file transfer, news groups, mailing lists, bulletin boards, chat systems, text or audio and video conferences, group calendars, work flow systems, collaborative writing systems, decision support systems as well as other elaborate systems for the support of work groups and teams.

The Prominence of ICTs in the Changing Roles of Teachers and Teacher Educators

Hyper Personal Communication is a construct that denotes communication which appears more desirable than what we tend to experience in face to face interactions. There are primarily four sources which contribute to the perception of a hyper personal experience: the sender has great control; the receiver can analyze the qualities in the sender; the channel, being synchronous or asynchronous, affects interaction and feedback can build an "Intensification Loop" between the partners in learning. Being in an actual classroom and interacting face-to-face with other students and students is the most effective way to learning. But still, the educators would highly benefit from having ICTs in their kit for teaching.

Asynchronous environments provide a means for students and teachers to discuss as well as collaborate ideas at different times and at different places. The power and diversity of ICTs supports learning through the modeling of online instructional material, the analysis of instructional experience, the experimentation in blended environments and practice in the laboratory to foster the promotion of professional experience. Of late, information technology has been a powerful vehicle that allows course instruction to be delivered to more people located in geographically dispersed places. Automation and computer mediated learning have made educational opportunities more available and affordable. The ICT learning is classified in to three types of communication:

1. *Content-related*

- Ask or answer a question
- Share information
- Express and idea or thought

2. *Planning of Tasks*

- Plan work, allot tasks, coordinate joint efforts and review drafts
- Negotiate and resolve conflicts
- Assessment and evaluation

3. *Social Support*

- Express emotional support and Use emoticons
- Provide technical support
- Talk about things other than class work

Higher education including open and distance learning is essential for social and economic transformation. Quality in education is a combination of exceptional high standards; perfection and consistency; fitness for purpose; value for money and transformation capabilities. The areas of quality concern in ODL are curriculum, design, content and organization; teaching, learning and assessment; student progression and assessment; student support and guidance. Educational systems around the world are under increasing pressure to use the new Information and Communication technologies (ICTs) to teach students the knowledge and skills they need in the 21st century. The UNESCO World Education Report proposes that to effectively harness the power of ICTs to improve learning, the following essential conditions must be met:

- Students and teachers must have sufficient access to digital technologies and the Internet in their classrooms, schools, and teacher education institutions.
- High quality, meaningful, and culturally responsive digital content must be available for teachers and learners.
- Teachers must have the knowledge and skills to use the new digital tools and resources to help all students achieve high academic standards.

To accomplish this goal we require both a change in the traditional view of the learning process and an understanding of how the new digital technologies can create new learning environments in which students are engaged learners, able to take greater responsibility for their own learning and constructing their own knowledge. Thomas Kuhn suggests that revolutions in science come about when the old theories and methods will not solve new problems. He calls these changes in theory and methods a "paradigm shift." There is a widespread concern that the educational experiences provided in many schools will not prepare students well for the future. Many educators, business and government leaders believe that creating a paradigm shift in views of the learning process, coupled with applications of the new information technologies can play an important role in bringing educational systems into alignment with the knowledge-based, information-rich society. Shifting the emphasis from teaching to learning can create a more interactive and engaging learning environment for teachers and learners.

This new environment also involves a change in the roles of both teachers and students. The role of the teacher will change from knowledge transmitter to that of learning facilitator, knowledge guide, knowledge navigator and co-learner with the student. The new role does not diminish the importance of the teacher but requires new expertise and competence. Students will have greater responsibility for their own learning in this environment as they seek out, find, synthesize, and share their knowledge with others. ICTs provide powerful tools to support the shift to student-centered learning and the new roles of teachers and students.

The ICT methods help learners reduce stress and enhance their self-instruction and self-confidence through games and communicative activities. Learner's learning process can be analyzed and recorded in the data, enabling the instructors to support learner's specific needs in a meaningful way. Learning can be used in :

1. *Acquisition*–to provide a platform for natural communications;
2. *Learning*–to apply methods with rich hypermedia materials to facilitate learning;
3. *Monitoring*–to provide automated editing functions to monitor students, allot exercises and provide suggested corrections to them;
4. *Natural order*–to facilitate the process of natural order of learning;
5. *Input*–to provide choices to follow methods with automatic selection of questions and exercises; and
6. *Affective filter*–to allow individuals to work at their own pace and provide positive feedback to learners.

The ICTs enable us to :

- Find information through electronic database searches;

- Rapidly evaluate the source, credibility and timeliness of information;
- Quickly make navigational decisions, pursue internal and external links or revert back to further searching;
- Make on-the-spot decisions to save or catalogue information;
- Organize or keep track of information;
- Integrate, texts, graphics and audio-visual material into multi-media presentations;
- Write effectively in hypertext genres;
- Write for an audience on the worldwide web;
- Use effective strategies for immersion in integrated practice, overt instruction, critical framing and transformed practice.

With advances in technology, hyper-personal approaches allow a high level of information richness with sophisticated functionality for informational retrieval. Conversely, there are certain challenges in shifting the teaching from the traditional high contact environment to an ICT environment. These challenges come from :

(a) An insufficiency of technological infrastructure;
(b) Mixed levels of individuals technical sophistication in using computer enabled technologies;
(c) A need to understand and respect cultural differences;
(d) Mixed levels of learner's computer literacy.

When pupils work with ICTs, they often work collaboratively in groups or teams. Originating often as a solution to shortage of computers, the experience of group work brings new benefits, by stimulating pupils to develop the interpersonal skills necessary for life after school. Through engaging pupils in joint endeavours, ICTs can help to make the classroom a more inclusive environment. ICT has something to offer most pupils, whatever their individual capabilities, i.e., the "virtual mobility". The teacher becomes leader, helper, partner and evaluator, combining the traditional role of subject expert with that of a manager.

CONCLUSION

An effective learning course must incorporate significant interactions between learners and instructors, whether those interactions occur face-to-face as in traditional courses or in the online learning environment. Researchers are still divided on the actual benefits of ICTs in learning. Though some difficulties are obvious, some weigh the potential advantages against the pitfalls. But it is true that if the instructors can apply the appropriate instruction in their classes and support students in utilizing the tools appropriately, positive relationship will develop between students and teachers. However, since many software applications do not support in-depth learning, instructors should become fluent and critical users of technology in order to choose software applications that suit learner's needs and provide relevant information. The creation of teaching-enabled environments through effective use of ICTs in the classroom may indeed have the effect of releasing hidden potential amongst pupils. The challenge of integrating technology into schools and classrooms is much more human that it is technological.

REFERENCES

1. Daneil, Sir John and Kanwar Asha (2006); Quality Assurance for Open, Distance and E-learning (World Bank Seminar).
2. David Amritha Rajan and Gnana Soundari (2005); Best Practices for Quality for Higher Education.
3. Hughes, I. (2005); The role of teacher knowledge and learning experiences in forming technology-integrated pedagogy; Journal of Technology and Teacher Education, 13(2), 277.
4. MacDonald, J.(2006); Blended Learning and Online Tutoring: A good practice guide. Ashgate Publishing.
5. Simpson, N. (2006); Asynchronous access to conventional course delivery: A pilot project, British Journal of Technology.

Theme–III

Curriculum Design and Instruction for ODL Teacher Education Programmes

9

Internet Usage in Distance Delivery of Teacher Education Programmes

A. Vijayalakshmi
Academic Consultant, Dept. of Education, S. P. Mahila University, Tirupati
Dr. S. Vijaya Vardhini
Asst. Prof., Dept. of Edn. and HRD, Dravadian University, Kuppam, A.P.

ABSTRACT

Teacher education is an important area where distance education has been used extensively to provide pre-service teacher preparation, upgrading of academic qualifications, and in-service continuing professional development in particular subjects, content areas and instructional methods. Many examples, from both developing and developed countries, show that teacher training at a distance may reach large groups of teachers and may have profound impact on the development of national education systems. Examples include distance learning initiatives in countries such as China, India, Nigeria and South Africa to prepare new teachers or upgrade skills of the existing teaching force. The use of open and distance learning for teacher education is therefore a crucial strategy when expansion or quality improvement is needed in the public education system.

Distance education may play an increasingly important role during this decade in helping address the growing shortage of teachers, educational administrators and other educational professionals experienced in both developing and developed countries. A particular advantage of distance education is that it makes teacher preparation and professional development programmes accessible to indigenous peoples and others located in remote, rural areas that do not have convenient access to higher education institutions and where there is often a shortage of well-prepared teachers and other educational professionals. The current and emerging communication and information technologies provide unique opportunities to continue the professional development of teachers and other educators.

Within open and distance learning, technologies are used for two contrasting purposes to distribute teaching material and to stimulate learning by means of one-way or two-way communication. An appropriate technology needs to be found to distribute material to students. In the case of physical teaching material, such as books or audio cassettes, material has to be carried direct to students or to a point from which they can collect it. It may be possible to use existing channels of communication with teachers for this purpose, or to rely on the post, or to set up a dedicated service. Broadcasting, by radio or television, videoconferencing and computer communication all offer means of delivering teaching material to learners without these physical arrangements.

Teaching involves more than distribution. Well-designed printed materials, cassettes, or broadcasts are usually designed to promote learning, often by stimulating an active response from the learner. In choosing technologies, therefore, the policy maker has to consider not just how materials will be distributed but how they can be designed to facilitate learning and to resolve tensions between these two aims. Television, for example, may look the best medium for showing a simulation in engineering but is inappropriate if the only available television hours are at an inconvenient time or on a channel which does not reach most of the learners.

Developed countries are using the Internet as the principal or supplementary means of providing both pre-service and in-service teacher education. There are a growing number of high quality Web-based professional development resources available for educators globally. The Web provides teachers with rich instructional and information resources to enhance their instruction and professional skills and the possibility of on-demand, just-in-time professional development without leaving their classrooms.

The Web also provides opportunities for online mentoring and support of novice teachers during their first year of teaching and to develop online communities of practice. Virtual Web based environments for teachers enable them to seek help from other teachers, locally, nationally, or globally in solving classroom problems, sharing lesson plans and materials, interacting with experts in particular fields, and in planning collaborative curriculum development projects.

Distance education may also play a major role in upgrading the knowledge and skills of teacher educators both in higher education and educational agencies. Web-based resources and tutorials may assist teaching faculty and teacher educators in upgrading their knowledge and skills in areas such as the new technology tools for learning in order that they may infuse and model the use of technology in the courses they offer to future teachers.

It is recognized that in many developing countries access to the Web in local schools is not possible. However, the Web may provide an important resource for teacher education institutions and agencies that provide professional development to teachers in the country. Communication between teachers and learners is a necessary component in distance education, as in all other forms of education. Communication technologies distribute messages in text, still and moving images, and sound. Knowledge-generating messages may be communicated to large numbers of learners, by broadcasting or accessed on demand through audio/video players or Internet. Thus, new Internet devices will make it possible for larger numbers of people to share a common learning experience, to enable an individual learner to have a unique personal interaction with a teacher or with another learner, no matter where located. Since they do not depend on physical access, these experiences can be of much higher quality than were possible before.

Communication serves two purposes. One is the distribution of information. This delivery system may comprise both distribution of pre-packaged material and transmission of synchronous or broadcast programmes, lectures etc. The second role of communication is the crucial component of all education which is the interaction between teachers and learners, and, where possible, between learners also. In some forms of distance education this learner interaction is practically non-existent, but in most cases it is considered important and may be provided in different ways. Often students meet together physically in groups, sometimes connected with other forms of local support. New technologies allow the organization of virtual groups and in countries where access to the Internet is common, this is the fastest growing approach to distance teaching.

A classroom teacher, writing on a blackboard, and getting questions from students does all three at once. In open and distance learning we may use print to present material, the mail to distribute it, and face-to-face tutorial sessions for feedback and dialogue, a variety of computer-based technologies, including the distribution of sample lesson plans on CD-ROMS, setting up exchanges by computer conference between teachers' colleges, encouraging the interactive use of computer-based learning materials, encouraging the use of web-based materials, and using computer conferencing to encourage discussion among learners.

Finally, distance education and the new tools for learning may serve as a catalyst for changing teaching practices, the roles of teachers and students as part of an overall strategy for systemic change of the educational system to reflect current knowledge on human learning and to help the educational system be more responsive to local and national needs as well as global trends.

10

Research in Language Teacher Education : Indispensable for Broadening the Knowledge Base of ESL Teachers

D. Vishwa Prasad
Asst. Prof., Maulana Azad National Urdu University, Hyderabad

ABSTRACT

It is pertinent and comes of the age that we discuss research in teacher education. We all know how important school education is in today's world. I firmly believe that school education lays the foundation for the knowledge based society. In order to realize the dreams of knowledge based society, as has been the call of the Prime Minister of India, Dr. Manmohan Singh, through school education, we need stronger and effective teacher education programmes–be it in the face-to-face mode or distance mode.

There are three important domains which have gained a lot of prominence: science and technology, economics, and language teaching/learning in the wake of globalization. We throw light on various issues of school education in teacher education, that's important, but seldom have we cared for language teaching issues–English as a Second Language (ESL)–in teacher education research. This paper has touches upon some of the important aspects of ESL and what research in language education could offer us to improve our understanding of second language teacher education.

Introduction

One of the important challenges for teaching ESL is the use of our increasingly sophisticated concepts in the area of language education to inform our understanding of the abstract and concrete phenomenon of teaching in the real world. At this juncture, improving the ESL teachers understanding of the learner needs of the world will require intensive study of variables affecting the learner's acquisition of English as the *second* language.

The 21st century society is laying emphasis on trade and commerce and has been paving the way for globalization for more than three decades. This situation really has given a lot of fillip for the English language education and English in particular. Hence, there is a crying need to draw programmes which are in tandem with the needs of the learners. In the whole process of drawing a potential ESL programme, a few pertinent questions crop up like: what does research say about teaching ESL and the beliefs that the ESL teachers hold regarding those research findings.

There may be dozens of questions, which may sound pleasing to our ears, addressing the objectives of the programme, materials that should be used, evaluation systems etc. but the most prominent point in the whole of second language education system is that of a teacher, and the programmes, which prepare them are even more important.

To cite an example, without a hint or a shadow of a doubt, we know that learner is at the centre of the teaching-learning process, but if the teacher is not willing to change his/her beliefs regarding various aspects of teaching, none of us can do anything, no matter how good the curriculum is. Hence, teacher education should reflect upon the research related to teacher beliefs, which unveils the belief systems of the English language teacher.

Role of Language Teacher Education Research in Improving/Understanding of ESL Teaching

The relationship between teaching and research is often ignored most of the time. SL teacher education research informs us of the practice in the teaching of English as a second language enabling practicing teachers, to make sound decisions about the educational activities that will best serve the learners taking into account the differences like socio-cultural, religious, intellectual etc., among learners of ESL. Besides, SLTE research honours human complexity, acknowledging the many influences that shape teachers beliefs.

Research in SL teacher education also stimulates discussion among researchers, teachers and all those who are involved in teaching and learning of the English language. Besides, it challenges assumptions, and raise new questions related to teaching of ESL. In responding to such difficulties, researchers often resort to multiple disciplines like: English studies, education, linguistics, anthropology, gender studies, sociology of education, philosophical foundations of education, social inclusion and exclusionary perspectives, etc., to portray problems and to help the learners. For example, recent research, focused on the ways in which teachers and teacher candidates understand the subjects they teach, reveals that they often have misconceptions or gaps in knowledge similar to those of their pupils.

Research offers clear, complete explanations of a particular issue and explains how a given study contributes to our understanding of SL teacher education. When provided with explicit information about the assumptions and beliefs guiding the work, we can draw upon studies informed by a range of theoretical orientations and use multiple ways of seeing to enrich our understanding of the learners.

In turn, teachers of English are also changing their attitude and they are no longer passive to published research. With the help of research, they are actively determining implications for classroom practice, and are conducting their own classroom-based inquiries to share with the SL teacher community. Hence, teachers of ESL approach research with an eye to enrich their understanding of their own students as they develop strategies appropriate to their learners.

In addition, research studies can help pre-service and practicing teachers recognize how to relate their specific questions and concerns about teaching of English as a second language. Published research studies present findings of particular inquiries from a particular perspective. Therefore, teacher educators of ESL ask pre-service and practicing teachers how they approach research in a critical fashion - learning to evaluate research involves asking questions related to those studies. Research probes into questions like: What does the study assume about how English as a second language is learnt? How is the study designed? How do the findings fit with the experience as a teacher of ESL? What new questions does the study raise for us? Etc.

Teachers who study and critique research, do so in terms of questions that emerge from their teaching. They continually ask, "How will what I learnt from this study help my students?" Such applications base their research in practice and translate the theoretical into the real. Teacher educators should help pre-service in this process by asking them to read and critique research studies they encounter in terms of their own classroom questions and concerns.

As teachers begin to apply the research of others to their own classroom contexts, they inevitably come up with their own questions: "Does the research I am involved in address the issues about my classroom?" "If not, how I might find the answers to my questions?" As teachers ask such questions, they begin the kind of reflection that leads to the generation of their own research—often as teacher/practitioner researchers. Teacher educators who promote an inquiry-based approach to teacher education expect teachers to think of themselves as reflective practitioners who understand the need to study continually their own approaches. Practicing teachers who ask questions and then systematically study their own teaching generate new research about teaching.

The emphasis on research-based practice makes it imperative that teachers understand not only how to use research to help their students learn but also how to critique the claims made by researchers outside the classroom who use research as a means of influencing or even over-riding teacher decision-making.

Therefore, research in teacher education is a cord, which connects all the characters - researchers, learners, teachers –

in a play called SL teacher education. And it in turn provides us a better understanding of the role of research in the development of new knowledge.

I opine that significant change in teachers' beliefs is likely to take place only after changes in student learning outcomes are evidenced. The teachers might study dozens of learning and teaching theories, day and night, but not all of them might dovetail with their beliefs. I assume, each one of us has different learning styles and might have a special preference for teaching strategies and these are in mind at every given time as we like them. And we tend to extend those preferences even to our second language classrooms, mildly worried about the target language culture, usage, and idioms etc. and the preferences of the majority – learners.

I shall give an analogy; a salesperson always keeps in mind that the utmost satisfaction of the customer is more important than his own. He puts a new item on display. And he uses sharp-edged persuasive demonstration of a product to make the customer buy it. If the customer doesn't succumb to his words in the first instance, he tries once again. If the customer is not convinced even then, the salesperson picks up hints from customer's conversation and finds out his tastes as in what the customer is interested in and now for sure, the customer is in line with his words to buy his products. Now the salesperson is happy, as it is in the selling of a product, his happiness lies. Every weekend he checks his stock of the new products and if they are insufficient, he places orders for some more along with a new product. This is how business goes on.

Teachers are more or less like salespersons, the customers are the learners, speech of the salesperson is the belief that a teacher carries, and the products are the latest research findings, stock verification is being reflective about the whole business of teaching.

What do we understand by it? The changes in student learning result, of course, from specific changes teachers have made in their classroom practices, for example, a new instructional approach, the use of new materials or curricula, or simply some modification in teaching procedures or classroom format. Whatever the case may be, the significant change in the beliefs of teachers is contingent on their gaining evidence of change in the learning outcomes of their students. (Guskey, 1986) For this to happen a teacher has to be a reflective practitioner.

CONCLUSION

Research is the soul of human race, and we have to keep the embers of research vigour alive to edge towards ideal knowledge based society. We have to shoulder the responsibility of getting ourselves renewed with firsthand knowledge about the learners' interests and how well our methods/approaches suit their tastes and needs. Most of the present day programmes are built upon a constructivist theory, requiring the teachers to continuously go through the literature, understand, conceptualize, and adapt it to our contexts. Research or dealing with it in language teacher education would assist us in developing effective curriculum and address various issues related to teachers–writing objectives, preparing and presenting materials, methods teachers employ, evaluation they take refuge in, beliefs they dwell in, qualification they possess, culture they belong to etc.– with quite indemnity. Hence, research has strong implications for teaching and learning. I believe that this type of a brass tack is critical for the success of any language teaching programme, especially English as a second language.

REFERENCE

1. Guskey, Thomas R. (1986), Staff Development and the Process of Teacher Change, Educational Researcher, Vol. 15, No. 5, 5-12.

11

The Role of ODL Teacher Education Curriculum in Challenging National Issues

J. Komaleswari
Academic Consultant, Distance Education Center, SPMVV, Tirupati
A. Gayatri
Ph.D. Scholar, Dept. of Education, S.V. University, Tirupati

Introduction

It is universally acknowledged that education is an effective means for social reconstruction and offers solutions to the problems of society. Education of teacher need to strengthen and stress upon the main attributes of profession. It is recognized that formal professional training need to be incorporated in Open and Distance Learning (ODL) teacher education in challenging national issues. Moreover it is necessary to become a good teacher as it caters to the development of one's personality and shaping of communication skills and commitment to a code of conduct.

ODL Teacher Education Vs National Issues

The education of teacher contributes for the education of entire nation and to overcome the issues of the contemporary. In ODL teacher education, the teacher trainees are already exposed to the community at gross route level and able to identify the issues with teacher education. The following are the some of the challenges:

1. *Economic Issues*: The major economic problems of the country are poverty, unemployment and low rate of growth and productivity, which have led to the compulsions of the backward economy. Education can help to find solutions if it is properly coordinated with manpower needs. Indian society needs education with special emphasis on science and technology, vocational inputs and realistic work experiences.

   ODL teacher education curriculum has to promote such attitudes as are necessary for the emergence of new economic order. Along with the vocational competencies and skills, a new work culture will have to be created which necessarily involves the inculcation of dignity of work, the spirit of self-reliance and scientific temper among students. The courses of ODL teacher education need to be enriched to enable teachers to understand the attributes of modernity and development.

2. *Social Issues:* Castism, communalism and regionalism are some of the problems in the body politics of the society which misguide the youth. Increasing delinquency, violence, terrorism and fissiparous tendencies are threat to the national integration and social cohesion. On the other side, the explosion of population is not only neutralizing the economic gains but also creating many problems led to child labour, child marriage, untouchability, gender inequality, violation of human rights ect. In globalization contest, man has disturbed the harmony and equilibrium resulted in environmental degradation, pollution and economical equilibrium. The role of ODL teachers and teacher educators is widened and strengthened in addressing the above issues.

3. *Problems of Cultural Reconstruction:* Education is the process of transmission of dynamic and responsive components of cultural heritage and its continuous enrichment. There is a need to reinterpret the Indian culture in its distinct identity and composite strength.

Its capacity to absorb the sublime from the other cultures needs to be highghted. The ODL teacher education curriculum should be need based in cultural reconstruction and to bring positive cultural change in the society.

4. *Crisis of Values and Morality:* There has been a persistent erosion of values in the society. There are situations where the values imparted and inculcated in schools are not generally practiced in society. It is through education and as of necessity through ODL teacher education programmes that task of inculcating values can be substantially accomplished. However, the moral education is essentially co-native in character and demand immediate decision and action. Through committed teachers, the art of ensuing moral development in a secular, multi-religious and multi-ethnic society needs to be cultivated.

Factors Responsible for the Quality ODL Teacher Education Curriculum

There are many factors responsible for assurance of quality of ODL teacher education programme in challenging national issues. These are:

1. *Factors with in the Education System:* Maintenance of educational standard against the pressure of increasing enrolment, relevance and quality of school education, efficacy of school functioning, need of social and economical groups of the society and of the minority communities, rush for urbanization of perceived urban orientation of educational system and inflexibility to respond to rural, tribal, and regional requirement.
2. *Isolation of ODL Teacher Education :* ODL teacher education institutions which considered 'islands of isolation' have gradually developed linkages with schools, peer institutions, universities and other institutions of higher learning as also the community. It is observed that in day-to-day functioning the

teacher educators often tend to lose contact with content areas relevant of their own disciplines resulting into gaps in communication and latest information. However, much remains to be done in this direction.

3. *Strategies for Breaking the Barriers:* The critical analysis regarding the role of teacher education curriculum in challenging national issues helped in bringing the new vision to ODL teacher education. In this context, strategies developed in bridging the gaps enlisted here.
   1. Total trust in the capabilities of institutions and organizations and organizations to develop an indigenous, comparable and area specific curriculum has to be the guiding principle.
   2. ODL teacher education has to be integral part of educational and social system and must primarily respond to the requirement of the school system.
   3. It is no longer conventional and static but should transform itself to a progressive dynamic and responsive system.
   4. National values and goals need to be meaningfully reflected and their inculcation attempted with care and caution.
   5. Theoretical and practical components need to be balanced appropriately.
   6. The theory and practice of ODL teacher education gas to be enriched with the latest research findings not only in the field of education but also in the allied disciplines and areas.
   7. Continuous in-service orientation to acknowledge the latest educational developments and social and cultural issues.
   8. Teachers who are professionally committed and prepared to present a value based model of interaction with their learner.
   9. It is essential to develop identified competencies to

prepare effective teachers and equally important to develop commitment and build capacity to perform as integral part of ODL teacher education.

4. *Spectrum of ODL Teacher Education Institutional Functions:* In the light of bringing change in the curriculum of ODL teacher education towards challenging national issues, respective institutions play a vital role. Resolution of specific functions listed below will have to be undertaken by different institutions according to availability of resources.
   1. Develop capability to provide for both ODL and in-service teacher education.
   2. Provide training and orientation programmes to the functionaries of alternative educational strategies aimed at achieving universal elementary education and eradication of illiteracy.
   3. Organize programmes for heads of schools and school complexes and supervisory staff.
   4. Offer courses for community leaders, voluntary agencies and parents.
   5. Undertake research and experiments with innovative educational ideas.
   6. Offer counseling and guidance services.
   7. Act as resource center for education for specific area.
   8. Provide academic support to schools and other agencies engaged in education.
   9. Organize need-based programmes for educational administrators, planners, curriculum designers, evaluators etc.

CONCLUSION

Education is an effective means for social reconstruction and offers solutions to the problems of society. Education of teacher need to strengthen and stress upon the main attributes of profession. The role of ODL teacher education in challenging national issues in economical and social development, cultural reconstruction and crises of values and morality are the major concerned. The other factors with in the education system and isolation of teacher education are also influencing the ODL teacher education curriculum. Many strategies are developed for breaking these barriers in challenging national issues. More over the role of ODL teacher education institutions need to be widened and strengthened to bring success in ODL teacher education curriculum.

REFERENCES

1. Biddle, Susan (2006), Attitudes of Education, Journal of Science Technology, Vol. 73, No. 3, pp. 52-56.
2. Bruce Joyce (1985), Teacher Education in India-Observations on American Innovations Abroad, Educational Research, Vol.14, No. 8, pp. 3-9.
3. Keegan D. (1990), Open Learning: Concepts and Costs, Success and Failures. In Atkinson Rand Me Beath C (Eds.), Open Learning and New Technology, Mursoch University Publication, pp. 230-243.
4. Moore M.G. and Kearsley G. (1996), Distance Education- A Systems View, Belmont CA Words Wortn.
5. Verma Chary (2007), Improving Quality of Elementary Education of Monitoring Professional Competencies of Teachers for Inclusive Education.

12

Integration of ICT for the Quality Teacher Education

Shaik Subhan
Lecturer, Ghulam Ahmed College of Education, Hyderabad (A.P.)
M. P. Dayal
Principal, College of Teacher Education (TW), Bhadrachalam (A.P.)

Introduction

Teaching is becoming one of the most challenging professions in our society where knowledge is expanding rapidly and much of it is available to students as well as teachers at the same time (Perraton, Robinson and Creed, 2001). Now-a-day's explosion of technology made the students as consumers of knowledge. Teachers no longer wear the same old hat. New demands are being made on teachers to use the technology creatively (Teeler and Gray, 2000). Recent developments of innovative technologies have provided new possibilities to teaching profession but at the same time have placed more demands on teachers to learn how to use these technologies in their teaching.

In India we have nearly 350 odd universities and 18000 colleges are providing higher education to about 10% of relevant age groups. This is extremely inadequate in a country where the demographic dividend by the way of young population of about 550 million youth is a much talked about asset. To raise the enrolment rate to 15% more by 2015 there is a need to establish nearly 50 national universities. In this context to fulfil the needs of the nation the open and distance education plays a crucial role to provide quality education.

For the attainment of quality in education, today a verity of ICTs can facilitate not only delivery of instruction but also learning process itself. Moreover, ICTs can promote international collaboration and networking in education and professional development. There is a range of ICTs options- from Videoconferencing through multimedia delivery to wedsites which can be used to meet the challenges teachers face today. In fact, there has been increasing evidence that ICTs may be able to provide more flexible and effective ways for lifelong professional development of teachers. Undoubtedly ICTs has brought about many challenges and opportunities for education.

ICT integrations in institutions is being as a necessity and is growing exponentially. The pervasive use of technology in all spheres of life, the knowledge economy and the paradigm shift together, generate demands on the institutions to adopt ways that help inculcate 21st century skills amongst students.

What are the 21st Century Skills?

EnGauge of the North Central Regional Educational Laboratory (U.S.) has identified what it calls "21st Century Skills," which includes :

1. Digital age literacy (consisting of functional literacy, visual literacy, scientific literacy, technological literacy, information literacy, cultural literacy, and global awareness).
2. Inventive thinking (adaptability, curiosity, creativity, risk taking).
3. Higher-order thinking (critical thinking, problem solving, sound reasoning and judgment).
4. Effective communication (teaming, collaborative working, interpersonal skills, personal and social responsibility and high productivity).

The potential of ICTs to promote the acquisition of these skills is tied to is use as a tool for raising educational quality, including promoting the shift to a learner-centered environment. Incorporating various methodologies like activity-based learning, problem-based learning, project-based learning and effective technology integration in everyday class room practices will lead to promote 21st century skills among students.

How ICT Helps to Promote These Skills?

In technology rich student-centered classrooms, there are many observable changes :

1. There is shift from whole class to small group instruction.
2. Coaching occurs rather than lecture and recitation.
3. Teachers work with weaker students more often rather than focusing attention on brighter students.
4. Students are more actively engaged.
5. Students become more cooperative and less competitive.
6. There is an integration of both visual and verbal thinking instead of the privacy of verbal thinking.

By integrating technology with constructivist methods, such as problem-based learning and project-based learning, teachers are more responsible for and active in the learning process (Grant, 2002).

Impact of ICT on Teacher-Educators and Student Teachers

1. It acts as the gateway to world of information and enables teachers to be updated.
2. For professional development and awareness of innovative trends in instructional methodologies, evaluation mechanism etc.
3. For effective implementation of certain student–centric methodologies such as project–based learning which puts the students in the role of active researches and technology becomes the appropriate tool.
4. It is an effective tool for information acquiring–thus students are encouraged to look for information from multiple sources and they are now more informed then before.

5. It has enabled better and swifter communication; presentation of ideas is more effective and relevant.
6. The dissemination of ideas to a larger mass now seems possible due to technology.
7. Student-teachers are transformed into self learners.
8. ICT creates awareness of recent methodologies and thus teacher educators feel empowered.

ICT Training Inputs for Teachers and Teacher Educators

For the successful implementation of ICT, teacher trainees, teachers and teacher-educators need to be trained in the following dimensions. The commercially available training programs are designed to provide exposure only to system software, some of the application software and the basics of internet.

1. *Awareness phase:* The input should be to make the teachers aware of the importance and possibilities of ICT–the current trends and future projections.
2. *Learning theories and technology integration:* Traditional and modern view of learning, shift from teaching to learning, constructivism, role of ICT in lifelong learning.
3. *Basic hardware skills:* Hands on experiences in operating (a) the PC and laptops. (b) storage devices. (c) input–output devices. (d) display devices.
4. *Understanding system software:* Features of desktop, starting an application, resizing windows, organizing files (Creating, editing, saving and renaming), switching between programs, copying etc.
5. *Using application/productivity software:* Word processing, spreadsheet, database, presentation, publishing, creation of Portable Document Format (PDF) files, test generation, data logging, image processing etc.
6. *Using multimedia:* Exposure to multimedia CD ROMs in different subject, installing programs, evaluating

CD ROMs, approaches to using CD ROMs, creating multimedia presentations.

7. *Using internet: e-mail, communities, forums, blogging, wiki:* subscription to mailing lists, e-mail and internet projects, web searching strategies (navigating, searching, selecting, and saving information) videoconferencing, designing web pages, freeware and shareware, evaluating website resources, virtual fieldtrips, learning opportunities using the web, and netiquette.
8. *Pedagogical application of ICT tools:* Specific use of application software in different subject, appropriate ICT tools and pedagogy, unit plan integrating ICT tools, approaches to managing ICT-based learning groups, assessment of learning, electronic portfolio and assessment rubrics, creating teacher and student support materials, supporting students with special needs.
9. *Introduction to open source software:* Concept, types, advantages, working on open sources application software.
10. *Social, legal, ethical and health issues:* Advantages and limitations of computer use, privacy violations, copyright infringement, plagiarism, computer security (hacking, virus, misuse, abuse and staying safe) healthy use (seating, light, sound, radiation, exercise)
11. *ICT for professional and personal productivity:* ICT for administration, record keeping, reporting and transfer of information, attendance, research, careers in computers and professional development opportunities.

As an advanced training website development, installation and use of server based applications, training in course management system, e-learning course content development using various authoring tools, audio/video/image editing, animation etc. can be introduced.

Teacher Educator's Initiatives

Whatever may be the inputs in the training and however well designed it is, the transformation can't be achieved without the leadership, commitment and initiatives of the teachers and teacher educators, both could take up initiatives like:

- Self-learning using the tutorials available on the net or print medium.
- Hiring an ICT expert by a group of teachers/teacher educators.
- Enrolling for online professionally development courses. There are many websites offering free training modules.
- Enrolling for the best commercially available ICT training programs.
- Coaching by a colleague-mentoring.
- Attending ICT training courses, seminars, conferences and workshops.
- Communities of teacher' collaborative groups to integrate ICT into their curriculum (same subjects, different subjects, same school/college, different school/ college).
- Online learning by means of videoconferencing, discussion forum, chat, blogging etc.
- Visiting institutions where the ICT is already being integrated.
- Action research trying out various models of technology integration and publishing the result of the same.
- Exploring the possibility of faculty exchange program to get placed in an organization where the ICT integration in already in place.
- Keeping up-to-date with the latest developments in ICT through journals, magazines, newspapers and the internet.
- Teacher educators modeling the ICT integration in their academic work.

- Planning and implementing ICT in-service training programs for schoolteachers-the best way to learn is to teach.
- Creating a pool of ICT competent past teacher trainees and involving them in the training programs.
- Designing and implementing self financing certificate course in ICT for in-service teachers.

CONCLUSION

UNESCO planning guide for ICT in teacher-education cities three key principles for effective ICT development in Teacher Education that were put forward by the Society for Information Technology and Teacher Education:

1. That technology should be infused into the entire teacher education programme, implying that ICT should not be restricted to a single course but needs to permeate in all courses in the programmes.
2. That Technology should be introduced in context. Accordingly, ICT application like word-processing, databases, spread-sheet and telecommunications should not be taught as separate topics rather encountered as the need arises in all courses of Teacher-education programmes.
3. That students should experience innovative technology supported learning environment in Teacher-education programmes. This requires that students should see their lecturers engaging in technology to present their subject their subjects utilizing power point or simulations in lectures and demonstrations. Students should also have the opportunity to use such applications in practical classes, seminars and assignments.

The application of these three principles will be a milestone towards effectively integrating ICT in Teacher-education.

13

Methods of Teaching Telugu : Regular and ODL Teacher Education Programmes

V. Hema Kameswari
Lecturer, St. Ann's College of Education for Women, Hyderabad

ABSTRACT

Due to globalization, liberalization society's demands are diversified. New work order has changed political economy. Many missions have launched both by the Government of India and Government of A.P. towards preparing professional and Humane Teachers. Some of them are - OBB, NCF-2005, NKC, SSA, RVM and NCR-2009, Right to Educations also enacted by the Government.

Conventional approaches give a lot of importance to direct teaching which is controlled by the curriculum and the teacher. The role of the teacher in acquisition model is that of facilitator. The new theory of language teaching is need-based intervention of the teacher where learners are encouraged instead of transmitting the content from the text book what is required is providing a variety of experimental programmes for transmitting well-defined curricular statements. It is also very important to create dynamic texts than static texts which are flexible in nature.

New approach deals with flexible learning methods for interacting with the learners in multiple ways. It should be in non-formal way. It should promote co-operation not competition where teachers exercise their role as democratic leader. Mothers (mother's talk) makes use of a language is organic communication.

> **"The aim of Teacher education should be to turn out true servants of people who will live and die for the country's freedom"**
>
> **– Gandhiji**

Teacher education programme is multiplex, multicultural. It sets body of knowledge, skills and understanding according to the needs of the public understanding not just in classrooms but beyond the classrooms.

Due to globalization, liberalization society's demands are diversified. New work order has changed political economy. Many missions have launched both by the Government of India and Government of A.P. towards preparing professional and Humane Teachers. Some of them are - OBB, NCF-2005, NKC, SSA, RVM and NCR-2009, Right to educations also enacted by the Government.

In order to account all these challenges and bring equity and equality in education there is a need to look into the modes of education. At present the demand of the day is to produce productive products, whether it may be the conventional or distance mode.

There is an urgent need to compare the structure curriculum framework, the transactional strategies, the output of both Conventional Vs Distance mode.

This study should be focused on the skills to be developed in the future generations. The traditional under both conventional and Distance mode is obsolete needs a face lift. This study may help to understand the position and nature of both the systems.

At present world needs competency based, task oriented, skillful, accommodative, humane citizens. This comparison may lead us to explore the criteria of the system, how such skilled learners could be produced, who could take the mission ahead.

This can be done by youth. As a representative of Andhra Pradesh to promote Telugu language and to put it into practice, in optimum level-I have selected the sub theme 'Regular and ODL Teacher education programmes since the language is a close companion to human beings.

Language is a bio-logically triggered of behaviour. It cannot be improved only through teaching or practice. The Teacher should take care of the above fact. They should give more emphasis on the construction of language by the learners. The language teaching should be modified from teaching to acquisition of language. It is a shift from behavioural model of teaching to constructive model.

Language Teaching is not totality of language facts but it is a system. It cannot be learned but it can be acquired. The teacher should make the student to perform various language skills effectively.

Teaching of language facilities not I-language but to deal with E-language, I-language means innate, internalized or individualistic language where as E-language refers to manifested form of language. The first one deals with mental aspect of world and the second one refers to the social aspect of it; tactic, knowledge, skill based approach.

Language is perceived as innate property of human mind not comes out from outside. Acquisition of language should take place none consciously. The learning rules of grammar we mean the learning process. A modern theory of language depends upon the grounds that the language should acquire through insightful theory construction.

Conventional approaches emphasized on the role of repetition in the process of learning a language but not on the recurrence which involves involuntary memory. Acquisition is a process of organic growth and it is not analogous to the brick laying process by internalizing cluster of language facts as a whole.

Conventional approaches give a lot of importance to direct teaching which is controlled by the curriculum and the teacher. The role of the teacher in acquisition model is that of facilitator. The new theory of language teaching is need-based intervention of the teacher where learners are encouraged instead of transmitting the content from the text book what is required is providing a variety of experimental programmes for transmitting well-defined curricular statements. It is also very important to create dynamic texts than static texts which are flexible in nature.

New approach deals with flexible learning methods for inter-acting with the learners in multiple ways. It should be in non-formal way. It should promote co-operation not competition where teachers exercise their role as democractic leader. Motherse (mother's talk) makes use of a language is organic communication.

National curriculum document recommends the incorporating of multiple intelligence theory conceived by Howard Gardener in teaching learning process. Vygotsky was far more of an interventionist in his view of the teacher's role. According to Vygotsky, social interaction plays a vital role in the learning process. He emphasizes the role of "shared language" in the development of thought and language which stands for social interaction. According to Vygotsky language is a very vital communicative system to develop human personalities so question arise in my mind which learner from which mode are fruitful in assimilation and enhancing their personality through frequent usage of language.

Looking into the curriculum of Telugu language teaching in conventional and distance modes an effort made to analyse the draw backs and revise the modular which will accelerate the process of Telugu language learning applicative skills.

As a primary research test now I am looking for Telugu language position, usage and status at 1st degree level both in conventional universities (Dual mode) and distance educational institutions. To study the quality input 1 prepared a questionnaire as a tool with following areas.

The quality input in:

1. The objectives of Telugu language Teaching of Both Modes (Regular and Distance mode)
2. The curriculum which has prescribed
3. The content in the Text book
4. The teaching learning process
5. Quality in teaching learning experiences
6. The evaluation procedure.

REFERENCES

1. Module for Language Teaching by SSA.
2. National Curriculum Framework for Teacher Education.

Theme–IV

In-service Training to Teacher Educators in ODL System

14

In-service Teacher Education Programmes—A Study on Dr. BRAOU

Chandrakala
Assistant Professor, Department of Education, Dr. BRAOU, Hyderabad
Dr. G. Paul Ratnakar
Assistant Professor, Department of Education, Dr. BRAOU, Hyderabad

ABSTRACT

Quality of Education is directly linked with quality of teacher. The Open Learning System (OLS) has earned a worldwide reputation for its productive programmes/courses, for its outstanding learning/teaching process through the self-learning programme materials and for the academic support it provides for its student. Up to 1950 there was no serious discussion on the quality of education and in those days it was commonly believed that teachers gave importance to their profession. Teaching profession involves dedication. Teaching profession is a part of teachers affective or emotional reaction to their experience in an educational setting. It can be seen as a part of learned in-service training to teacher educators in Open distance learning.

In educational process, a good and affective teacher occupies a place of tremendous importance. Teaching at present has made the work of the teacher more challenging and difficult. Instead of having concern for himself only with a few pattern of effective presentation of subject matter, the modern teacher's responsibility is to see that everything that goes on in the classroom is for all-round development of the child. The role of the teacher in nation building is universally recognized. According to crow and crow "A good teacher and the quality of his teaching has always been of paramount to a free man and to the society." Teacher pave the was for enlightened society. So, effective teachers do it effectively. An effective teacher may be understood as one who helps in a envelopment of basic skills, understanding, proper habits, desirable attitude, value adjustment of the students.

Introduction

Distance education or distance learning, is a field of education that focuses on the pedagogy, technology, and instructional system designs that aim to deliver education to students who are not physically "on site" in a traditional classroom or campus. It has been described as "a process to create and proved access to learning when the source of information and the learners are separated by time and distance, or both." In other word, distance e learning is the process of creating an educational experience of equal quality for the learner to best suit their needs outside the classroom. Distance education courses that require a physical on-site presence for any reason is considered a hybrid or blended courses of study. This emerging technology is becoming widely used in universities and institutions around the globe. With the recent trend of technological advance, distance learning is becoming more recognized for its potential in proving individualized attention and communication with students internationally. The most widely cited pedagogical theory of distance education is that of transactional distance.

Concept of Distance Education and Open Learning

One of the most significant developments in the field in the education during the last two decades has been the acceptance, spread and growth of distance education through open learning system in most parts of the world.

The terms distance education and open learning have been used in different contexts with some what different meanings. Distance has been defined as an educational process in which a significant proportion of the teaching is conducted by some removed in space and/or time from the learner. Distance education programmes have often used a combination of educational media, old and new, varying from print to broadcasts to audio and video recordings, and included opportunities for face-to-face study as well as learning from recorded material.

The term open learning has been used to refer to the process of making learning available to learners no matter who they are or where they wish to study. The term open has been taken to imply open access for students regardless of their previous qualifications or age. International experience shows that distance education and open learning tend to complement each other.

The term distance education is a fairly recent one, but the concept it expresses is 150 years old. It gained formal recognition in 1982 when the four decades old International Council for Correspondence Education (ICCE) changed its name to the International Council for Distance education (ICDE). This was an acceptance of the fact that distance education as no longer primarily associated with the printed word and had successfully incorporated the use of multi–media in the teaching-learning process.

Distance education is now internationally recognized and accepted as an alternative channel for providing broader access to education in a cost-effective manner; wider and diversified curricula and a means for continuing life-long education. Increasingly new categories of clients are seeking better education; the young who for one reason or the other are not able to join a college or university; adults who want to acquire a diploma or degree; professionals who want to keep pace with technological change; persons required to discharge responsibilities for which their formal education does not equip them; those who do not want to get uprooted from their environment and not want a disruption from their responsibilities at home and/or in their offices; and those who look for education at their door step. Many of these categories may not fit in with the normal admission criteria and find that their aspirations may not be fulfiled through the conventional system of education.

This is also a time of convergence between the worldwide need to extend and develop educational opportunities and the development of new communication technologies viz. sophisticated printing methods, audio based technology, video technologies; computer based technologies, and satellite communication, making it possible for learners to get access to the world's knowledge from the remotest and most inaccessible areas.

Objectives of Open Universities

The objectives of Distance Education at the tertiary level are :

- To provide an alternative cost-effective non-formal channel for tertiary education.
- To supplement the conventional university system and to reduce the pressure on it.
- To provide "second chance" education to those who have had to discontinue their formal education or could not join regular colleges or universities owing to social, economic and other constraints.
- To democratize higher education by providing access to large segments of the population, in particular the disadvantaged groups such as those living in remote and rural areas, including working people, women and other adults who wish to acquire and upgrade their knowledge and/or skills.
- To strengthen and diversify the degree, certificate and diploma courses related to employment and necessary for building the economy of the country on the basis of its natural and human resources.
- To provide continuing and life-long education to enrich the lives of the people.
- To provide an innovative system of university level education, which is flexible and open in terms of methods and pace of learning, combination of courses, eligibility for enrolment, age of entry, conduct of examination and operation of the programmes with a

view to promoting learning and encouraging excellence in new fields of knowledge.

Major Benefits of Use

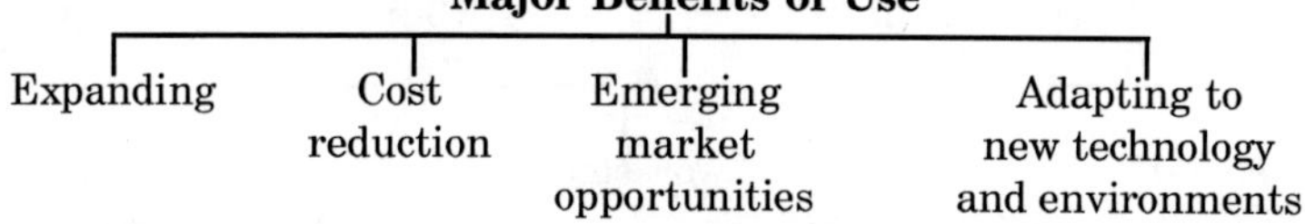

Distance education can reach underserved populations of students who cannot attend a school that offers the educational services they desire, perhaps because they live too far away.

Distance education can turn predication of content into a repeatable and durable learning tool that does not require as much infrastructure. As most material can be packaged in an easy to deliver "just-in-time" format, the expanding payroll of educational institutions becomes unnecessary. Distance education fuels the public's need for lifelong learning in education by providing access to learners not in the traditional age group. Educational institutions may adopt distance education as a mean to adapt to the rapid changes in technology being used in education today. In this way there are so many universities in the education field i.e., IGNOU, Dr. BRAOU, NALANDAOU, KOTAOU, MAHARASTRAOU, BHOJOU, MKOU, OSMANIA OU etc.

The Dr. B. R. Ambedkar Open University offering the programmes for In-service training to teachers in ODL system, like M.Ed., B.Ed., B.Ed (Special Education) and will soon launch the Certificate Programme in ECE and Certificate programme in Literacy and Community Development.

M.Ed. Programme

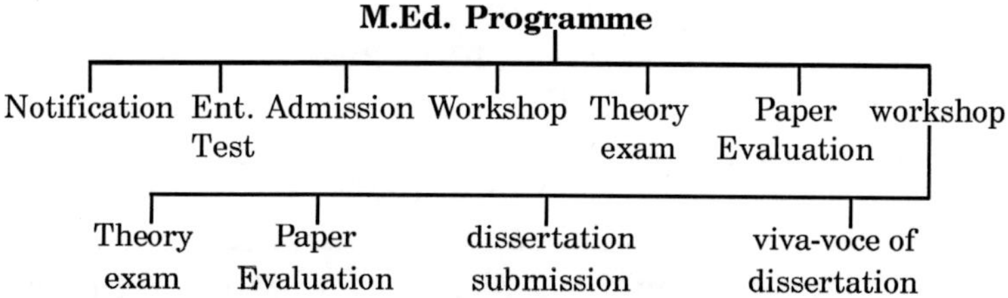

B.Ed. Programme

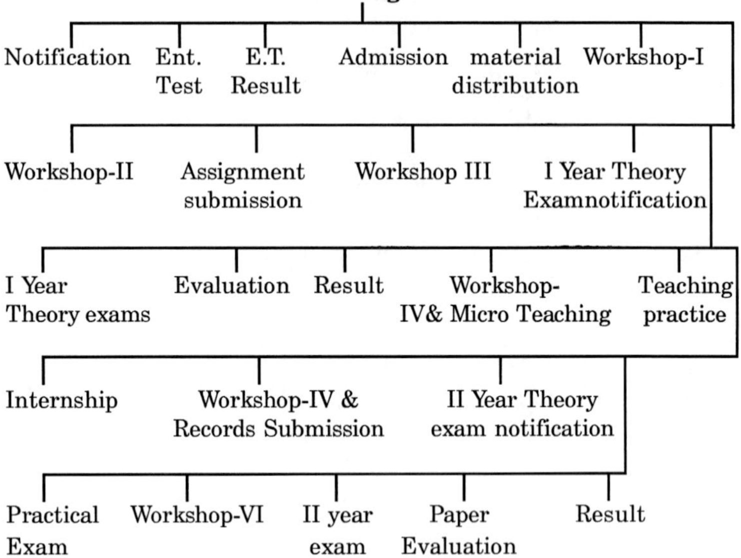

B.Ed. (Special Education) Programme

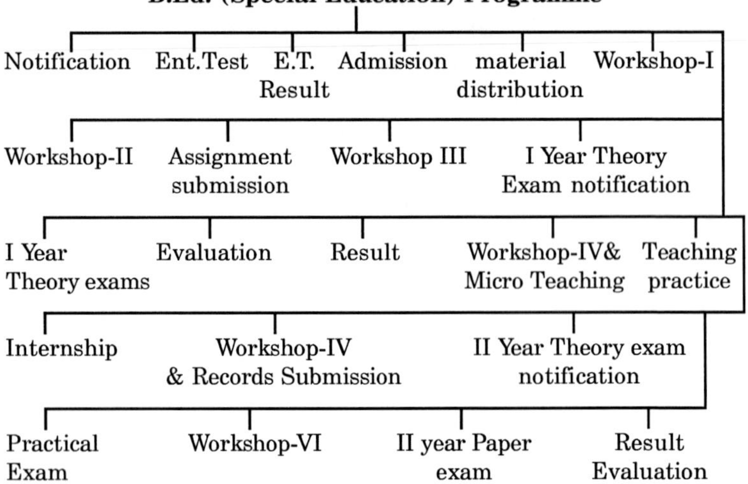

Supervision and Monitoring by the Department of Education for Every time

Sequence of activities and functions of the different branches involve in effective implementation of programme, like Student Service Branch, Marital Production, Examination Branch etc. These are helping to In-service trainees to gain the Certificates and the Academic Staff will develop the programme. Like Entrance Test, Admissions, Contact with Students, Observing and Monitoring and Evaluation of the Papers etc. Programme Centrers Activities are Academic Couselling, Workshops conducting, classrooms arrangement and Guidance etc. Coordinator will take care of the Programme Centre and Counsellors are taking the classess. All programme activities are happening only in Programme Centrers. In these days what ever happens here, overall Departments, Branches and Centrers are maintaining intercom relationship in between all together to have a done work/activities.

15

Components and Quality Enhancement of In-service B.Ed. Programme– A Study on SPMVV

Dr. G. Suneetha Bai
Assistant professor, Dept. of Education, SPMVV, Tirupati
Dr. T. G. Amuthavalli
Assistant professor, Dept. of Education, SPMVV, Tirupati

ABSTRACT

This study was intended to investigate the opinion of women teacher trainees on different components of In-service B.Ed teacher training programmes through distance education and to receive suggestions for improvement of the ongoing In-Service B.Ed. training proramme through distance education. Sample of the study consisted of 100 women teacher from Sri Padmavathi Mahila Visvavidyalayam, Tirupati in Andhra Pradesh. A questionnaire with 30 questions related to 10 different components of teacher training was prepared by the investigators. The results of the study revealed that all the learners expressed that micro teaching practice helped in their classroom teaching and to develop their teaching skills. Further all the learners are satisfied with admission process and programme instructions, resources like delivering lessons, discussions, feed back and supervision of demonstrations provide by the resource persons. 32% of in-service teacher trainees expressed difficulty in writing lesson plans. 56% of learners felt that lesson plans are very lengthy.

Introduction

Open and Distance Learning (ODL) takes place when a teacher and students are separated by Physical distance and technology. Open and distance learning has emerged as a powerful instrument for augmenting opportunities for higher education. In fact, open and distance learning is the only alternative to meet the increasing demand for lifelong continuing education and rising aspiration of people for better quality of life.

Distance education approach provides to a great deal of opportunity both in terms of qualitative improvement and quantitative expansion for in-service education and training of teachers at all levels. This is helpful for training large number of teachers with limited time and also it is employed in the field of teacher training programmes correspondence education, independent study, distance teaching and learning, open learning and education, self learning and study, distance study etc. It promotes the professional growth of teachers where the physical contact and direct participation of teachers in their in-service education programme is not possible Distance education facilitates the in-service training (or) Orientation of teachers by providing required facilities at their doorsteps.

Distance education may be defined as a mode of education in which instruction is provided without any contact between teachers and students. Today distance education employs an integrated combination of means such television, radio, audio cassettes, computers and printed materials.

Generally, the idea of professional education through the Distance Education mode was mooted by the report of the education commission (1964-66). On teacher education programmes through Distance Education, the education commission had visualized its major role in terms of in-service training for teachers at different stages. The National Policy on Education (1968) focused on promotion of teacher education programmes through correspondence courses. A similar stand has been taken by the National Policy on Education (1986), regarding the role of Distance Education in the promotion of education of various kinds of in-service persons especially teachers at the primary, secondary and higher education stages. USSR (1967-1971) had recommended in favour of adoption of correspondence courses for in-service teachers.

The comparison between curriculum frameworks of distance education with that of the face-to-face training programmes has created confusions regarding role perceptions of trainees in distance education situations. Mostly they perceive their role as mechanical in obtaining a degree or certificate. It is very challenging to develop an appropriate role perception of trainees as distance education learners, especially in the context of managing self-study, activities, Practicum, group activities, evaluation and feedback for self development etc. The training curriculum of Distance Education programmes must have scope for proper orientation of trainees regarding these aspects.

In-service teacher education programmes aims at upgrading professional competence of teachers and acquainting them with new knowledge and skills that would facilitate the acquisition and use of new knowledge, whenever curriculum changes take place, it is imperative that a comprehensive plan of in-service education be developed and implemented. This would enable the teachers to understand the curriculum changes both in letter and spirit. In-service programmes have to be organized to re-orient and update teachers competencies and prepare them for further professional growth especially in terms of reflection, innovation and commitment. These programmes would enable student teachers to learn how to lead a change and at the same time be a part of it. In-service education has an added impact when supported by teachers' own self directed life long learning. This symbiosis resulting into teachers becoming reflective practitioners.

The most important issue for school reformers to address is how to provide high quality in-service training programmes through distance education that are necessary to produce effective schools particularly for by increasing the effectiveness of teachers. The present investigation tried to survey the opinions of women teacher trainees on different components of in-service B.Ed. teacher training programme through distance education and to receive suggestions for improvement of the on going in-service B.Ed. training programme through distance education and to give suggestions to teacher educators to Quality enhancement in In-service teacher training programmes.

Objectives

1. To find out the opinion of trainees on different components of In-service B.Ed. teacher training programme through distance education.
2. To receive suggestions for improvement of the ongoing In-service B.Ed. teacher training programme through distance education.

Method of the Study

Normative survey method was suitable for the present study.

Sample Selected

Sample consisted of 100 in-service women teacher trainees of Directorate of Distance Education from Sri Padmavati Mahila Visvavidyalayam (Women's University), Tirupati in Andhra Pradesh were selected randomly for the study.

Tool Used

A questionnaire with 30 Yes or No type questions related to 10 different components of in-service B.Ed. teacher training programme through distance education was prepared by the investigators and was used for the collection of data.

Statistical Techniques Used

The collected data was analysed using simple percentage and description.

Results and Conclusion

Objective-1

To find out the opinion of trainees on different

components of in-service B.Ed. teacher training programme through distance education.

Table 1
Percentage of Responses on Different Components of In-service B.Ed. Teacher Training through Distance Education

Sl. No.	*Components*	*Percentage of Responses*	
		Yes	*No*
1.	Microteaching Practice	100	0
2.	Admission Process and Programme instructions	100	0
3.	Study Material	80	20
4.	Lesson Plan Writing	32	68
5.	Lesson Plan length	56	44
6.	Assignments and record works	52	48
7.	Resource Persons	100	0
8.	Prior Preparation for personal contact programme	60	40
9.	Accommodation during personal contact programme	80	20
10.	Cooperation of the administrators during practice teaching	90	10

Table-1 shows that percentage of responses and these indicates the following findings :

1. All the learners expressed that micro teaching practice helped in their classroom teaching and to develop their teaching skills.
2. All the learners are satisfied with the admission process and programme instructions.
3. 80% of teacher trainees expressed that study material is easily understandable remaining 20% felt difficulty in understanding the material.
4. 32% of teacher trainees expressed difficulty in writing lesson plans.
5. 56% learners felt that lesson plans are very lengthy and 44% teacher trainees satisfied with lesson plans.
6. 52% of teacher trainees had family problems/ constraints to complete the assignments and record works.

7. All the learners were satisfied with resources like, delivering lessons, Discussions feed back and supervision of demonstrations etc., provided by the resource persons.
8. 60% of learners could not go through the study material before personal contact programe because of professional and social responsibilites.
9. 80% of women teacher trainees expressed that Hostel and accommodation facilities during contact programme classes were very poor.
10. 90% of learners expressed that they had received good cooperation from the Headmasters/Principals/ Headmistress during teaching practice.

Objective-2

To receive suggestions for improvement of the ongoing In-service B.Ed. training programme through Distance Education.

Suggestions by the In-service B.Ed. teacher trainees to improve the ongoing in-service teacher training programme :

1. Teacher educators should try to use innovative methods of teaching.
2. Almost all the teacher trainees suggested providing computer literacy and techniques of teaching different types of learners.
3. Effective use of information and communication technology in in-service teacher training institutions can prove the quality. Teacher educators should be trained to use the technological innovations to make their teaching more suitable in the modern context.
4. Community education, work education and computer education should be given more scope and weightage.
5. Obsolete course content be reduced and repetition of content units be deleted.
6. Integration of pedagogy and content should be visible in classes conducted by teacher educators.
7. Mother tongue should be used as medium of instruction.

8. One full paper should taught by one teacher only.
9. Training programmes should be evaluated by authorities so that further changes can be done in these training programmes.
10. Curriculum should be reconstructed according to the needs of the society and learners.

Suggestions to teacher educators for quality enhancement :

1. There is an urgent need for a comprehensive review of the curriculum of in-service B.Ed. teacher training programme curriculum should be more dynamic and flexible and should incorporated the neglected aspects like physical and yogic education.
2. The training curriculum of Distance Education programmes must have scope for proper orientation of trainees regarding the aspects like self study activities, Practicum's, group activities, evaluation and feed back for self development.
3. Teacher educators should use approaches like activity method, demonstration etc., teacher educators should follow the same method of teaching as they expect from the student teachers in the real classroom situations.
4. Lecture method may be avoided and demonstration-cum-discussion method may be followed.
5. More emphasis should be given to the strategies of teaching.
6. Teacher educators should continuously refresh their content knowledge particularly before they go to the class.
7. Teacher educators must regularly use ICT aids and other teaching aids.
8. The consortium approach should also be evaluated optimize resource utilizations at D.E. Institutions level as well as at the traditional institutions level.
9. It should be linked with a holistic framework of the future of the teacher education system.

10. Fresh thinking among teacher educators and experts of Distance Educations is very essential for quality improvement of Distance Education teacher education programme.
11. Distance education should evolve specific strategies for quality improvement keeping in view local specificity trainees back ground, availability of resources and support from external agencies/institutions.

REFERENCES

1. Dulumoni Goswani (2007), Student Teachers' Perception of Quality Teacher Education, Anweshika, Indian Journal of Teacher Education, Vol.4, No.1, NCTE, New Delhi.
2. Government of India (1968), National Policy on Education, New Delhi, MHRD.
3. Government of India (1996), Education Commission Report, New Delhi.
4. NCERT (1971), Education and Development, Report of the Education Commission Report, 1964-66, New Delhi.
5. NCERT (2002), Indian Educational Abstracts, January 2002, Volume-2, Number-1, New Delhi.
6. Talwar, M.S. (2003), Quality Management in Teacher Education-By Teacher Educators Cultural and Educational Forum (TECEF), Bangalore.

16

In-service Education—Need and Importance

Dr. R. Ramudu
Lecturer, S. K.University College of Education, Anantapur, AP
K. Adilakshmi
Deputy Librarian, Zilla Grandhalaya Samstha, Anantapur, AP

ABSTRACT

Teacher education programme is consists of the facts, theories, principles, methods, techniques, philosophy etc. concerning the teaching profession. It aims at providing knowledge of theories, principles, law, facts and others regarding teaching activity to the prospective teachers who enter into the filed and apply the given knowledge in their real professional life. But after a period of time, their knowledge lags behind as knowledge in the fieled of teacher education is increasing day-by-day. One finds changes in society, its values, norms etc. The field of technology is increasing day-by-day. Again after a period of time, the teacher forgets whatever was taught him during his training period. Thus teacher Education is a life long process. Life long learning should be the motto of every teacher. If he stops learning, he degenerates.

Continuous learning is essential in order to improve the quality of teachers and educational system, as "the strength of an educational system must largely depend upon the quality of its teachers. However, enlightened the aims, however up-to-date and generous the equipment however efficient the administration, value of the children is determined by the teachers." While in the words of H.G. Wells, "Teacher is the maker of history. The history of a nation is written in its schools and the schools cannot be very different from the quality of their teachers." Rabindra Nath Tagore has rightly remarked: "A teacher can never truly teach unless he is still learning himself. A lamp can never light another lamp unless it continues to burn its own flame. The teacher who has come to the end of his subject, who has no living traffic with his knowledge, but merely repeats his lesions to his students, can only load their minds. He cannot quicken them. Truth not only must inform but also must inspire".

In-service Teacher Education

The idea of In-service education has emerged to take care of the need of some sort of provision which may make the teachers up-to-date with respect to the knowledge of his subject of teaching, methods and techniques, innovative ideas in each sphere of his academic life.

In-service education is continuing education of teachers and other educators. In commences after initial professional education is over it which leads to the improvement of professional competence of educators throughout their careers. It is designed to promote the continuous professional development by providing planned and systematic instruction within an educational setting. It denotes planned efforts to promote the professional growth and development of teachers. It includes all those courses and activities in which a serving teacher may participate for the purpose of extending his professional knowledge, interest or skill. Teacher education institutions can extend their services out side their premises through Extension services the visits of their staff for consultations, lectures, or conducting courses, or through lending of books and equipments. As these are extended beyond the physical limits of an institution and aim at prompting the professional growth of teachers by adding to their repertoire of skills and knowledge, they are called extension services.

Definitions of In-service Training

(1) M. B. Buch, "In-service education is thus a programme of activities aiming at the continuing growth of teachers and educational personnel in-service". It is the sponsoring and pursuing of activities which bring new insight, growth, understanding and co-operative

practices to the members of teaching profession and arouse them to action to improve themselves in every possible manner. It include all activities and experiences participated in by the educational personnel in education during their services. These activities are planned and organized by various agencies to help the educators to improve as persons and to mature as professionals.

(2) Cane (1969), In-service Teacher Education is "all those activities and courses which aim at enhancing and strengthening the professional knowledge, interest and skills of serving teacher." According to this definition In-service has the following significant components:

(i) Professional knowledge.

(ii) Skill aspect not only what he is to do but also why.

(iii) Attitude towards profession.

(iv) A code of conduct on ethics of profession.

(v) Professional skills, such as–administrative skills, management skills, organizing skills, leadership skills etc.

(vi) Interest towards teaching profession.

(vii) Courses meaning the provision of such experiences based on sound pedagogical and empirical considerations as are well related to research findings.

(viii) Activities such as seminars, symposium, workshops, discussion, brain storming etc.

In-service Teacher Education is primarily meant for regular serving teachers. It includes such new courses whose fruitfulness and validity have been tested. In subjects the serving teachers to such activities which may enhance their professional knowledge, interest and attitude so that they may be able to maximize their pupil's learning and themselves derive maximum inner satisfaction and sense of achievement.

Improtance of In-service Education for Teachers

(1) *The University Educations Commission Report (1949)*— It is said, "It is extraordinary that our school teachers learn all of whatever subject they teach before

reaching the age of 24 or 25 and then all their further education is left to experiences which is another name for stagnation. We must realize that experiment before reaching its fullness and the teachers to keep alive and fresh become a learner from time to time.

(2) *The Secondary Education Commission Report*—It highlighted importance of in-service education in these words – "However, excellent the progamme of teacher training may be, it does not by itself produce an excellent teacher. It can only anger the knowledge, skills and attitudes which will enable the teacher to begin his task with a reasonable degree of confidence and with the minimum amount of experience".

(3) A teacher has to play different roles of which each requires different kind of knowledge, attitudes, skill etc.

(4) After a period of time, a teacher generally forget whatever he is taught in his pre-service training.

(5) The enthusiasm and morale of a teacher generally decreases as the time passes.

Need for In-service Education

(1) *Education of the Educator*–It continues throughout his professional career in a planned manner.

(2) *Educational Extension*–It contributes to the qualitative improvement of Education.

(3) *The Pre-service Training Provided to the Teacher*–It is not adequate for the rest of his professional career for discharging his duties efficiently.

(4) *Changing Areas of Human Endeavour*–These changes demand corresponding changes in education and the educator. All these new developments, innovations and changes necessitate corresponding changes to be brought about in educational objectives, curricula, textual content, teaching methods, instructional materials without delay so that education remains dynamic, up-to-date and responsive. Educational extension prepares in-service teachers and other

educators for bringing these required changes in education.

(5) *Improvement of Competence*–In order to bring about changes in education, corresponding to the changes in other related areas, it is necessary to improve the competence of the teacher in terms of his knowledge skills, interests, and aptitudes as an essential means of improving education.

(6) *Need of change*–In addition to mass scales changes to be brought about in Education from time to time, individual teachers and small groups of school may feel the need of bringing about certain changes and aspire to solve certain specific academic problems. Educational extension is capable of helping these individuals or groups in meeting their academic needs and in solving their academic problems.

Objectives of In-service Education

(1) To provide incentive to the teachers to function more efficiently.

(2) To help the teachers to know their problems and to solve them by pooling their resources and wisdom.

(3) To help the teachers to employ more effective methods of teaching.

(4) To help the teachers to get acquainted with modern techniques in education.

(5) To broaden the mental outlook of the teachers.

(6) To up grade the teachers knowledge and understanding of the contents.

(7) To increase the professional efficiency of the teacher.

CONCLUSION

A large scale and coordinated programme of continuing education for teachers of all levels should be organized by university pre-education institutions and pre-associations.

Visualizing our limits of resources, it is advisable to arrange for each teacher in initial stages a programme at the rate of 3 months continuing education in every five years of completed service.

A fundamental policy may be evolved at national level to make adequate provision to involve every teacher in their professional growth. In India, primary level teachers by and large, have not availed of such facility of continuing education in the past. Something concrete must be done for them.

The NCERT has suggested that every state should prepare a three-tier plan of continuing education. The first tier will consist of teacher education followed by the second tier of the headmasters and secondary school teachers who will be trained by key persons trained in first tier. Lastly, the third tier consisting of primary school teachers will have to trained by both the first and second tier trainers.

To meet the needs of teachers belonging to different categories the programme of continuing education should be varied in nature. Planning of continuing education should follow a comprehensive approach based on understanding of needs of schools, needs of teachers and problem developments in the near future. Realistic in their approached the organizers should expect gradual changes in participating teachers.

There is need of developing a theoretical framework of continuing education through deeper thinking and pooling of ideas. At present it is considered as a mixture of adult education, teacher education extension education and continuing education etc. and has ultimately lost its entity. An effort may be made to set up independent centers of continuing education.

REFERENCES

1. Amidon, Edmund J. and Hough, John B. (1967), Interaction Analysis Theory, Research and Application, London: Addison Wisely Publishing Company.
2. Andesron, Edmund J. and Hunter, Eligabeth (1967), Improving the Teaching analysis of classroom Verbal Interaction, New York: Halt Rinehart and Winston, Inc.,
3. Buch, M.B. and Santhanam, M.R. (1972), Communication in Classroom, CASW Faculty of Education and Psychology, M.S. University of Baroda, Baroda-2.

Theme–V

Regular and ODL Teacher Education Programmes

17

E-learning for Innovative Learning

Dr. P. Lakshminarayana
Head Master, MPUP School, Namala, C.K. Palli (Md), Anantapur
Dr. V. Govinda Reddy
Principal, Sri Sairam College of Education, Pondicherry

ABSTRACT

Change is the key element for the twenty first century that poses many challenges and enormous pressure on our daily life, work and society. Political, economical, social and technological environments are changing significantly and rapidly. Information and Communication Technologies (ICT) transform all aspects of education and Distance Education (DE), which is a rapidly growing segment. The advent of the Internet as a means of information access and distribution and the explosive growth of the World Wide Web (Web) have transformed distance teaching from a broadcast mode to an interactive one. Faculty and librarians are all at the crossroads and being pressured to increase their productivity and to change instructional strategies to accommodate changes and educational reforms.

Educational reforms which have been implemented in several countries in the last ten years have assigned to teachers a central role in the improvement of education in schools. Teacher education became, then, one of the most important issues in the reformist agenda. At the same time there seems to be an agreement among politicians, media agents and the population in general that having qualified teachers in all classrooms is the surest way to improve education.

Quality teacher education looks for quality performance. It should be recognized that advances in education depend largely on the qualification, ability of the teaching staff in general and on the human, pedagogical and technical qualities of the individual teacher (status of Teachers, ILO, 1966).

Furthermore, there is a general expectation that responsibility for preparing qualified and competent teachers rests primarily with teacher education programs at higher education institutions. This means that teacher educators are now assumed to be the spearheads in educational reforms.

What is E-learning?

As technology continues to change at a rapid pace, e-learning has become an important priority of corporate education. E-learning is a term used to describe using computer technology to deliver instructional material for learning. Content may be delivered by web-based training, computer-based learning, virtual classrooms, and digital classrooms (Ashmalla, Mohamed, and Ghobashy, 2001; Shankar, 2007). Various devices may also be used to deliver training such as workspaces, portable computers, cell phones, Palm Pilots, and iPods.

"E-learning combines improved computer capabilities, improved telecommunications infrastructures and improved pedagogical techniques to improve training offerings cost-effectively" (Grollman and Cannon, 2003, p. 45).

Approaches of E-learning

E-learning is frequently discussed in the context of synchronous, asynchronous, or blended method learning. The choice of method depends on the content and speed required for learning.

Synchronous Learning Approach: Synchronous learning stands for an instructor-led, online virtual classroom that occurs in "real-time." Trainers and students "meet" at a specified time in a virtual classroom and are able to communicate directly with one another. Examples of this include: virtual classrooms, audio/video conferencing, Internet telephony, and two-way live satellite broadcasts of lectures to students in a classroom (Bachman, 2000).

Asynchronous Learning Approach: It is more flexible in

that it does not require simultaneous participation of all learners and instructors. Asynchronous learning allows people to learn at anytime, anywhere, at their own convenience. This can include just-in-time training where a person gets exactly the training he or she needs to perform a task, when they need it. Asynchronous learning usually uses multimedia to make learning more interactive and engaging for learners. Examples of this include: self-paced courses via the Internet or CD-ROM, interactive tutorials, videotaped classes, streamed audio/video Web presentations, Q and A mentoring, online chats and discussion groups, and e-mail and listserves (Bachman, 2000; Zhang and Nunamaker, 2003).

Blended Learning Approach: Many institutions are now using technology blended with more traditional training methods for their employees (Pulley, 2005). Blended learning can be defined as using a combination of face-to-face and online media for learning. A blended approach to learning allows instructors to use self-paced instruction, along with live collaborative teaching. Some people benefit more from a blended delivery method than e-learning alone because they are able to have direct human contact (Brodsky, n.d). An example of the blended approach might include combining extensive e-learning modules with online support, collaboration, and coaching. A specific example would be a institution having interactive training sessions that allow employees to engage in hands-on practice after listening to presentations, as e-learning continues to grow, collaborative learning and interaction among users will likely be more successfully blended into the learning process (Grollman and Cannon, 2003).

Innovative Learning Techniques (ILT)

A. Internet: The Internet as a medium of learning is explored to the maximum for the creative use and positive impact of such knowledge on the learning process. Topics from recent advances in the subject are allocated to them. Through Internet search, the students acquire the latest know how on the assigned topics and compile the projects in the form of a brochure. Web-based Instruction (WBI) is defined broadly as any form of innovative approach for delivering instruction to a remote audience in which the Web is included as a tool (Relan and Gillani, 1997). Presently, several Web sites have been developed to provide learners with access to instructional resources from a distance. However, Hill (1996) noted that, most course-based or learning sites simply post course materials. In such instances, use of the Web falls far short of the potential this medium affords. According to Casey (1998), currently used Web models of learning can be identified as one of the followings:

1. *The Web as Source of Information:* This is the simplest use of the Web. It is used as a convenient place to store supporting information for traditionally offered courses.
2. *The Web as Electronic Book:* Many institutions have moved to use the Web to present information in a more structured way for teaching process. Students use the screen to read materials, activate multimedia demonstrations, and take self-correcting quizzes or other activities. The course material is mostly factual information, which is to be learned from the Web page and any accompanying media. There is no interaction between teacher and the students through the Web.
3. *The Web as Teacher:* Some Web-based courses include some form of personal communication between students and other students via the use of e-mail and perhaps chat rooms.
4. *The Web as a Communication Medium between Teacher and Students:* In this model, students learn from the teacher but "through" the Web and not "from" the Web. Thus, the Web acts as the communication medium for the necessary interaction. A model such as these aims to mirror a face-to-face learning environment, within which the students will be able to establish some form of human relationship with the teacher. (Ruksasuk, 1999). According to Reeves (1997), the WBI has a rich mix of media

features and the pedagogical dimensions to deliver. The aim of Web-based education must surely be to develop a model, which will enable a relatively large proportion of the student population to learn relatively easily and successfully (Casey, 1998).

B. Computer-assisted Learning (Learning Through CD-ROM): The opportunities associated with the development of computer-based technology in contributing to effective science education have grown exponentially within the past decade. The multimedia software available on CD-ROM plays a powerful role with applications in labs and lectures, tutorials and project work.

C. Seminars: To have interaction, weekly seminars are held and all the students are required to participate actively. The best speaker of the seminar from the entire batch is given an award. The awards are given to inculcate a competitive spirit among the students and bring the best out of the students.

D. Virtual Laboratories: Virtual laboratories detail the preparation, essential equipment, and method relevant to the practical and students then actively perform experiments themselves with simulated responses. Virtual laboratory presents a range of equipment on-screen and may offer a very high degree of interactivity. Training through audiovisual aids can play an important role in medical education.

E. Students as Project Coordinators: The department inculcates leadership qualities in students. The students actively participate as coordinators of the on-going departmental research projects, by which they are encouraged.

F. Teleconferencing: It is a new mixed model approach for DE combining satellite teleconferencing with hands-on activity session. It was developed to adjust for many of the disadvantages associated with DE and traditional in person training. The mixed model used live teleconference speakers, video clips, interactive call-in sessions and local sessions.

G. Telematic Education: Enables students to access teaching programmes and learning materials at a more flexible time, place and pace, and results in many flexible learning opportunities. Quiz -after all the above techniques, the most encouraging one could be the conducting quiz for the students at various rounds (six). The first round, consisting of question-answers, is based on simple recall of factual information. Rounds II and III, consisting of Jumbled Words, Multiple Choice Questions (MCQs) and Graphs and Flow Diagrams to indicate missing links are based on interpretation of information from charts, graphs, or flow diagrams or interpretation from two concepts that have a relationship. Rounds IV, V and VI, having Match the Following, Ascending Order, Trace the Path and Rapid-Fire Questions are based on testing primarily the application of knowledge to the solution of a specific problem and the fitting together of a variety of elements into a meaningful whole. The quiz conducted for students inculcates in them team spirit, leadership, better organizing abilities and interest and better comprehension of the subject. The Quizzes help in improving memory power, scientific nomenclature, and vocabulary and active learning through integrative reasoning, which helps in improving intellectual power.

Advantages and Disadvantages

e-Learning advantages and disadvantages are important to consider when making instructional and learning decisions. Many organizations and institutions provide different forms of training and instruction to their employees or learners. Typically they provide needed training by sending people to school, holding in-house training classes, or providing manuals and self-study guides. In some situations it is advantageous for them to use e-learning or other forms of e-learning instead of the traditional training. Other times it is disadvantageous. As with anything else, there are benefits and limitations, as well as pros and cons. There are many advantages to online and computer-based learning when compared to traditional face-to-face courses and lectures. There are a few disadvantages as well.

Advantages of E-learning

- Class work can be scheduled around personal and professional work.

- Reduces travel cost and time to and from school.
- Learners may have the option to select learning materials that meets their level of knowledge and interest.
- Learners can study wherever they have access to a computer and Internet.
- Self-paced learning modules allow learners to work at their own pace.
- Flexibility to join discussions in the bulletin board threaded discussion areas at any hour, or visit with classmates and instructors remotely in chat rooms.
- Different learning styles are addressed and facilitation of learning occurs through varied activities.
- Development of computer and Internet skills that are transferable to other facets of learner's lives.
- Successfully completing online or computer-based courses builds self-knowledge and self-confidence and encourages students to take responsibility for their learning.

Disadvantages of E-learning

- Unmotivated learners or those with poor study habits may fall behind.
- Lack of familiar structure and routine may take getting used to.
- Students may feel isolated or miss social interaction.
- Instructor may not always be available on demand.
- Slow or unreliable Internet connections can be frustrating.
- Managing learning software can involve a learning curve.
- Some courses such as traditional hands-on courses can be difficult to simulate.

Knowing e-learning advantages and disadvantages helps with learning software selection as well as online distance learning programs structure and selection. It is important to know the merits and demerits of e-learning to make a decision.

The vast movement towards e-learning is clearly motivated by the many benefits it offers. However much e-learning is praised and innovated, computers will never completely eliminate human instructors and other forms of educational delivery.

Advantages of E-learning to the Trainer or Organization

Some of the most outstanding advantages to the trainer or organization are:

- Reduced overall cost is the single most influential factor in adopting e-learning. The elimination of costs associated with instructor's salaries, meeting room rentals, and student travel, lodging, and meals are directly quantifiable. The reduction of time spent away from the job by employees may be the most positive offshoot.
- Learning times reduced, an average of 40 to 60 per cent, as found by Brandon Hall (Web-based Training Cookbook, 1997, p. 108).
- Increased retention and application to the job averages an increase of 25 per cent over traditional methods, according to an independent study by J.D. Fletcher (Multimedia Review, Spring 1991, pp. 33-42).
- Consistent delivery of content is possible with asynchronous, self-paced e-learning.
- Expert knowledge is communicated, but more importantly captured, with good e-learning and knowledge management systems.
- Proof of completion and certification, essential elements of training initiatives, can be automated.

Teacher Eduation for the Future

In my view, teacher education - rather than teacher training - needs to change in the near future. Some experts say it is too late to begin the changes, as we need new competencies in teaching right now. However, if teacher education follows its best tradition, and it remains practical, flexible and child-centred, there is a hope that the next generation of learners will get the support and skills they need in life during their schooling years from their own teachers.

The need of a generation of teachers who aim to develop learners instead of teaching them, who help their pupils to become independent (learning to learn), who provide students with motivation and interest for life-long learning and urge them to become autonomous learners, is essential in the education of the future.

REFERENCES

1. Anderson, J. and Glen. A., (2003), Building Capacity of Teachers/ Facilitators in Technology-Pedagogy Integration for Improved Teaching and Learning [Online]. Available from UNESCO Bangkok at: http://www.unescobkk.org/fileadmin/user_upload/ict/ebooks/ICTBuidling_Capacity/BuildingCapacity.pdf [Accessed 9 April 2009]
2. Barron, D.D. (1990), The Use of Distance Education in United States Library and Information Science. History and Current Perspectives. Education for Information. 8, 325- 339.
3. Bothma, Theo J.D. and Snyman Retha (MMM) (2000), Web-Supported Teaching in the Department of Information Science at the University of Pretoria: A case study, paper presented in 66th IFLA Council and General Conference, Jerusalem, Israel, 13–18 Aug., 2000.
4. Brine, Alan and Feather, John (2002), Supporting skills development – LTSN-ICS, paper presented in 68th IFLA Council and General Conference Bangkok, Thailand, 18 – 24 Aug., 2002.
5. Casey, D. (1998), Learning "From" or "Through" the Web: Models of Web Based Education.
6. Communications of the IIMA 78, 2005, Volume 5, Issue 4.
7. Natarajan M., Innovative Teaching Techniques for Distance Education.
8. Shuleman, L. S. (2004), The wisdom of practice: essays on teaching and learning to teach. San Francisco, Jossey-Bass, pp.1-14.

18

How to Teach in a Changing World?

Dr. Najma Unnisa
Associate Professor, Ghulam Ahmed college of Education, Hyderabad.

ABSTRACT

The rate of expansion of knowledge appears to be increasing and technology has enhanced access to information worldwide. Education for the new millennium therefore needs to enhance individual's ability to assimilate, evaluate and apply the available information. Indeed globalization which is affecting the economy, culture and information, the internalization of relations and the increasing mobility of individuals, a complete revolution in communication media and the massive advent of computerization into daily life and into the world of work represent a challenge and an opportunity to the education system. This globalization in the present century calls upon the teachers to change their roles to meet the future challenges and demands of the society. Hence the author in the present paper throws light on the radical change in the role of the teacher in future due to the impact of ICT.

Education in the modern age seeks to preserve, transmit and advance knowledge, and is committed to bring a change for the betterment of society. The importance of education lies in the fact that it is considered as a power full instrument of social change and progress as has been underlined by various experts, committees and commission in India and abroad.

The hallmark of the present century is the knowledge explosion and hence there is an urgent need for the teachers to equip themselves with the latest developments in their areas of specialization.

A Profession with Competing Demands

There are nearly 60 million teachers around the world today. They are also up against competition in his/her own field. Following the development of information services and new modes of communication; the teacher has lost his/her kind of monopoly as a supplier of knowledge. Consequently teaching and learning are no longer a protected area of competence of the teaching profession, but are gradually opening to other private or public sectors. New teaching and learning theories are challenging the teaching capacity of large number of educators who have been trained and who practice traditional approaches to education. New ways of acquiring knowledge and new delivery system threaten the teaching profession, such as multimedia, including CD-ROMS, with sophisticated devices for self-learning at one's own pace. This means that we are already in a world where the teaching profession will require radical adaptations to new skills and new demands.

Some have already predicted that the teachers will disappear due to the advent of these new possibilities. It is unlikely, but the role of the teacher will, on the other hand, evolve and become perfectly adapted to the new skins and new needs.

New Tasks (Teaching and ICT)

Finally globalization, by relying heavily on New Information Technology (NIT's) generates additional demands for the teacher's skills. The important technologies in education that made the communication revolution and information age a challenging era for educators are:

1. Computer.
2. Artificial intelligence.
3. Computer Assisted Instruction (CAI).
4. CD-ROM.
5. Dial access.
6. Educational T.V.
7. Edu-sat (Educational Satellites).

8. E- Mail.
9. Tele conferencing.
10. Tele lecture.
11. Tele tutorial.
12. Tele seminar.
13. Video.
14. Interactive video.
15. Video conferencing.
16. Digital resource.
17. Virtual universities.
18. Internet.

Changes in the Schools

The National Curriculum Framework (2000 AD) prepared by NCERT has observed, "That revolution in new technologies constitutes a fundamental challenge converting information society into knowledge society". It further states that, "new technologies have tremendous potentials to revolutionize education, dramatically transforming schools".

The following changes are expected on account of use of ICT:

1. Ending monopoly of formal education and formal schools.
2. Transforming existing educational provisions.
3. Influencing globalization of education.
4. Changing the existing curricular programme.
5. Bringing a new generation learning material.
6. Encouraging networking of schools.
7. Planning education in an electronic environment.
8. Making computer as an integral part of the schooling process and not merely a subject of study.
9. Shifting traditional learning environment to a climate of values that encourage exploration, problem solving, and decision making.
10. Replacing didactic classroom teaching to participating, decentralized and interactive learning.

11. Changing traditional instructional method to strategies that unify knowledge.
12. Replacing mastery of fixed body of knowledge to understanding a web of relationship between parts of a whole.
13. Searching for pattern and connection in place of linear sequential reasoning.

When these tremendous changes occurs then what could be the suitable method to teach in the future. Here I am mentioning a few methods that could be the most suitable methods to teach in the future.

Methods of Teaching

1. *Doing method:* These consist of assignments, committee work, guided experience and project work.
2. *Individual study method:* Under these method I may mention the Dalton plan, programmed learning, CAI, use f internet, etc.
3. *Discovery method:* These methods are based on all the three dimensions; learner activity, experience and experimentation by the learner, and cognitive understanding. Simulation primarily comes under this category. The main emphasis of methods in this category is on problem solving and providing necessary framework to the learner, so that while solving the problem the learner is able to learn the rationale and logic of what he has done.
4. *Encounter method:* Carl Rogers popularized the term "encounter". Since the emphasis is on providing experience through confrontation or through encounter, and not through cognitive understanding, these methods are effective for change in basic behavioural patterns and developing new ways of looking at things. Role play also involves some amount of encounter.

CONCLUSION

The rate of expansion of knowledge appears to be increasing and technology has enhanced access to information worldwide. Education of the new millennium therefore needs to enhance individual's ability to assimilate, evaluate and apply the available information. Indeed globalization which is affecting the economy, culture and information, the internationalization of relations and the increasing mobility of individual's, a complete revolution in the communication media and the massive advent of computerization into daily life and into the world of work represent challenge and an opportunity to the education system. Thus globalization in the present century calls upon the teachers to change their roles to meet the future demands of the society.

19

Regular and ODL Teacher Education Programmes– Challenges and Prospects

Ch. Sandhya
Academic Consultant, Department of Education, Dr. BRAOU, Hyderabad
Dr. L.V.K. Reddy
Assistant Director, Student Support Services, Dr. BRAOU, Hyderabad.

ABSTRACT

Education at the school level has special importance because these are the years when human mind is most impressionable. A majority of the students are under the care and influence of Pre-Primary, Primary and Secondary school teachers during the most formative years of their lives. That places a tremendous responsibility and confers a great privilege to all teachers at these levels. It is the teacher who build the nation through what they do in the class room, hence responsible to bring about the moral, ethical and humanistic development of the child.

It is imperative that teaching for various stages of education, right from Primary level to higher level requires different kinds of skills and professional competencies on the part of teachers. This has serious implication for teacher education programmes. All these programmes have to be designed on the basis of the set of general objectives for teacher preparation with sufficient latitude for catering the needs of teaching students at different levels of Education. Teachers have to be given special training to operationalise the educational programmes. The quality of training has a predominant role in the teachers' performance and student learning.

At present the demand of the day is to produce useful, fruitful and meaningful products whether it is in Conventional or in ODL mode. Conventional approach gives a lot of importance to direct teaching which is controlled by the curriculum and teacher. The role of the teacher in acquisition model is that of facilitator. Where as in Open Distance Learning there will not be any direct contact but the learner will experience flexible learning methods in multiple ways. Innovative model of Teacher Education Programmes have to be implemented through which we can over come the challenges in maintaining the quality of Teacher Education and produce highly talented teachers not only for our country but also to other countries.

"We are convinced that the most important factor in the contemplated educational reconstruction is the teacher...his personal qualities, his educational qualifications, his professional training and the place that he occupies in the school as well as in the community".

—Secondary Education Commission - 1952-53

Different Programmes of Teacher Education

1. *Teachers of Early Childhood Education:* There is no systematic training programme to train teachers of ECE. Very few institutions are offering diploma in ECE which is not recognized by NCTE.
2. *Teachers of Primary Education:* The DIETS under the Public Sectors and about 150-200 Private Colleges of Education which are permitted to run D.Ed./TTC training programme, to prepare teachers for Primary level.
3. *Teachers of Secondary Education:* The University departments, IASEs and CTEs under public sector and Private Colleges of Education offering B.Ed. Programme, to train teachers in all core subjects and in English. To teach Indian languages we have Pandit Training Institutions, mostly in private sector.
4. *Teachers of Higher Secondary/Senior Secondary (+2) Education:* We do not have any specific training programmes for this level in our state.

5. *Teachers of Physical Education:* The D.P.Ed. B.P.Ed. and M.P.Ed. are being run by both Government and Private Colleges of Physical Education.
6. *The Drawing, Music and Crafts etc., Teachers:* Very few institutions under private managements are providing training on these trades.

An Insight into the Curriculum

If we look into the curriculum for the above Teacher Education Programmes, we find lot of over lapping or repetition both in Foundation and Pedagogy courses. Although either the psychological principles or the sociological principles that are to be kept in mind by the Primary Teacher and the Secondary Teacher are different, the syllabus under these courses at all levels—D.Ed. B.Ed. and M.Ed. appears to be the same at least to the extent of 70%. Similarly, the methods of teaching, the strategies of classroom management, the methods of evaluation and styles of teaching are supposed to be significantly different from one level to other level, the syllabus in methodology (pedagogy) papers appears to be more or less the same.

The B.Ed. and M.Ed. Programmes are taken care of by the Universities for Curriculum Development, Evaluation and Certification. The D.Ed. and Pandits Training Programmes are under the control of State Government Department of Education. The SCERT develop the curriculum for these programmes and Directorate of State Board of Examinations conduct evaluation and issue certificates.

The B.P.Ed. and M.P.Ed. courses are developed by the University Departments of Physical Education and Universities conduct evaluation and issue certificates/degrees to the successful candidates. For D.P.Ed. SCERT develops the curriculum and State Board of Examinations conducts the examinations. In the case of Drawing, Music and craft teachers the State Board of Technical Education coin the courses and conduct the examinations. Thus the Universities, state Department of Education, State Department of Technical Education are in the field of providing Teacher Education Programmes through the institutions of their own and also through the colleges/institutions under Private managements.

Gaps in the Existing System of Teacher Education

1. The Senior Secondary Education (+2) is exists as a separate entity in our State. The required qualification for the appointment of teacher at +2 stage is only Master's Degree in the concerned subject as in the case of degree college lecturers. Where as the situation is totally different in other States and across the country. The +2 is included in the school system and PG trained teachers are recruited to handle the classes.
2. Recently in our State, The Department of School Education is appointing School Assistants in English and Physical sciences in all the secondary schools. Thus, the secondary schools are provided with subject experts in all core subjects and languages. No teacher has to handle classes in more than one subject. Then "Where is the need to have two methodology courses at B.Ed level?" Why can't we focus on one?
3. Training in utilizing the modern technology is not provided through the present programmes of teacher education, which is a must in present scenario.
4. We require more number of Primary teachers who lay the foundation for the child at the beginning, but we expanded the colleges of Teacher Education. The Government of AP issued a GO twice stating that only D.Eds are to be recruited at primary level but the situation is reversed because the Government could not stick on to the GO and thereby large number of B.Ed. qualified persons are recruited as Secondary Grade teachers to handle Primary classes.
5. About 200 B.Ed. colleges were permitted to run D.Ed. course with an intake of 50 students. To run B.Ed. or D.Ed. there should be devoted and well trained faculty to train youngsters. Out of 600 and odd colleges in the state not even 25% of them are fulfiled with the objective of having the devoted faculty on full time basis.
6. Apart from the above issues the colleges of Education are not having attached Model School. There is no proper supervision or monitoring the teaching practice/

block teaching and the student teachers go to their neighbouring schools and manage their practical in most of the cases. Thus B.Ed. training has become mostly theoretical oriented. The thirst on the competency development among the student teachers is almost ignored.

Suggestions

To overcome the gaps there is a need to develop a well designed model of Teacher Education Programmes and be implemented by both Central and State Governments of the country.

1. All Teacher education Institutions are to be recognized by NCTE and affiliated to th respective Universities or State Departments.
2. D.Eds. are to be recruited at the Primary level and B.Eds. at Secondary level.
3. Instead of having two methodology courses at B.Ed. level why cant we have one and focus on that.
4. The methods of teaching Economics, Botany, Zoology, Physics, Chemistry, Political Science and Geography etc...are to be introduced at B.Ed. level to produce teachers for +2 with appropriate qualifications.
5. The Faculty selection and appointment in the Colleges of education should be made transparent.
6. NCTE and Universities should insist upon establishing a model school attached to every College of Teacher Education.
7. Every teacher should be trained in using the variety of devices available both to update his knowledge and to use them in day to day class room interactions....like computers, Internet and CDs etc. since modern technology is widely used in the field of Education every teacher should become a computer literate.
8. *Integrated Teacher Education Programmes:* To identify students who are successful at 10th and +2 class exams and those who are willing to be teachers in their carrier, should admit them in the institutions of teacher education to prepare them as Pre Primary, Primary,

Secondary, Higher Secondary teachers, Teacher educators, Administrators and Researchers. This kind of Integrated approach will certainly develop professional zeal among perspective teachers and the quality of those teachers is clearly visible in their entire carrier as they learn the subject to teach.

E.g. : RIE established by NCERT are conducting such integrated Teacher Education programs for the past two decades.

9. *University of Teacher Education:* To bring all teacher education programmes under one roof Universities of Teacher education have to be established in all States.

CONCLUSION

It is high time to think seriously about the issue to bring back all the programmes of Teacher Education to the expected standards and quality. As we all know that without quality teachers we cannot improve the quality in any programme of Teacher education. The role of teacher is so important in the maintenance of quality.

Teaching is a noble profession and unfortunately the institutions of Teacher education are not being treated as professional institutions on par with other professions like Medicine, Engineering, Agriculture, Management Studies etc., Innovative model of Teacher Education Programmes have to be implemented through which we can over come the challenges in maintaining the quality of Teacher education and produce highly talented teachers not only for our country but also to other countries. It is the greatest challenge before us.

It may be an extreme step to revitalize the Teacher Education but it is an urgent and essential policy decision to be considered by both Central and State governments.

REFERENCES

1. Teacher Education/Programmes and Institutions in India: Growth and development.— IGNOU study material for M.Ed. Programme.
2. Tilak, Jandhyala B.G. (2007), Inclusive growth and Education–On the approach to the Eleventh Plan, Economic and Political Weekly.
3. The Hindu Speaks on education, editor N. Ravi, September 1997.

Theme–VI

Quality Parameters of ODL Teacher Education Programmes

20

Strategies for Qualitative Improvement of Teacher Education through Distance

Prof. G. Vijayalakshmi
Dept. of Education, S.P. Mahila Visvavidyalayam, Tirupati, A.P.

ABSTRACT

The conventional system of education is inadequate to provide teacher education for growing educational needs of our country. In this juncture, the system of distance education has emerged as an effective alternative to the traditional system of education including the teacher preparation. The quality of learning mainly depends on the quality of teaching. Quality of teaching again depends on the quality of preparation in teacher education. Untrained, under-trained and ill-trained teachers employed in schools will be a real havoc to both our children as well as potential human resource of our country. In distance mode of teacher preparation the in-service teacher is our primary concern and unless the learning style meets individual requirements, it will not be possible for that institution to claim that it has achieved total quality.

The paper mainly discusses the need for teacher education through distance and its quality enhancement. In view of the relationship between objectives of teacher education and procedures of implementation of the program, strategies for qualitative improvement of teacher education are suggested.

The conventional system of education is inadequate to provide teacher education for growing educational needs of our country. In this juncture, the system of distance education has emerged as an effective alternative to the traditional system of education including the teacher preparation. In olden days teaching was done by any literate. It is important to note that the teaching is not all what the teachers think, do and express, but it is the thing that makes a student to think, do and express. So teaching is very comprehensive task. This requires exposure from professionals due to ever increasing complexity and minute specialization. Ensuring quality in teacher education is what the student teacher requires but not what the teacher education institution provides. So quality characters of teacher education are more difficult to define since it is determined by the institution at the giving end including the facilities available, teacher educators, job opportunities etc. and the student teachers at the receiving end in turn the students at different levels.

The quality of learning mainly depends on the quality of teaching. Quality of teaching again depends on the quality of preparation in teacher education. Untrained, under-trained and ill-trained teachers employed in schools will be a real havoc to both our children as well as potential human resource of our country. In distance mode of teacher preparation the in-service teacher is our primary concern and unless the learning style meets individual requirements, it will not be possible for that institution to claim that it has achieved total quality. The institution should ensure that learners experience a varied range of teaching and learning styles so that their chance of success will be maximized. So the student teacher should pass through a standard process or a set of processes and to meet their specifications. It is a holistic and value driven process. To some extent it is a mid career enrichment program for in-service teachers. Every one working in the institution, management, the interpersonal relationships with other institutions and interdependence, standards, commitment, every relationship, every aspect and every process, every facility, evaluation procedures etc. contribute for its quality. Moreover the quality and importance of teacher as an instrument of change and progress have been emphasized by various experts, commissions and committees on education. So it is important to plan with great care the various dimensions of distance channel viz. human and material resources, material production, contact program, evaluation and feedback. Accordingly there is need to plan the objectives of teacher education program by taking all the above factors into consideration.

The program of teacher education has the following objectives :

1. To enhance and ensure the professional efficiency of in-service teachers for gainful employment and to upgrade their professional qualifications.
2. To learn while earning without availing leave or without interrupting their teacher career.
3. To supplement the contribution of conventional system in providing teacher education.
4. To provide a chance for teachers, who had to discontinue their formal education for various reasons.
5. To provide access to in-service untrained or under-trained teachers by providing opportunity at their door step to improve qualifications in their own field.
6. To keep abreast of the latest methods and techniques in the process of school management.
7. To understand the learner and learning process and to use and integrate the latest communication technology in their teaching learning strategies.
8. To train teachers to provide better guidance and counseling to their students.
9. To improve teaching learning process by including non-print material also.
10. To develop understanding of various psychological principles and apply to the real situations.
11. To know the emerging trends in the field of teacher education.
12. To familiarize and use appropriate evaluation techniques and grading of students.
13. To posses competence to teach subjects of their specialization.

14. To impart knowledge and understanding of various methods and practices required to plan and organize learning experiences.
15. To develop competencies to organize various co-curricular activities.
16. To develop proper role perception and functions of teachers in emerging scenario and as an agent of social change.
17. To facilitate research among in-service teachers.
18. To make the in-service teacher to identify the weaknesses for further improvement.

The following are the strategies suggested in view of the above objectives under two broad categories.

A. Strategies Administration

1. Since emphasis is on learning, there should be clear goals and high expectations regarding teacher preparation. So there should be a continuous improvement in the curriculum.
2. There should be orientation to faculty before starting the course.
3. Student teachers may be selected on the basis of entrance examinations.
4. Selection of number of school subjects language/group/ two subjects or one subject etc. by the student should be clear.
5. Orientation program for a short duration may be planned for students immediately after admission to explain the nature of course material, nature of process, expectations from the students, evaluation procedures, feedback mechanism etc. either by an expert or senior faculty member.
6. Preparation of self instructional material for the students and timely dissemination of the material.
7. Orientation program for course writers regarding the structure, topics, subjects and evaluation procedures. Self evaluating exercises and assignments are to be given at the end of the lesson.

8. Input evaluation is to provide information regarding how to employ the resource to achieve program objectives. Process evaluation is to identify the defects if any in the procedure and possibility for its betterment. Product evaluation measures and interpret the attainment during or after the program. It is the quality of outcome. So evaluation should be a continuous process and the results of evaluation should be discussed with the authorities and students.
9. Making to attend the counseling session/contact program/orientation program compulsory.
10. There should be a panel of instructors to receive worked out lessons, correct errors and give constructive suggestions in accordance with the needs of individual student teacher.
11. Observation of a minimum of five lessons by experienced teachers/peer lessons in each methodology subject should be made compulsory.
12. Supervision and discussion on at least five lessons by the concerned methodology teacher.
13. Test construction and administration, interpretation of results should be made compulsory. Send observers preferably from nodal centre/B.Ed. colleges during examinations.
14. Teaching learning material preparation and use is to be made compulsory for each and every in-service candidate.
15. Physical education program should be made familiar and organized by the student teachers without any exception.
16. Making 60 (2 sessions) days contact program attendance compulsory. There must be clarity of objectives, process during each of the program and learning outcomes for the students.
17. The minimum duration of Block Teaching Program and insisting on 20 school working days, counselling sessions and interaction with the teachers during the

program will be useful. Feedback mechanism from the students for modification and guidance if necessary will be of great help for improvement.

18. Supply of assignment questions to trainees in advance for proper completion in time and interaction with students during the program will help for better understanding.
19. Equipping the library for professional development of teacher educators as well as students.
20. Students should be encouraged to borrow books from the library to make comprehensive study as they are expected to be up-to-date and enhance their knowledge.
21. Since these teachers are prepared for various purposes, there should be inclusion of some topics in the curriculum related to special children, physical education, language teaching etc. besides different procedures to be adopted may be useful to meet their requirements.
22. Interaction with other institutions offering B.Ed. program through distance may facilitate to compare and modify the course structure in all respects. Suggested modalities may be implemented for betterment from time to time.

B. Strategies Faculty

1. Staff should be provided with suitable environment including the systems and procedures to perform their duty properly and effectively. Besides this there should be continuous staff development program.
2. Staff need encouragement and recognition of their successes and achievement and motivate to greater success to highten self esteem and empowerment.
3. Senior teachers quickly return to traditional ways of teaching and hesitant to adapt new methods and approaches is a major barrier. Since the original role of providing knowledge in the form of lecture is split

into that of study unit author and the counselor, staff should be motivated to adapt new approaches as there is difference in regular and distance channels of instruction.

4. Teachers should be empowered to give them the maximum opportunity to improve the learning of their own and their students.
5. Arranging faculty improvement programs to acquire skills to edit the content of course material including addition/modification of new knowledge and skills on online course delivery, clarifications etc.
6. Arrangement is to be made to get experts from different fields. Staff of university departments or colleges of education may be invited to deliver lectures to the students during the program to provide expert exposure in different areas.

REFERENCES

1. Mohd. Akhbar Siddiqui (1991), In-service Teachers Education, Ashish Publishing House, New Delhi.
2. Parmaji (Ed.) (1984), Distance Education, Sterling Publishers Private Limited, New Delhi.
3. Pradeep Kumar Johri (2005), Modern Distance Education, Anmol Publications Pvt. Ltd, New Delhi.
4. Rao, V.K. (2003), Quality Education, APH Publishing Corporation, New Delhi.

21

Development of Teacher Education in India

Dr. K. Krishna Reddy
Asst. Prof. of Economics, Dr. BRAOU, Hyderabad.
Dr. G. Dayakar
Asst. Prof. of History, Dr. BRAOU, Hyderabad.

Teaching is a profession – indeed a noble one, conceptually and ideally. And it is also different form other professions because of its multitude of dimensions. Teachers are the largest professional group engaged in human development activities. Only in the case of teaching there is much more that is required to be accomplished than in the case of other professions. Training of the practitioners is considered to be one of the important characteristics of a profession. Therefore, in order to benefit the teachers to their roles, a sound professional training is needed. Induction training and continues education thereafter equips the teachers with adequate knowledge and skills to perform their professional functions. Hence the training of the teachers assumes special importance. Professional training of a teacher implies his mastery in knowledge of the subject, in pedagogy and teaching techniques, in his/her love and dedication for his/her best to the world of learning and to the whole world along with it and march ahead to the future.

Training of teacher is an important component of Teacher Education. Teacher Education covers in its ambit the whole gamut of activities involved in the accomplishment of the teaching profession. Teacher Education denotes a real and holistic perception of teacher for that task they are required to perform and to continuously upgrade their professional skills. Pre-service training programmes are the major activities involved in it. Teacher Education has come a long way to reach the present destination. There were many important landmarks which need to be headed to really understand the present position. In this paper an attempt has been to trace those landmarks.

To origin of teacher education can be traced back to early 19th Century. State initiatives for teachers training was ensured in 1815 which is one of the earliest recorded views in support of the training need of schools teachers. The school societies of presidencies of Calcutta, Madras and Bombay were in receipt of grants from the East India Company for providing training to the teachers engaged in missionaries. Sir Thomas Munro, the then Governor of Madras in 1826 submitted a detailed proposal for establishment of training schools in each Collectorate with a continuous supply of trained teachers.

Consequent upon the Wood's Despatch of 1854, teacher education had a humble beginning. Wood's Dispatch described "The great deficiencies in the facilities for teacher training and desired to see the establishment with as little delay as possible of training" (Wood's Despatch, 1854). As a result first training school 'Normal School' for training of primary school teachers was established in Madras Presidency in 1856. Later on, in other presidencies also such schools were established thus making the official acceptance of teacher training as an integral part of Indian education system. In 1881-82, within 25 years of establishment of first training school, the number of Normal Schools went up to 106. The total enrolment in those schools was 3886, making an average of 35 odd students in each training school.

In 1882, the Indian Education Commission, for the first time recommended training for secondary school teachers, examination in both theory and practice of teaching and training should be precondition for permanent employment in Government and aided schools. As a result by the end of 19th Century, six training colleges were established in Madras, Lahore and Kurseong (1886), Allahabad and Jabalpur (1890) and Rajamundry (1894). Of these, the schools at Madras and Rajamundry had their origins in normal schools which were upgrade to colleges when Licentiate in Teaching (LT), equivalent to a degree was introduced.

The recommendation of the Government of India Resolution of 1904 had a far-reaching influence on teacher training in India. The major recommendations are:

1. Practice school should be attached to each training college.
2. Training courses for undergraduates should be of two years and for graduates should be one year leading to a university degree.
3. Every possible care should be taken to maintain a connection between training college and the school.

Besides, it also emphasized on infrastructure of the teacher training institutions.

The Government resolutions, 1913 have been considered another significant development of teacher education. It states, that under the modern system of Education no teacher should be allowed to teach without a certificate that he has qualified to do so. The concept of demonstration school, a school attached to a training college for experimental work and creating a university department for systematic research have been emphasized by the Sadler Commission, popularly known as Calcutta University Commission which was established in 1917-19. the Commission also suggested that education should be included as a subject of study in intermediate, B.A. and M.A. degree examinations in-service educations of primary teachers to attract and retain better quality of teachers are the consequence of the recommendations of the Hartog Committee in 1921.

In January 1943, the Central Advisory Board of Education adopted the report of the committee on Recruitment, Training and conditions of service of teachers. The report suggested vital changes in the existing system. The recommendations are – the normal periods of training for preprimary teachers should be two years, for junior basic teachers (middle) three years, for non graduate in high school two years, and for graduates in high schools one year.

Increased duration of training of three years for senior basic teachers refresher courses for in-service education of teachers and campus selection are the major developments of teacher education as a result of recommendation of the Sargent report in 1944 the report recommended "suitable persons for teaching jobs should be picked up during the last two years of their high school course and they should be given stipends for receiving teacher training" (Report of the Post-war Educational Development in India, 1944, p.13).

In 1947, at the eve of independence, there were 648 training schools with enrolment of 39,000 students. The number of secondary training colleges all over the country was 42 with an enrolment of about 3,000 teacher trainees.

Indian University Education Commission (1948-49)

The Commission did not substantially deal with the teacher education in a policy framework. However, in the field of professional education, the commission recommended:

- That the courses be remodeled and more time given to school practice and more weight given to practice in assessing the students' performances.
- That suitable schools be used for practical training.
- That students be encouraged to fall in with the current practice of a school and make the best of it.
- That the courses on the theory of education be flexible and adaptable to local circumstances.
- That the students be encouraged to proceed to the Master's Degree only after some years of experience of teaching.
- That original work by professors and lecturers planned on an all-India basis.

The Constitution of India

According to Article 45 of Indian Constitution under

the Directive Principles of State Policy states, "the state shall endeavour to provide, within a period of ten years from the commencement of the constitution, for free and compulsory education for all children until they complete the age of fourteen years". Keeping in view of the Constitutional mandate there was a dire need of restructuring and strengthening the teacher education programmes in the country, which has a pivotal role in achieving the intended objectives of national reconstruction.

Secondary Education Commission (1952-53)

The Secondary Education Commission suggested the provision of two types of teacher training institutions:

- For those who have taken the school leveling certificate, for whom the oeriod of training was recommended to be two years.
- For graduates for whom the training may, for the present, be of one academic year, but extended as a long-term programme to two academic years.
- Designing new programmes of teacher education to implement the recommendations of multi-purpose education.

It also maintained that the teacher trainees should receive training in one or more of the various extra curricular activities;

Teacher training colleges should arrange refresher courses, short-internship courses in special subjects, practical training in workshops and professional conferences.

Establishment of NCERT (1961)

The establishment of National Council of Educational Research and Training (NCERT) in 1961 was a major step taken for the development of school education which involves teacher education also. Amongst the significant contributions of NCERT are:

- Revamping of elementary and secondary teacher education curriculum.
- Recognizing of student teaching and evaluation.
- Institution of All-India Surveys on teacher education.

- Focus on continuing education of teachers through establishments of centers of continuing education.
- Recognition to contribution to education by outstanding school teachers and teacher educators through a scheme of national awards.

Indian Education Commission (1964-66)

The Indian Education Commission popularly known as Kothari Commission. This commission recommended that is:

- The isolation of training institutions should be removed.
- The quality of training programmes and expansion of training facilities should be improved.
- Continuing professional education of all teachers be provided for.
- Suitable agencies for the maintenance and development of teacher education should be established.
- The schools and their staff should be guided by the teacher education institutions in their neighbourhood in planning their activities and using improve methods of teaching.
- There should be extension deportment in each teacher education institution.
- Internship programme should be initiated by the teacher education institutions.
- Internal assessment should be introduced and emphasized as a regular feature.

Non-statutory National Council for Teacher Education (NCTE-1973)

The Government of India taken a resolution for the non-statutory NCTE was setup to maintain standards and norms in teacher education. It evolved a document called as "teacher education curriculum—a framework" with the involvement of UGC panel and teacher education which was the first attempt to revamp teacher education pertaining to all stages of education. The unique teachers of this frame work were:

- Teacher education was made task-oriented and less theoretical.

- The instructional weightage was foundation course-20% content-cum-methodology and practice teaching a including related practical were 60% and working with community 20%.

The National Policy on Education (1986) after the followed by "the challenge of education" was released by department of education MHRD, which provided a policy perspective based on ground realities and an over view of development in teacher education during 1950-83. This document emphasized that the number teachers increased from 7.5 lakhs more than 32 lakhs ending an annual growth rate of 4.6%. The percentage of trained teachers from 56.1 (1949-50) to 88.4 (1982-83) during this period.

The national commission and teachers recommended the following in respect of education of teachers which are also incorporated in the National Policy on Education (NPE) 1986:

- Teacher education is a continuous process and its pre-service and in-service components are insufferable.
- The District Institutes of Education and Training (DIETs) be established with the capability to organize pre-service and in-service courses for elementary school teachers and the personal working in non-formal and adult education sectors.
- At the national level, the National Council for Teacher Education (NCTE) be established which will have the power to accredit each institutions of teacher education, phase out the sub-standard institutions, provide guidance regarding curricula and methods.
- Networking arrangement be created between institutions of teacher education and university departments of education. (NCTE 1999).

Acharya Rammurty Committee (1990)

The Government of India appointed Acharya Rammurty Committee (1990). The committee examines various aspects in teacher education and recommended some important point that is:

- The first degree course on teacher education should not be given through correspondence mode.
- More institutions should be encouraged to introduce four year integrated courses the pattern of regional colleges of education.
- the practice of using teacher training institutions as dumping ground for unwanted or trouble some staff should be stopped herewith.

Establishment of Statutory NCTE (1993-95)

The Government of India established National Council for Teacher Education (NCTE), a statutory body by an Act of Parliament (Act 73, 1993) in 1995 with the objective of achieving planned and coordinate development of the teacher education system in the country. This is considered to be one of the land marks in the history of teacher education in India. Soon after its inception the NCTE was entrusted the following responsibilities:

- Undertake surveys and studies relating to various aspects of teacher education and publish result thereof.
- Make recommendations to the central and state governments, universities, university grants commission and recognised institutions in the matter of preparation of suitable plans and programmes in the field of teacher education.
- Lay down guidelines in the respect of minimum qualifications for a person to be employed as a teacher in schools or in recognised institutions.
- Lay down guidelines for compliance by the recognised institutions, for starting new courses or training, and for providing physical and instructional facilities, staffing pattern and staff qualification.
- Lay down standards in respect of examinations leading to teacher education qualifications, criteria for admission to such examinations and schemes of courses or training.
- Examine and review periodically the implementation of the norms, guidelines and standards lay down by

the council, and to suitably advise the recognised institutions.

- Formulate schemes for various levels of teacher education and identify recognised institutions and set up new institutions for teacher development programmes.
- Take all necessary steps to prevent commercialization of teacher education.

CONCLUSION

The early 20th century witnessed a considerable political turmoil like Civil disobedience movement, Non Cooperation movement and Quit India movement. Though teacher education was not greatly effected during that period, but within disturb educational system, training of teachers could not get considerable attention, as it required. However, after independence the need for teacher education received vide reorganization, got differentiated into programmes for primary and secondary school levels and grew into a network of variety of institutions–normal schools, training colleges and departments of education in universities. As Eraut points out, "the power and status of professional workers depend to a significance extent on their climes to unique forms of expertise which are not shared with other occupational groups and which are valued by society". A teacher become a professional in real sense if he fulfils all the obligations and remembers that a profession is above the professional and in no case he should allow his human instincts and feelings to come in the way of his profession. Teacher education is undergoing rapid changes in India in keeping pace with the demands of learning and expectations of learners, community and society as a whole.

REFERENCES

1. Basil, Fletcher (1968), Universities in Modern World, Pergoman Press Ltd., London.
2. Chaurasai Gulab (2000), Teacher education and professional organizations, Authors Press, New Delhi.
3. Kavita Sharma A.(2003), 50 Years of University Grants Commission, UGC, New Delhi.

4. Jagnath Mohanti. (2004), Modern Trends in Indian Education, Deep and Deep Publication Pvt. Ltd., New Delhi.
5. Jaffar, S.M.(1972), Education in Muslim India, Idarah-i-Adabiyat-i-Delhi, Delhi.
6. Mukharjee. S.N, (1964), Education in India. Today and Tomarrow, Acharya Book Depot, Baroda.
7. Rawat, P.L. (1970), History of Indian Education, Ramprasad and Sons, Agra.
8. Uday Sankar (1984), Education of Indian Teachers, Sterling Publishers Ltd., New Delhi.
9. Underson, L.M. and Ching, M.(1987), Effective teacher education, international encyclopedia of teaching and teacher education, New York: Pergoman Press.

22

Parity Between Regular and Distance Education Teacher Education Programmes

Dr. D. Hassan
Asst. Professor, Dept. of Education, ANU Campus, Ongole, Guntur Dt., AP.
Dr. A. Amruthavalli
Asst. Prof., Dept. of Education, ANU Campus, Ongole, Guntur Dt., AP.

ABSTRACT

"Teacher Education" will play a vital role in developing the society. "According to Kothari Commission," the destiny of the nation will be decided in the class rooms only", the sentence is itself shows the importance of "Teacher Education". In our educational system we have many opportunities to continue our studies from anywhere in India. Studies through regular and studies through distance will make a big difference in their quality of learning. Especially in "Teacher Education" it should be compulsorily in Regular, because in distance education it is impossible to give instructions to the student-teachers by following the curriculum. In Teacher Education most of the training depends upon the internships of the student-teachers, but it is impossible to conduct internships to the student-teachers in distance education. The following are the advantages in Regular and distance learning in Teacher Education

Regular	Distance
(1) It is easy to cover the entire entire syllabus in the academic Year.	(1) It is impossible to cover the entire syllabus in the academic year.

(2) No. of working days are available	(2) Less no. of working days.
(3) No. of internship programmeswill be conducted.	(3) Less no. of internships will be conduct
(4) Student-teacher will able to develop all the skills in teaching the various subjects.	(4) Student-teacher will not able to develop all the skills in teaching.
(5) It helps to the all- round development of the student	(5) It does not helps to all-round development of the student-teacher.
(6) There is a chance to observe the interests, attitudes, aptitudes, abilities of the student-teachers.	(6) No chance at all to observe interests, attitudes, aptitudes, abilities.
(7) Chance to make the teachers useful to society by conducting N.S.S. Programmes and other programmes.	(7) Impossible to make teachers with social awareness.

Distance Learning is becoming popular day by day all over the world. In India, there are one National Open University, 14 State Open Universities and about more than hundred Distance Education Institutes in which numerous academic, vocational and professional programmes such as B.A., B.Com., B.Sc., M.A., M.Com., M.Sc., B.Ed., M.Ed., M.B.A., M.C.A., etc., are being offered. Thousands of students are enrolling in these programmes. For example, there are about 2.5 million students enrolled in Indira Gandhi National Open University (IGNOU) as on date. Although there is quantitative expansion in open and distance education system, there is an urgent need to provide learners effective and quality education. It is only possible through systematic development by carrying out programme evaluation. So, Indian Open Universities and distance education institutes should take onus to evaluate their programmes. Of course, they are paying less attention towards programme evaluation while it is one of the most important aspects in the field of distance learning. It is also necessary and most important that, Indian Open Universities should pay much attention towards programme evaluation. There are some research studies, which have been carried out in the area of programme evaluation. However, there is also an urgent need to evaluate their programmes.

Programme Evaluation in Open and Distance Education

Programme evaluation is an important aspect in open and distance education, which plays a vital and critical role. We all consider, open learning an innovative approach to education and training. We have to therefore check whether the aims and objectives of education and training offered through distance mode are achieved, whether or not our expectations are justified in the process of transaction of curriculum and in the use of resources? Therefore, there is a need for evaluating the components associated with a distance education programme. Part of the problem may lie in the way open learning has been defined at the general level as an approach to put right all the mistakes of conventional education and training which keep many people out of the system and make learning difficult for the few who get in. Open learning has so often been defined in terms of the desirable effects which are its goal, and which incorporate values it would be difficult to reject, like learner centeredness, flexibility and autonomy. Programme evaluation is regarded as the process that leads to judgment about the worth, effectiveness and efficiency of an educational programme. In a given institutional context, the aims and objectives of the programmes need to be matched with the overall aims and objectives of the institution as well. "Programme evaluation is necessarily concerned with the specific programme that has already taken place, i.e., it fairly deals with the retrospective findings, on the other hand, the results of such evaluation certainly feed to the long-term decisions of the programme and looked this way, a programme evaluation obviously contributes to planning of the programme.

Need and Importance of Programmed Evaluation

Programme evaluation is very much needed in open learning because:

(1) As with the provision of learning opportunities, it is

necessary to find out whether the means used have achieved their goal, and to prevent the danger for granted assumptions about their effectiveness.

(2) It provides the basis for responsive and therefore learner-centered provision.

(3) It is integral to the improvement of quality in open learning which is still very much in the research and development phase.

(4) It has an important development role, not only for the quality of the learners experience but for the competence of practitioners and the programmes and courses offered by organizations.

(5) It contributes towards understanding how people learn and in particular how to help adults learn while fulfiling other social and work roles for which they are responsible.

(6) It is an important mechanism for effective programme implementation and management and may be required by external bodies and clients.

Some Other Issues of Open and Distance Learning

1. Quality of the Study Materials and its Content

The Open and distance learning students mainly depend on the study materials given by the universities and corresponding institutions. They were mainly relying on the contact classes to be conducted by these institutions. The more comprehensive the curriculum, the more comprehensive would be the study materials. This would also pave way to create more employment for student community. The course content should be intermittently linked to the learning objectives and the learners' characteristics, knowledge, skills and experiences. In order to facilitate easy flow of knowledge it would be appropriate to provide content in a phased manner. The content so provided should be accurate and relevant should be supported by examples and case studies.

The students may be asked to give the constructive feedback on the course content, contact classes and also on the course coordinators. The feedback thus collected could be used to review the programmes. The employer and also other stakeholders may be involved for the review of the programmes. Their suggestion certainly helps to keep the pace of the programmes and its relevance. We may ask the following questions :

- Does the material meet institutional instructional objectives and student learning needs?
- Can the learner access it/get permission to use it in a reasonable amount of time?
- Whether study material is available in a local language?
- Will students have access to the use of new technology?
- Can institution provide instructional and technological support?

2. Contact Seminar Classes

Many of the universities are conducting contact classes for the benefit of the students. The seminars and workshops aimed at enhancing the competencies, writing and communication skills of the students. These seminars should be necessarily handled by local and national experts chosen from the academic worlds for their expertise and outstanding teaching ability. The topics should cover a wide range of subjects to suit the needs of the students who enrolled a particular course of study.

However, the present pattern could be further refined by giving specific focus to group work activity and more thrust on practical aspects. This would pave way for more skill oriented outcome of students and enhance their employability in the market.

3. Use of ICT in ODL

Most of the CCI of Conventional Universities are in the first generation level. The standard of printed material needs to be improved. The State level institutions are in the second level. The IGNOU by and large used third generation tool and has made modest beginning with internet.

Parity between the Curriculum of Regular and Distance Education Programmes

The open and distance learning may initiate steps to have the credit transfer of courses and this may be accepted by the regular universities for continuation of the programme. It ensures and encourages the students to study further and become a good citizen. There should be a co-ordination in the distance education programmes and regular programmes regarding the course content and its evaluation. These facilities the regular and correspondence course institution students on par with their subject knowledge and content.

Management of Interruptions and Renewal

Often the students discontinue their study due to unavoidable reasons. It may differ from person to person and place to place. This issue makes the students to continue the programme at a later stage in their life. It may be planned and made easy to the students to take an oath in the beginning to complete the course in a stipulated time (5 years) and may be extended in extreme circumstances to one more year. The dropout in the ODL is due to lack of correspondence from the universities and also the frequent change of address of the learner. Looking at the student's perspective these options may be extended to them. There is a great need to computerize the records and also the use of ICT in State Open University and Correspondence Course Institutions.

How Open and Distance Education to be Imparted?

The selection of modes of instruction in open and distance education is made on the basis of structure of the system and receptivity of knowledge by the learner. They are elaborated as under :

(a) Structure of Open and Distance Education

- Openness leads to provide freedom to the learner for having aces to learning through variety of ways. Learner's convenience remains in the focus.
- Element of flexibility is another important aspect that helps the learner to adjust himself to thee system and

thus complete the course without much strain and difficulty.

(b) Receptivity of Information/Knowledge in Learning

Here two factors are kept in view to transfer information/ knowledge to the learner.

- Distance (from face-to-face to distant learning through teleconferencing, T.V. Radio, Internet, etc.).
- Utilizing maximum number of sensory channels for learning (viewing, listening, touching, smelling and tasting).

Emerging Trends in ODE

It is more than ever clear that open and distance learning will be an important element of future educational training systems. It is approaching acceptance within mainstream of education and training in such a way that it will make up part of the repertoire of most educational institutions in the future. The following trends in ODE are getting space in the literature.

Application of New Technologies

The emergence of new forms of distance learning based on new information and communication technologies in particular, those supported by the Internet and using the World Wide Web, have significant pedagogical, economic and organizational implications.

Globalizing Perspectives

Furthermore, there is a significant trend towards intensifying globalization. Institutional and inter-governmental co-operation is increasing, and the global classroom has been realized in quite a number of projects, particularly in connection with emerging global communication networks. Governmental leaderships concerning network development and access will have to play special role in this sphere.

Future Possibilities

Future of ODE is directly linked with the nature and

forms of emerging technologies. In the process we will have to be ready to design and redesign structures and processes, of ODE. Let us look into future possibilities in the background of the following :

Internet and Web-based Education

The emergence of the internet and related networks such as the world wide web has had and will increasingly have radical effect on the transformation of education and training in all sectors.

The web offers a world wide forum in which to teach courses that can be dynamically updated in ways never before possible. Each student has an enormous range of resources available, free from limitations of time and space. There remains considerable work to be done concerning searching and shifting techniques within these resources for learners and teacher alike.

Economics of Open and Distance Learning

The cost structures in open and distance learning are quite different from cost structures in conventional types of education. Capital investments usually substitute for high recurrent costs, making economies of scale of decisive factor Large distance-learning programmes may produce graduates at considerably lower costs than conventional institutions.

UnESCO Initiatives in Open and Distance Learning

UNESCO's initiatives in open and distance learning are based on its overall priority to ensure the right to education for all. While the use of distance education was given early support by the organization, new developments in information and communication, technologies, in particular the internet and the World Wide Web have radically increased the demand for lifelong education but also provided new means to meet the demand. Facing the educational challenges of the 21st century, UNESCO continues, through its support of open and distance learning, to contribute to the construction of knowledge societies in a lifelong learning context.

(a) Adult Needs

Great attention is given to open and distance learning n order to meet the educational needs of the adult population and this.

(b) Deprived Groups

UNESCO continues to strengthen the role of open and distance learning in the diversification of educational delivery systems. Support is also given to open and distance learning to meet the special needs of the disabled, migrants, cultural and linguistic minorities, refugees, populations in crisis situations, who cannot be efficiently reached by traditional delivery systems.

(c) Teacher Education

Great importance is attached to open and distance learning in teacher education, notably, for in-service teacher training but also for the training of teacher educators. National and sub-regional initiatives are encouraged and supported through UNESCO chairs and inter-university cooperation.

(d) Higher Education

The potential contribution of open and distance learning to the development of higher education is fully recognized and supported by UNESCO. In their efforts to make wider use of distance education to expand access to advanced learning and improve its efficiency, member states are assisted, among other things, by providing them with support in the initiation and development of open university schemes and other higher education programmes making use of distance education.

(e) Human Capacity Building

In its efforts to support its member states to make wider use of openand distance learning, UNESCO gives priority to national capacity building, including activities to enhance policies, planning, administration, financing, personnel, production, technologies, and other capacities essential to the establishment and management of efficient open and distance learning systems.

Global Corporation in ODL

In line with its mission to serve its member states, UNESCO gives great importance to international, interregional and regional co-operation for the promotion of open and distance learning. Co-operation is pursued with intergovernmental organizations such as other UN system agencies, the commonwealth of learning, the World Bank, the commission of the European union, the organization for economic cooperation and development, regional development banks, private and public sector partners, non-governmental organizations, notably, with the international council for Open and Distance education which are competent to act in this field.

CONCLUSION

Distance learning is especially valuable as a way to give these older learners access to expertise and an opportunity to share their own experience and thinking with others. It is thus a good way to deliver lifelong learning, to students who are likely to have well defined goals and to be more motivated than the younger full-time campus student. The usage of computer makes administration more efficient may also raise the overall quality of education. For instance, if teachers spend less time on administrative tasks, they will have more time for teaching and for preparing materials. So using ICTs to improve administration may pay off rather well.

The open and distance learning system need to take up accreditation process on a war footing. This will not only ensure qualitative achievement of the open and distance education system but also give a new impetus to the employment avenues to the students who pass out.

REFERENCES

1. AIU (2004), Hand Book on Distance Education, New Delhi: AIU Press.
2. Garg, Reddy, Pandey, Open and Distance Learning in India, IGNOU's contribution to Indian society, University News, Vol. 42, No. 46, p. 104.

3. Keegan, D. (1986), The Foundation of Distance Education, London: Croom Helm, p. 4.
4. NAAC (2001), NAAC-DEC Manual for self-study for open universities and Distance Education Units, published by NAAC, Bangalore, India.
5. NAAC (2007), Hand Book on Assessment and Accreditation– NAAC Publication, Bangalore, India.
6. Panda S. (I991), Programme Evaluation in distance education: A perspective and proposed agenda of actions' in educational technology, Third year book, Vol. I, AIAET, New Delhi, pp.168-181, quoted in IGNOU (2006), STRIDE Hand book 12; Programme Evaluation in Open and Distance Education, IGNOU, pp. 9-11.
7. Tiwari, S.K. et. al. (2008), An evaluation on orientation programmes of the academic staff college (ASC), BHU with reference to other ASC's in India. University News, Vol. 46 (44).
8. Trust and Priorities of UGC during XI plan; http://www.ugc.ac.in/notices/UGC reviews.pdf (Accessed on 28-09-07).

23

Quality Improvement in Teacher Education

P. Renuka
Asst. Prof., Dept. of Education, Sri Padmavathi Mahila Visvavidyalayam, Tirupati.
Dr. P. S. Pragathi
Asst. Prof. of Education, Sri Padmavathi Mahila Visvavidyalayam, Tirupati.

ABSTRACT

The future society in India shall be a knowledge-oriented, technology driven and fast changing society. The teacher shall be required to continuously update their stock of knowledge through a well organized mechanism of in-service programmes. To improve the efficiency of teachers and to make them acquainted with the modern developments in each subject, it is very necessary to have reorientation courses regularly. The teacher education curriculum and training programme should be upgraded as per the changing requirements of the modern world in order to face the challenges of the 21st Century more efficiently by our would be teachers. Teacher is the hub of any educational process. Educational programmes are bound to fail, if the quality of teachers is compromised. Hence, the teacher education programme is of utmost importance.

The programme of teacher education requires much improvement. Linkage between teacher training institutions, educational institutions and university departments needs to be improved. Different Commissions have made several recommendations. Unfortunately by and large not many are implemented. The quality of teacher training institution remains, with a few expectations, either mediocre or poor. So, there is an urgent need to improve the quality of Teacher Education in our country.

Teacher is the top most academic and professional person in the educational pyramid. The teacher is essentially a nation builder. He is the torchbearer of the human race. On him depends the future of the whole mankind? Professional competence and consciousness of teachers are the keys to the delivery of quality education. Even if an educational system possess adequate material resources and excellent administrative personnel, in the absence of efficient teachers, the programme of education becomes a case of wastage of time, economic resource and valuable human resources. Without good teachers even the best system of education is bound to fail. With good teachers the defects of the system can be largely overcome. Teacher is the hub of any educational process. Educational programmes are bound to fail, if the quality of teachers is compromised. Hence, the teacher education programme is of utmost importance.

The Education Commission (1964-1966) has stressed "Investment in teacher education can yield very rich dividends, because the financial resources required against the resulting improvements in the education of the millions". For the assessment and accreditation of the institutions offering teacher education and higher education, the UGC established the National Assessment and Accreditation Council (NAAC) with its headquarters at Bangalore in 1994.

In 1996, National Council for Teacher Education (NCTE) has been established. The NCTE has laid down certain norms and standards for granting recognition to the institutions offering teacher education. The establishment of this statutory body has undoubtedly been one of the significant moves towards achieving uniform standards in teacher education across the country. The NCTE has tried to improve the quality of teacher education programme but the development has been restricted to infrastructure only. To get permission from

NCTE, the institutions have created a separate blocks with some essential equipments and books etc. Only improvements in the physical facilities and infrastructure cannot improve the quality of teacher education.

HURDLES IN TEACHER EDUCATION PROGRAMMES

- Difficulty in getting staff for the colleges of education.
- Scarcity of the eligible candidates, who passed SLET/ NET.
- Difficulty in bringing uniformity by overcoming the regional disparities.
- Lack of teachers' commitment to the profession.
- Lack of commitment on the part of staff and students.
- Poor management of institutional resources.
- Lack of ability to use locally available resources.
- Shortage of duration (9 months) of B.Ed. and M.Ed. courses.
- Lack of co-operation from the practicing schools.
- The problem of maintaining quality in internship programmes.
- The problem of maintaining balance between arts and science graduates.
- The difficulty in establishing correlation between theory papers and practicals.

Directions for Improving the Quality in Teacher Education

Curriculum

For the improvement of quality in teacher education, the curriculum should be revived at regular intervals of time. Needs of the society are to be given due weightage at the time of revision of curriculum. The current Teacher Education Programme is heavily dominated by theory, with less attention paid to the more important practical and functional part of the classroom teaching. Every time a change is incorporated in the teacher education curriculum, unfortunately more theory is added to it without removing the dead wood.

Teaching Competency

The teacher education progrmames for developing teaching competencies are not comprehensive and adequate. There is a wide gap between teaching competencies in practice and teaching competencies expected. The following are some of the areas, where improvement is needed:

- Training in effective methods of teaching.
- Training in handling of hardware materials.
- Training in advanced communication skills.
- Training in the preparation and use of software materials, tape script, transparencies, Power Point presentations.
- Training in curriculum development, textbook analysis and documentation.
- Training in handling of physically challenged children.
- Training in laboratory skills, for which physical and life sciences, social sciences, psychology and computer education laboratories should be strengthened.

Teaching Practice and Internship

At present, the time devoted for teaching practice is not adequate. The available guidelines to conduct teaching practice programme are inadequate. It has become the weakest component of teacher education programme. The schools should be given clear guidelines for their co-operation in conducting teaching practice and internship.

Value Orientation

Quality is not merely a measure of efficiency; it also has a value dimension. The attempt to improve the quality of teacher education will succeed only if it goes hand in hand with step to promote social justice. Various commissions and committees from time to time have made strong case for the orientation of teacher education programmes towards the development of values and have suggested curriculum for this. The value orientation in teacher education programme is not a simple matter of inclusion of an additional course but percolation of it in the whole curriculum with a concern for value development.

Technology

The development of new technology and communication, explosion of information, increasing relevance of education, national and international understanding and peace in all walks of life, new demands are being made on the teacher. Adaptation of technology is the most significant challenges now confronting teachers, schools and teacher education. Changing technology is part and parcel of the rapidly changing social, cultural, political and economic times in which we live and it is clear that development of technology is a key driver of education.

The use of new techniques of education particularly educational technology in schools has an impact on students and its success depends only on the quality and ability of the teachers handling the education system mainly the school education system. Teachers have to be trained to handle new educational technique and to manage it effectively in the teaching learning system. So it is the responsibility of the teacher education system to provide necessary training inputs to the teacher trainees.

Encouragement for Research and Innovation

Teacher education should have ample freedom to undertake research and innovative work. Teacher education is a continuous process and its pre-service and in-service components are inseparable. Apart form teaching, teachers perform several other functions i.e., facilitating learning by offering remedial help to learners, seeking parent's co-operation and making them aware of their responsibility, seeking community support to strengthen teaching-learning, participating in other professional activities related to educational planning, educational development, etc. All these functions are to be performed effectively by acquiring relevant knowledge and skills.

CONCLUSION

The future society in India shall be a knowledge-oriented, technology driven and fast changing society. The teacher shall be required to continuously update their stock of knowledge through a well organized mechanism of in-service programmes. To improve the efficiency of teachers and to make them acquainted with the modern developments in each subject, it is very necessary to have reorientation courses regularly. The teacher education curriculum and training programme should be upgraded as per the changing requirements of the modern world in order to face the challenges of the 21st Century more efficiently by our would be teachers.

The programme of teacher education requires much improvement. Linkage between teacher training institutions, educational institutions and university departments needs to be improved. Different Commissions have made several recommendations. Unfortunately by and large not many are implemented. The quality of teacher training institution remains, with a few expectations, either mediocre or poor. So, there is an urgent need to improve the quality of Teacher Education in our country.

REFERENCES

1. Agarwal, J.C. (1996), Development and Planning of Modern Education, Vikas Publications, New Delhi.
2. Aggarwal, J.C. (1996), Educational Reforms in India, Dobal House Publications, New Delhi.
3. National Curriculum Framework (2005), Draft Report, NCERT, New Delhi.
4. NCTE (1998), Policy Perspectives in Teacher Education - Critique and Documentation, NCTE, New Delhi.

24

Enhancing the Quality in ODL Programmes

Dr. T. J. M. S. Raju
Principal, KPN College of Education, Gantyada, Vizianagaram Dt.
Dr. S. N. Rao
Asst. Professor, Dept. of Education, EFL University, Hyderabad.
Dr. T. Sharon Raju
Asst. Professor, IASE, Andhra University, Visakhapatnam.

ABSTRACT

In present system of education, the open as well as distant learning programmes are increasing in every university. Comparably all universities establish the distance education programmes and at the same time the admission rate of joining students in the distance education programmes is also increased.

This is happened because the living expenses of an average man have increased. So he has to work and he has to learn. The present paper deals with the some of the visible facts to improve the quality of open and distant learning programmes.

The distant learning programmes in every university were increased and the students are concentrating on the nearby universities for obtaining education. Mainly all the students are joining the traditional courses like B.A., M.A., etc., but ignoring the professional courses and diploma courses.

The professional courses or diploma courses are meant for the skillful personnel to enhance their professional skills. So they can get immediate jobs with high salaries. For example, if a student completed BA instead of joining MA better to opt for B.Ed. So the in-service teacher can benefitted more with the professional teacher degree. It can be helpful to the professional advancement.

(1) Appointment of Academic Councilors

The university has to appoint academic counselors for giving awareness programs of the courses conducted by the universities in the nearby colleges and social organizations. So every individual is a useful creature in this universe and everyone has unique potentialities to learn and exhibit. So according to the interests and measuring abilities of their skills, the academic counselor has to show a path to the each individual. So the counselor has to act as a guide and a mentor to mould the life of every individual.

(2) Printed Material and Media

The printed material about the courses i.e. prospectus of the course is giving only for the joining students. But those brochures or prospectus if circulated or distributed to every school or college then everyone should aware of every course.

So the selection to join the course is become easy for the students. Different universities are giving different courses. So based the interest and utility the students have to select their options by the print media.

(3) Improve the Websites of the Universities

Every university has their own websites. For the open and distant learning students about their courses or to clarify their doubts e-mail and chatting facilities should be improved. So by way of chatting students can easily understand from their native places. So the university has to appoint some computer programmers in this regard.

The second thing is to keep the reading material in their websites in MS word or PDF files for download of students. Recently the NCERT schools were also using this technique. Those who want the study material can down load from the websites. This will also reduce the burden to print the books and distribute to the students.

(4) Establishment of Public Demanded Courses

Instead of starting the traditional courses the university has to start the public demanded courses those are having need based to the society.

The courses like personality development and communicative English, Language skills, Diploma courses, Transport management, Teaching and learning courses, Vocational courses etc. should be improved by the university. For this a body should be established and the committee should be met every week or month to discuss about the improvement of every course, maintaining standards and taking the suggestions from scholars etc. should be maintained regularly.

(5) Conducting Meetings at Different Universities

The meetings for improve the quality the committee has to visit at different universities within the state and outside the state to observe and adopt the courses conducted by different universities and also the suggestions were taken by different experts at different areas.

So overall knowledge and innovative and creative ideas may exists for improving the courses and adopt useful courses from different universities.

The retired professors, educated parents and some social organizations should be involved to give their valuable suggestions for the improvement of courses to the university committee.

(6) Interlink with Other Universities

While running a particular course by the university there are so many problems to give contact program for the students by the university alone and it is a problem to attend for the whole group of students.

If the university link up with other university to organize or conduct a program then it should be become easier for the student to attend and the quality can also improved with limited group of students to attend.

The involvements of other university departments were also benefit more for the students to offer best quality of education.

(7) Organizing Seminars/Workshops/Conferences

Now and then the university has to conduct or organize the national seminar or conference to take the scholarly articles and papers for the benefit of their programs.

The themes of the particular seminars and the sub-themes should be noted according to their options like quality improvement. The material obtained by the professors or participants should be thoroughly reviewed and the information should be published. This information help the University a lot for improving the quality of open and distant learning programs.

(8) Taking Feedback from Students and Parents

After completion of the course the university has to take the suggestions from the successful completed candidates and their difficulties faced while the course is in action.

The feedback from the parents of the students about the fees, problems and about everything should be taken.

By reviewing all the information the drawbacks and the problems should be modified and the university has to enhance the quality according to the instructions and directions given by students and parents.

(9) Finance of the University

The financial benefit of the university is also an important thing for organizing the courses and also for appointment of new staff. So the university has to fix the fee according to the present day situation. At the same time the university has to see the average person into consideration to pay the fees in semester or yearly basis. The collection of fee amount in single payment should be very difficult to the average earning person.

So in fixing and collection of university fees the finance committee of the university has to think in a logical manner by showing humanity on students for all round development of the students. In fixing reasonable fees also helpful to the students to join and study in more number even from the average economic status families.

25

Quality Concerns in ODL Teacher Education

Shakera Parveen
Asst. Prof. of Education, Maulana Azad National Urdu University, Hyderabad
Shamim Ahmad
Asst. Prof. of Education, Maulana Azad National Urdu University, Hyderabad

ABSTRACT

This paper highlights the quality concerns in ODL teacher education and suggests various measures to enable the individuals and the organizations contribute for the 21st century knowledge-based society. To stimulate the ODL teacher education for promotion of quality, many interventions such as support mechanism, technology enabled infrastructure, standard contents, innovative instructional strategies, proper checks and balances, networking, need based programmes, effective governance etc. should be emphasized.

"Quality – you can't define it
But you know it
When you see it"

Background

Quality concern in any field of work is a necessary condition for success. It not only enhances the individuals' and organizations' competence but also contribute towards the overall development of the society. In non-conventional mode, we find that there are some objectives which aim at bringing quality in ODL teacher education. In order to bring quality assurance in ODL teacher education some necessary inputs are provided and it remains an under-researched area but what little research there is suggests that such alternative interventions are as effective as traditional-conventional teacher education.

Of the many educational issues, the quality concern has been the most crucial one especially when aiming at outcome based instructional strategies. As a mater of discussion on the issue, quality in ODL teacher education may be defined as a set of standards that offer innovations and best practices, thereby enabling individuals and institutions to transform the educational services for higher level knowledge, skills and experiences.

How best to use quality delivery to support teaching and learning in ODL teacher education provides the subject for developing knowledge society. How can today's institutions change to meet the quality concerns while providing teacher education through ODL. There are certain issues to be discussed in the paper with regard to quality concerns in ODL teacher education.

Towards Quality in ODL Teacher Education

The fundamental changes are observed in the ICTs role and that will profoundly has impact on academic institutions. Many insist that the instructional—teaching and learning environment must be dramatically restructured. The Daker Framework quotes "improve all aspects of the quality of education to achieve recognized and measurable learning outcomes for all—especially in literacy, numeracy and essential life skills". For the purpose of discussion, there has been, in fact, quality as a thrust area for institutions of higher learning and research. This becomes more crucial to the institutions offering teacher education programmes through non-conventional mode.

To stimulate the ODL teacher education for promotion of quality, many interventions are discussed, a few of them are mentioned below:

1. Support Mechanism

Support mechanism is regarded as the most significant intervention to strengthen the quality of ODL teacher education. It facilitates the learners to overcome the barriers of open distance and flexible learning. It is strong support mechanism that may be regarded as 'an agent of quality assurance' especially in providing teacher education through distance education. ODL teacher education, as part of quality assurance, must offer certain learner support services inclined to bring together relatively better experiences of learning, motivation, tutoring, counseling etc. Support mechanism in ODL teacher education is more significant from the quality perspective.

2. Technology-enabled Infrastructure

Technology-enabled infrastructure is just another powerful resource which has the potential to drastically change the teaching learning paradigms worth considering into ODL teacher education. For the purpose of quality assurance technological interventions—ICTs should be in place to strengthen the delivery services. ICTs can also be used in exploring huge data and interpreting them for various application purposes. Distance learners usually make use of technological tools, devices and other applications to enhance their learning.

3. Standard Contents

Designing and developing standard contents is considered to be important from quality perspective. In the ODL teacher education the pupil-teachers are provided with some self-instructional materials, which help them in day-to-day learning activities. It is suggested, however, to make sure that these materials not only address the needs of the learners but also meet the standards in terms of language, content, presentation and its learning in day-to-day life.

4. Innovative Instructional Strategies

Instructional strategies help in facilitating the educational aims and objectives effectively. Institutions aspiring for quality are expected to devise and make use of innovative instructional strategies. It is a fact that ODL itself is an innovative instructional strategy and within the strategy it rquires to apply certain innovative techniques and devices that enhance the over all performance of the organization.

5. Proper Checks and Balances

Checks and balances', usually used in governance and administration, have positive impact while managing any organization or system. It encompasses the proper delivery of goods and services at the same time it also protects the democratic processes and functioning of the system. The intent of checks and balances, here, is to deliver learning materials assuring that the learning process should not become passive and monotonous in the pursuit of learning, knowledge, skills and experiences. Those checks and balances also ensure that every systemic unit promotes the ODL teacher education.

6. Networking

In the changing scenario, networking tools are easy to use and are widely used by the public in general. The question, here, is why should not we use them in transforming the lives of the learners and institutions of ODL teacher education. Networking technologies should be used as an aid for learning a number of concepts and skill development strategies in the fast changing teaching and learning environment. Thus, enabling the learners and organizations to make use of various networking tools will ensure the coverage of a wide range of learning activities, thus, leading to quality assurance.

7. Need-based Programmes

Considering the changing requirement of the 21st century, ODL teacher education institutions are required to run the need based programmes and courses. ODL teacher education institutions have to examine whether the proposed programmes and courses are realistic for the societal needs. What is needed to incorporate is the consideration of changing pattern of need based academic and professional programmes and courses.

8. Institutional Commitment

Institutional commitment is an important issue of quality concern especially in ever increasing competitions among the providers of teacher education. Distance education organization has to re-organize its activities on par with excellence. In this backdrop, institutional commitment can make a difference. The focus, along with the institutional efficiency, be given on the attitudinal issue of institutional commitment.

9. Accommodating Best Practices

To sustain in the field, most of the ODL institutions have emphasized to accommodate the best practices. Best practices, here, refer to the management of work practices which, when effectively linked and utilized together, can be expected to lead best results in terms of quality, learner satisfaction, accessibility, flexibility, originality and cost-effectiveness.

10. Effective Governance

Governance is the most crucial aspect of any organization. An effective governance has greater impact on all the units of ODL. A majority of the ODL institutions are in the process of introducing technology based flexible governance. Effective governance also leaves its mark by ensuring the successful and widespread application of innovative strategies and best practices.

11. Meeting the Challenges

In view of the above, there emerges some challenges for providing quality ODL within the prescribed domain of teacher education. Before putting forward the various strategies for quality assurance it is important to have a clearly defined policy in place. With the help of well defined policies ODL teacher education institutions can attain fully the potential of new technologies, innovative strategies and other related resources and infrastructure.

CONCLUSION

ODL teacher education without quality considerations does not have the opportunity to form the bonds on par with other institutions and programmes nor does it have to accommodate innovations and best practices for its stakeholders. As the paper illustrates, quality interventions with sincere commitment and dedication to make a positive difference in teacher education programmes through ODL. However, consistency in assuring quality is to be maintained throughout the programmes and courses. Lastly, it is concluded that 'quality, like excellence, is not a destination as much as it is a never ending journey'.

REFERENCES

1. Dange, J.K (2009), Online Learning: A new way of Education, Neelkamal Publications Pvt. Ltd.
2. Keegan, Desmond (2004), Foundations of Distance Education.
3. Sidhu, B.K. (2009), Total Quality Management in Teacher Education, Neelkamal Publications Pvt. Ltd.
4. World Education Forum (2000), The darker framework for action, Paris, UNESCO.

26

Quality Roles of Teacher Educators

Najma Begum
Asst. Professor, Dept. of Education and Training, MANUU, Hyderabad.

ABSTRACT

In the fast changing world the role of the teacher too is changing as fast. The teacher needs to be conceived as a change agent and not as mere transmitters of knowledge and culture it means the education of teacher has to keep pace with changing needs and demands of the society. Now it is the time think on teaching. If kids can't learn the way we teach, we must teach the way they learn. It is need of hour to notice and try to implement the teaching in which they can learn easily.

Conventional, teacher centered pedagogies dominated current teaching practice in all subjects despite numerous research based assertion that promote more progressive student centered teacher education. As Pradhan (2003) rightly observed teacher education programme that are followed throughout the length and breadth of the country have manic static both in for of content over 100 years. The pedagogy that was introduced in the late part of 19th century is still continuing which obviously is no longer relevant.

Why teacher preparation programme are is not meeting the expectation of the society. There is an urgent need to review and reorganize the teacher education programme. Before talking about the specific issues related to the evaluation of the practical component, let us recall the basic purpose of any evaluation. It has three fold purposes to assess the ability of the student in a particular area. Find out common weakness and take necessary remedial measures to overcome these weaknesses.

Changing Roles of the Teacher and Teacher Educators

Education works best when it concentrated on thinking and understanding, rather than on rote memorization. Constructivism concentrates on learning how to think and understand. Children learn more and enjoy learning, as they are actively involved in authentic and real-world context activities, which give students ownership of what they learn; even students learn how to articulate their ideas clearly as well as to collaborate on tasks effectively by sharing in-group projects. This is essential to success in the real world, since they will have to cooperate and navigate among the ideas of others.

It is important for the students to know their progress using self-assessment techniques. Even though we are emphasizing a shift in the teaching-learning process from teacher-centered to learning-centered, in reality the teachers are still following the same old traditional methods of teaching.

As we all aware that basic aim of teacher education programme is to train teachers who can become effective and efficient, professionally and academically qualified so as to promote learning and also contribute in shaping all round personality of children. As Teaching practice is an integral part of the teacher education programme. It is geared towards preparation of new entrants into teaching profession. The exercise is to acquaint student teachers with practical knowledge of teaching and learning process including lesson plan preparation, presentation, class management, communication skills, evaluation and the required personality of professional teachers.

Conventional, teacher centered pedagogies dominated current teaching practice in all subjects despite numerous research based assertion that promote more progressive student centered teacher education. As Pradhan (2003) rightly observed teacher education programme that are followed throughout the length and breadth of the country have manic static both in for of content over 100 years. The pedagogy that was introduced in the late part of 19th century is still continuing which obviously is no longer relevant.

Now let us see the background of teaching practice briefly, the earliest attempt was made by Herbert. It included preparation, presentation and evaluation the impact of Tyler and Bloom by modeling practice teaching on the lines of cognitive objectives of knowledge, understanding, application, analysis and synthesis. It follows Ausbel and skinner made a contribution of meaningful learning, anchoring and assumption of concepts and principles of small steps and immediate reinforcement and feedback to the learner. The impact of Bruner and Piaget can be seen in moldering teaching on the principles of cognitive learning and structuralism. Besides these progress made in communication also made an impact on practice teaching. The use of teaching aids from models charts use of audio and video cassettes also changed the progress of practice teaching.

Most of the teacher education institutions suffer from lack of adequate facilities, and they do not adhere to the norms regarding physical facilities or provision of adequate staff. Colleges of education are generally either under-staffed or the staff are under-qualified. There are serious curricular deficiencies, and evaluation in teacher education is far from satisfactory. There is no uniformity in the duration of teacher education. This is particularly so in the case of teacher education related to the elementary level. In some States, there is only one-year programme while in others it is of two years' duration. Moreover, due to various reasons, academic sessions for B.Ed. are delayed, and in some cases, effective teaching lasts only for three to six months, although the number of working days in a teacher education institution is expected to be at least 220 in a year.

We also know that success of any institutional programme depends upon its evaluation procedure. At present our emphasis, generally remains an objective and comprehensive evaluation of student teacher in theory and teaching practice. The objective of practice teaching is to promote the prospective teacher a command over the necessary tool in the profession, control of techniques of class instruction and management skill and proficiency in the out of teaching.

The quality of classroom teacher depends upon the programme of practice teaching. So the programme of practice teaching is becoming more and more important in the preparation of good teachers. But today we find the majority of the student teachers who pass the B.Ed. exam with good marks lack the faire confidence and efficiency in the fundamental skill of effective classroom teaching.

To overcome this problem earlier national policy on education (1986) had recommended revamping of teacher education programme with an increased duration of internship/school attachment increased programme in view of the fact that practice period allotted is not adequate in terms of duration and experience gained what is done during the period is stereotyped material preparation during practice teaching having no relevance to realistic condition of school, need of all types of students are not taken care of during teaching and there is little scope for development of effective domain of the teacher.

Teacher education NCTE (1998) on the basis of field survey had observed that practice teaching remains to be a weak link in teacher training curriculum transaction. In order to accommodate practice teaching/school attachment programme of longer duration with the objective of meeting above gaps various committee and NCTE had recommended introduction of two years B. Ed. programme for secondary teacher and reforms in practice teaching.

Now let us talk what do we mean by an Effective teacher?

The objective of practice teaching is to produce effective teachers. Effective teacher is one who has sense of humor, ability to understand the students and their problems. And explain thing clearly (so that student can easily understand what is being taught), willing to help students (whom they need) and ability to be as fair as possible in dealing with them.

It is unfortunate that most of our teachers are still unaware of the immense possibilities that e-learning offers in ushering in an e-learning society in our educational setup. The teachers should be made aware of various tools and advantages of online teaching in order to bring about great changes in the field of education in the country at large.

Role of the Teachers

The introduction of e-learning in education has created a fear among the teaching community that the use of ICT in the process of teaching and learning would relegate the place of the teacher to some extent and eliminate teachers from the teaching scene. But the teachers, instead, should take it as a challenge and equip themselves with various ICT skills to face the changing needs and trends in education. They must enrich themselves with the knowledge of latest developments in the field of ICT and should play the following roles as "multi-facilitators" to learners.

- *Content facilitator*: Assisting learners understand the course content.
- *Process facilitator:* Facilitating online learning activities.
- *Adviser/counselor:* Providing individual counseling support to learners.
- *Assessor:* Providing grades and feedback on performance.
- *Administration:* Managing learner records.
- *Designer:* Devising worthwhile learning tasks.
- *Researcher:* Discovering new knowledge relevant to the subject taught.
- *Technologist:* Providing technical support to students and uplifting their technological environment in which the course is taught.
- *Concern for teacher:* The quality and efficiency of education depends to a great extent on the quality of teachers who truly add value to the students. Unless we have quality conscious teachers we cannot expect innovation or change in the quality of products of education. In India the teacher is considered to be the least development resources. We have hardly given the attention and consideration to select right kind of people for teaching profession and providing them the

best possible training and ensuring their status in keeping with the importance and responsibility of their work. Many teachers in colleges and universities are unable to conduct research which is necessary and don't have adequate knowledge of using information and communication technology, consequently using outdated method of teaching.

Professional development of teacher is a must for quality teaching in higher education. The professional development of teachers is mainly concerned with competencies, commitment and value frames associated with teacher work whereas in the present scenario, teaching work is confined only to lectures and dictating notes. If the teacher is concerned about his professional development it will automatically lead to quality teaching.

In this day and age of globalization and privatization with increased competition and to meet the new challenges of the 21st century higher education should be radically transformed. We should also keep in mind that quality can come only from quality teachers and quality infrastructure, under quality leadership. The present system demands more skilled teachers. Increase in number of students creates pressure on the part of training institutes to improve the teaching tack because students may have different intellectual and socio-cultural backgrounds.

The very fact that teaching is a profession entails that teaching is a specialized activity for which specialized knowledge/training is required through specialized institutions. A good institution will produce individuals who will be devoted to the profession and make their mark in the activities organized by them while going to the field. If examples with respect to engineering and medical institutions in India and abroad are considered, one will agree that the onus of getting good teachers lies on the institution that prepares the professionals. Further the institutions alone do not matter much; it is the teachers in the institutions who produce desired individuals. Teacher educators are responsible for producing quality teachers. Harvey (1993) and Atwood

(2007) point out that Quality processes tend to focus on 'core' aspects of education such as learning-teaching and course organization.

In other words teacher educators' way of organizing theoretical framework, practical sessions and skills development programme affect the future teachers. The activities suggested during training are carried to the classroom teaching in the schools. Researchers like Mc Affrey et. al. (2003), Rivkin et.al. (2005) and Rockoff (2004) found that teachers have a significant impact on the achievement of the students. However, research studies are to provide answer to the question if the teacher educators directly affect the teachers' classrooms behaviour or management of activities in the schools. Reasons for this could be many.

Teacher educators have never taken the aspect of professionalism very seriously. They have been criticizing the process of teacher education rather than providing answer to problem faced by them. However, NCTE was established in 1993 by the Act of parliament to give the tinge of professionalism to teacher preparation programme. Unfortunately instead of mending the system it caused some damage to the programme of teacher education. Obvious reason was lack of insight on the part of teacher educators to provide a good model of teacher education. Till date they have not been able to envision a good model of teacher education programme.

Existing teacher education problems were further aggravated by the privatization of teacher education institutions. Teacher educators never accepted the private enterprise in teacher education programme though they had been party in recognizing the private teacher education institutions (through NCTE) for the sake of fringe benefits bestowed by the private players. The situation deteriorated to such an extent that at particular time a committee was constituted by the Ministry of Human Resource Development to scrap the regulatory body of teacher education (NCTE). The situation was saved after a great hue and cry made by some right thinking teacher educators to reverse the decision. The developments like these have made it mandatory for the teacher educators to put their heads together and give a little thinking to their role in the changed set up under Liberalization, Privatization and Globalization.

The technology–based teaching is a new way of thinking in educational theory. It acts as a powerful enabling device to promote active learning and open new learning approaches, the use of new techniques that involve two-way student–teacher interactions, student-student interaction and interdisciplinary approaches is gradually flow-typical of traditional classroom-where a teacher addresses a group of passive learners. Apart from synchronous, face-to-face instructor–student interaction in a distance based teleconferencing; there is enormous potential for synchronous interaction between instructor and students via e-mails, videoconferencing online, etc.

Dave (1999) on the basis of job analysis of present day teachers identified five performance areas for effective teacher education programme. They are (1) performance in classroom.(2) school level performance (3) performance in our of school activities. (4) Performance related to parental contact and cooperation and (5) performance related to community contact and co-operation.

At present systematic training is generally not provided to teachers by many colleges of teacher education to perform several of these tasks in a professional manner. A teacher is after all, a professional practitioner mere for intensive and effective training must be provided to him/her in different performance areas. This should become essential and urgent ingredient of practice teaching for pre-service teacher education also should also find place in recurrent in-service teacher education programme. The role of the teacher will change giving up the 'expert' role to become more of facilitator.

CONCLUSIONS

Supervising teachers are expected to provide guidance and encouragement needed to prospective teachers but at the same time, allow them to experience the realities of teaching.

Maintain a high level of expectation of the student teacher in terms of professionalism, appearance, attendance and effort, share philosophy of education, suggest materials and strategies, provide appropriate information, help them to put their observations and teaching experiences into a positive perspective.

REFERENCES

1. Fourth survey of research in education (1983-88), Vol. II, NCERT, New Delhi.
2. NCTE (2004), Some specific issues and concerns of teacher education, NCTE, New Delhi.
3. Ruhela, S.P. (1999), Essentials of Educational Technology, Indian Publisher's Distributors, New Delhi.
4. Stephen. M. Alessi (1985), Computer based Instruction—Methods and development. Prentice Hall, New York.
5. www. reflectiveaction.com

27

Role of Apex Bodies in Quality Parameters of Teacher Education Programmes

Dr. M. T. V. Nagaraju
Asst. Professor and Head I/c, Dept. of Education,
Dr. BRAOU, Hyderabad

Pre-NCTE (Statutory) Period

Recognition and quality assurance in ODL based Teacher Education has always been a matter of concern to teacher education professionals and policy makers in the country. Initially, this responsibility was only with the governing structures within universities facilitated by the recommendations provided by the National Council of Educational Research and Training (NCERT) and the Panel for Education under University Grants Commission (UGC). The non-statutory National Council for Teacher Education (NCTE) was set up in 1973 by a resolution of the Government of India and was located in the NCERT mainly to provide recommendations to universities and teacher education institutions on curriculum development and transaction and related matters. It brought out curriculum framework for teacher education at primary and secondary levels and also adviser institutions on matters related to quality in teacher education. However NCTE, at that time being only a non-statutory body had only recommendatory role to play. This is evident from the fact that the proliferation and commercialization of B.Ed. correspondence/distance education programme by several dual mode Universities in the country continued in spite of the recommendations of NCTE against them during seventies and eighties. University Acts provided them adequate autonomy to launch and organize courses.

Establishment of a Statutory Body

The National Council for Teacher Education Act No. 73 of 1993 was passed in the parliament on 29 December, 1993. The Act provided "for the establishment of National Council for Teacher Education with a view to achieving planned and coordinated development of the teacher education system throughout the country, the regulation and proper maintenance of norms and standards in teacher education system and for matters connected there with". In the Act, "teacher education" means programmes of education, research or training of persons for equipping them to teach at pre-primary, primary, secondary and senior secondary stages in schools and includes non-formal education, part-time education, adult education and correspondence education. Under functions of the Council, the Act specifies, among other things, that the council may: "lay down norms for may specified category of courses or training in teacher education, including the minimum eligibility criteria for admission there of, and the method of selection of candidates, duration of the course, course contents and mode of curriculum."

"Take all necessary steps to prevent commercialization of teacher education." Although open and distance education was not specifically mentioned in the Act, the new Council got it rectified by a resolution that the term 'correspondence' shall also include other related modes such as open Universities and Distance education.

Role of Distance Education Council Under IGNOU

IGNOU Act of 1985 included a statutory body called the Distance Education Council (DEC) within Indira Gandhi National Open University (IGNOU) to regulate quality of open universities and distance education institutions. The statute states: Consistent with the duty of the University to take all such steps as it may deem fit for the promotion of the Open University and distance education systems in the educational pattern of country and for the coordination and determination of standards of teaching, evaluation research in such systems; and in pursuance of the objects of the University to encourage greater flexibility, diversity, accessibility, mobility and innovation in education at the University level by making full use of the latest scientific knowledge and new educational, technology, and to further cooperation between the existing Universities, it is considered necessary and expedient to establish a Distance Education Council as an authority of the University under Section 16 of the Act.

Facilitative Role of NAAC

The National Assessment and Accreditation Council (NAAC) is an autonomous organization established within UGC in 1994, on the recommendation of the National Policy on Education (NPE) 1986 and its sequential Programme of Action (PoA 1992).1t is the only external quality assurance body in India, its vision is to make quality the defining element of higher education in India through a combination of self and external quality evaluation, promotion and sustenance of initiatives.

Joint Efforts of NCTE, DEC and NAAC

Extensive discussions happened during late nineties between NCTE and DEC (IGNOU) on one side and NCTE and NAAC on the other. There were also concerns about each other's statutory power and extent of coverage.

NCTE was considered primarily responsible for recognition of teacher education courses leading to first Diploma and Degree in Pre-primary, elementary and secondary teacher education in campus based, part-time and distance education modes. Accordingly, NCTE has formulated Norms and Standards for recognizing Diploma in Elementary Education, Bachelor of Education, and Master of Education programmes offered by distance education mode.

DEC was mandated with quality assurance in all open distance learning course's including those for teacher education and hence, NCTE and DEC constituted a joint committee to Jointly execute the recognition task for teacher education programmes offered by ODL. An Memorandum of Understanding (MoU) was signed between NCTE and DEC of IGNOU in 2004 with a number of aims and objectives including: "carry out the various functions of NCTE, as mandated under its Act and ensure coordinated and integrated development of teacher education under distance mode in the country by maintenance of Norms and Standards"; and "jointly determine and implement the Norms and Standards to teacher education in distance mode, as laid down amended from time to time, for Diploma/Degree/PG level studies in the field of teacher education".

Similarly, NCTE also signed an MOU with NAAC. Both NAAC and NCTE are the outcomes of the recommendations contained in the NPE and PoA. While the enactment of the NCTE Act by the Parliament in 1993; marked the most purposeful and determined action taken at the National level to place teacher education at a high pedestal, the establishment of NAAC by the UGC in1994, signaled an equally lofty resolve in uplifting the quality of Higher Education including that of higher education offered by alternative modes such as open and distance learning. In fulfilment of the provisions laid down in the NCTE Act 12(k) "to evolve suitable performance appraisal systems, norms and mechanisms for enforcing accountability on recognized institutions" and for quality assurance of Teacher Education Institutions (TEIs), the NAAC and the NCTE have entered into an MoU for executing the process of assessment and accreditation of all TEIs coming under the provisions of the NCTE Act. The efforts of NCTE and NAAC to ensure and assure the quality of TEIs in the country are complimentary to each other. Combining the expertise of NCTE in teacher education and of NAAC in quality assurance expertise, the NAAC developed the methodology for assessment and accreditation of TEIs and the "Manual for Self appraisal of Teacher Educational Institutions".

The norms and standards for a teacher education programme through open and distance learning system formulated for D.Ed., B.Ed. and M.Ed. by NCTE constitute primarily aspects such as duration, number of intake, admission eligibility, admission procedure, infrastructure and human resources for teaching and learning related support, number of contact day/hours, quantum of practical work etc. DEC norms would also include the format and style of the self-learning materials and other study materials. These norms and standards basically define the minimum standard required for each programme to be recognized and this recognition is renewed periodically. The role of NAAC being quality assurance, it facilitates self-appraisal and external evaluation with an aim to support enhancing quality in various aspects of the institutional functioning. It gives considerable emphasis for institutional processes along with inputs and output performance.

With an assumption that there are several basic quality indicators in programmes and institutions which are common to all modes, NAAC along with the Commonwealth of learning brought out a 'Quality Assurance Tool-kit for Teacher Education Institutions' including institutions of open and distance learning. The Tool-kit was developed with the involvement of over 300 teacher education professionals from all over Commonwealth.

Way Forward

India has more than forty years of experience in offering teacher education programmes and courses using initially correspondence mode and later open and distance learning mode. Use of Information and Communication Technology (ICT) in combination with other non-electronic media started in mid-eighties and today India has the national ICT infrastructure adequate enough to launch programmes entirely though e-learning. ODL based teacher education especially for; in-service teacher education will develop and continue to provide training to many teachers and other personnel in the system.

In India, developments, in ICT infrastructure and connectivity are growing steadily providing access to majority of people in the country. ICT applications for open and distance education is being developed and provided by IGNOU and other open universities and other autonomous organizations. Technology and platforms for on-line, provision of courses are available. In the coming years we hope to see more development in innovative course designs with appropriate pedagogy or learning designs suitable to various kinds of learning and training using on-line platforms.

Face-to-face education/training and ODL based education/ training ware for a long time considered parallel modes with definite characteristics. Hence, institutions offering only one of these modes were called single mode universities/ institutions to differentiate from dual mode universities/ institutions which offered courses through both modes. When there has been flexibility in dual mode institutions for students to combine course study from both the modes these were called as mixed mode institutions. This classification continues in many countries. However, with the development and use of ICT in both face-to-face and ODL modes, the differentiating characteristics are getting blurred. There are universities where the students although stay in the campus, learn most of the time thorough distance learning techniques including on-line learning .There is definitely a trend towards convergence of the both the modes.

There is definitely an increasing trend of shift of control of learning from the providers to the learners. Earlier models of ODL such as the correspondence courses and distance teaching universities are essentially institution or provider controlled. The open universities did try to create more flexibility in the course delivery and learner support facilitating more and more focus on the individual learner. With appropriate technologies, becoming accessible and cheaper to the learner, the possibility of each learner planning and organizing his or her learning in one's own way is increasing. This is bound to happen in teacher education too especially in ODL based in-service teacher training where each teacher would be able to identify the required competencies one wants to develop and enroll in courses accordingly through on-line or blended modes. He or she should be able to complete the course at one's own pace mostly learning with the support of Open Education Resources (OERs), interact with other teacher and experts through synchronous and non-synchronous online interaction and practice by applying the learning in one's own teaching and other school based activities. All these would facilitate him/her to have collaborative reflective practice leading to development of the relevant competencies.

Quality assurance in ODL based teacher training is another area. This would attract more attention in the coming years. It is hoped that the NCTE, DEC and NAAC will work more closely to make sure that quality is never sacrificed along with encouraging the adoption of innovative designs and technologies for teacher training. The focus today by agencies like NCTE and DEC is to provide standard models and frameworks of quality curriculum and transaction systems expecting all institutions to follow that. While this is required, agencies should encourage and foster creativity and flexibility for innovative curriculum and systems to emerge and flourish. Prescribed norms and standards are important, provide what is to be encouraged is to follow the spirit of those requirement rather than forcing institutions to follow them mechanically.

REFERENCES

1. Menon M., Rama. K., Lakshmi T.K.S. and Bhat V.D. (2007), Quality Indicators for Teacher Education, Bangalore, NAAC/COL.
2. NAAC and COL (2007), Quality Assurance Tool Kit for Teacher Education Institutions, Bangalore, NAAC.
3. NCERT (1990), A Report of the NCTE Committee on Teacher Education Programme through Distance Education Mode, New Delhi, NCERT.
4. NCTE (2005), Act, Rules and Regulations (updated up to 30 September, 2005) New Delhi, NCTE.

6. Report of an Expert Committee of NCTE (1995), Different Modes of Education used for Teacher Preparation in India - A Study, NCTE, New Delhi.
7. Report of the UGC Delegation to study evening and correspondence courses 1971, New Delhi.
8. Siddiqui.M.A., Sharma. A.K., Arora. G.L., Teacher Education (Reflections Towards Policy Formulation), NCTE, New Delhi, pp. 272-277.

28

Quality Concerns in Teacher Education–Agencies, Indicators and Enhancement

L. Chinna Reddeppa
Lecturer, MNR PG Teacher Education College, Hyderabad
Dr. K. S. Prabhakaram
MNR PG Teacher Education College, Hyderabad

Introduction

In the present day society one thing is constant that is change. It has changed the societies dramatically. Ancient was changed to medieval, medieval to modern, modern to super modern and what the next-supersonic. How long this wave would continue. Everywhere the change is there, changing the society, life style of the people, market structure, education, culture and what not. With the changing times, the position, status and the role of a teacher have undergone a change from the highest stature (Guru Brahma, Guru Vishnu, Guru Devo Maheshwara) in ancient times to the present stature (Guru friend, Guru facilitator, Guru adapter).

The development of one's education system depends on its planners, administrators, educationists and the teachers. Keeping all the other things constant, one thing i.e., teachers can be manipulated to make an education system developed. This is why it is said that a good mass of teachers can change the fate of a society. It has also been reflected in the Report of Education Commission (1964-66) as the commission begins its report with this statement "the destiny of India is now being shaped in her classrooms".

Concept of Quality

It is very difficult to give a comprehensive definition of quality. Quality is not an act, it is a habit. It generally signifies the degree of excellence. It is the totality of featurers and characteristics of the product, process or service that bear on its ability to satisfy stated or implied needs. When we describe human being as product, the description cannot encapsulate all the characteristics of teachers or learners in the same way, as one would describe the quality of commodities. Hence, the definition of quality varies depending upon the individual, institution, educational situation, social and national context.

Quality Concerns

Teacher education program is an integral part of educational system, which is directly linked with the society. Its scope and objectives have become larger in the modern society. The major factors of quality concerns in teacher education are input, process and product factors.

Input Factors

Input factors involve all the physical infrastructure such as building, equipment, library books, laboratory, playground etc. It also includes student's entry behaviour such as their family background, socio-economic status, academic achievement, their interest, need etc. Teachers' entry behaviour such as their academic and professional background, socio-economic status, their attitude towards teaching profession, interest etc., are also considered as input factors.

Process Factors

A teacher education programme is said to be successful if its outcomes are maximized amongst the trainees in terms of development of necessary skills, values and attitudes. Quality lies in its processes, out put is the result of processes. A process is a particular course of action intended to achieve the desired results. Good quality inputs coupled with weak processes may not lead to desired outcomes. On the other hand, good quality processes coupled with minimum desirable inputs may lead to desired outcomes.

Product Factors

Product factors are the desired outputs of a given course of instruction. It determines whether objectives of a particular course of instruction are being achieved or not. They are students' academic achievement, commitment to teaching profession, efficiency in learning, personality development etc.

Agencies of Quality Assurance

Various agencies are involved for assuring quality in teacher education, the significant ones are as follows:

(a) National Council for Teacher Education (NCTE)

The National Council for Teacher Education (NCTE) became a statutory body by an act of Parliament in 1993.The main objective of the NCTE is to achieve planned and coordinated development of the teacher education system throughout the country. It is also involved in the regulation and proper maintenance of norms and standards in teacher education system. It is mandatory for the existing and new institutions to seek NCTE recognition after fulfiling the NCTE norms. Further these recognized institutions have to submit the Performance Appraisal Report (PAR) annually. On the basis of PAR, actions are taken to withdraw the recognition in case of violation of norms and standards.

In 2000, the council also developed "Curriculum Framework for Quality Teacher Education" for upgrading the quality of teacher education programmes at par with international standards. NCTE being aware of the importance of Information and Communication Technology (lCT), has made ICT literacy a compulsory part of B. Ed. course.

(b) National Assessment and Accreditation Council (NAAC)

All over the world, since the 1980 the expansion of the system of higher education was coupled with mounting criticisms about the quality of education. As a result of this, establishment of quality assurance agencies has become a common phenomenon worldwide. India has joined this trend in 1994. The primary objective of establishment of NAAC is to assess and accredit institutions of liberal arts, sciences and other disciplines in order to help these institutions to work continuously to improve the quality of education, through self evaluation of performance of an institution and/or its units based on self study and peer review through defined criteria. The three stage process for assessment and accreditation as follows:

1. Preparation of the Self-appraisal Report by the teacher education institution for submission to NAAC;
2. Validation of the Self-appraisal Report by peers visiting the institution; and
3. The final decision of NAAC based on the Self-appraisal Report and the recommendations of the team of peers.

(c) Universities

The university is responsible for providing affiliation to the teacher education institutions situated in its jurisdiction. It also designs curriculum, coordinates for quality teaching, and conducts examination. It also prescribes norms for certification of faculties. It is also engaged in capacity building through faculty development programme and research.

(d) Institutions of Teacher Education

Teacher education institutions create appropriate infrastructure for providing quality teacher education and grants admission against management seats. It organizes teaching as per prescribed curriculum of the affiliating university. It is also engaged in appointing faculties and overall management of the institution. It also coordinates with the affiliation university, NCTE and the State government, in all matters regarding teacher education.

Quality Indicators

In order to assess the quality of teacher education institutions, certain quality indicators are to be considered.

NAAC (2004) has identified seven core indicators for quality teacher education as follows :

1. Curriculum planning and design, which includes goal orientation, curriculum development, programme options, academic flexibility and feedback mechanism.
2. Curriculum transaction and evaluation which includes admission process, catering to diverse needs, teaching learning process, teacher quality, evaluation of teaching, evaluation of learning and examination reform.
3. Research, Development and Extension, which includes promotion of research, research output, publication output, consultancy, extension activities, participation in extension and linkages.
4. Infrastructure and learning resources which includes physical facilities, maintenance of infrastructure, library as a learning resource, computers as learning resources and other facilities.
5. Student Support and Progression which includes student profile, student progression, student support and student activities.
6. Organization and Management which includes goal orientation and decision making. Organization structure, powers and functions of functionaries, perspective planning, human power planning and recruitment, performance appraisal, staff development programmes, resource mobilization and financial management.
7. Healthy practices which include total quality management, innovations, value-based education, social responsibilities and citizenship roles, overall development and institutional ambience and initiatives.

Enhancing Quality-Some Suggestions

The skill development of student teachers should be on par with their counterparts abroad. With liberalization of economic activities, the demand for teacher education at nationally comparable and internationally acceptable standards has increased. This demands the teacher education institutions to be innovative, creative and entrepreneurial in their approach to skill development among the students.

Although skill development is crucial to the success of the teachers in the job market, skills are of no value in the absence of an appropriate value system. Teacher education institutions have to shoulder the responsibility of inculcating the desirable value system among the student teachers commensurate with social, cultural, economic and environmental realities at the local, national and universal level.

Our teachers are still uncomfortable with the use of technology in the classroom. They should be trained to use the technological innovations that are readily available. Effective use of information and communication technologies in teacher education institutions can improve the quality of teacher education.

In order to manage the expanding work and complex nature of the problems of teacher education, every State should have a separate Directorate of Teacher Education. Such Directorate will also be responsible for manpower planning with respect to recruitment of various levels of teachers in the concerned State.

The assessment procedure of NCTE, NAAC and the University should help the teacher education institutions to know its strengths, weaknesses opportunities and threats. It should provide the funding agencies with objective and systematic database for performance funding.

School curriculum is becoming more and more complex. Many new areas of knowledge are getting into the curriculum. In this situation, one-time teacher training of a particular duration may not serve the purpose. There should be continuous in-service programme organized both through face-to-face and distance mode in order to make the teachers cope with the latest developments.

Each teacher is expected to involve in undertaking action research for qualitative improvement of classroom teaching. They should also be involved in developing teaching and learning (print and non-print) instructional materials, psychological tools etc. This will help the teachers in updating their knowledge and skills continuously as well as improving their self-esteem.

Teacher workshops and seminars which can benefit teachers at all levels and the most effective in-service programmes tend to be the ones that teachers request. Colleges of Teacher Education can arrange centers where teachers can come together with other teachers and perhaps with other useful persons to do things that will help them teach better.

REFERENCES

1. Mishra, 2004, Privatization of Higher Education Policy Prospective and Role of Regulatory Bodies.
2. NAAC 2004, NAAC a decade of dedication to quality assurance. NAAC Bangalore.
3. NCTE - Policy Prospective in Teacher Education, Critique and Documentation NCTE, New Delhi.

29

Quality Assurance, Challenges in ODL Programmes

Shamshaad Begum
Asst. Professor, Dept. of Education and Training, MANUU, Hyderabad

ABSTRACT

Open distance learning programs are essentially continuing education programs for the employed with a goal of participation in the human development.

The distance learning model is a 'person centered' form of continuing education, where the educational goals of a degree program are strongly integrated with the work environment of the student.

Open and Distance Learning (ODL) aims at providing need-based quality education to large and heterogeneous groups of learners at affordable cost.

In this system learning outcomes are prescribed similar as formal and distance mode learning. ODL produces self-instructional materials (SIM), arranging personal contact programs, conducting examinations and offering student support services throughout the study period.

The institutional models of open universities are designed to effectively respond to the growth and development of ODL particularly to meet the educational requirements of the regions, for which they have the mandate.

ODL systems contribute to human capital formation and pave the way for higher education and for making the economy globally competitive.

Open distance learning programs are essentially continuing education programs for the employed with a goal of participation in the human development.

The on campus education (formal education) involves the university as the pivotal element and the students being processed through it, the distance learning programs involve the student as the pivotal entity around which the university, the work environment and the educational programs revolve. Mostly the distance learning model is a 'person centered' form of continuing education, where the educational goals of a degree program are strongly integrated with the work environment of the student.

Generally the learning environment of a student under the distance learning program consists of three broad facts:

(1) Create academic environment.

(2) Impart structural guidance and conduct planned evaluation of assignments bringing closer the educational needs and the manpower development needs.

(3) The work environment of the student employee where theory is forced to be seen continuously against the backdrop of practice in his job, while strengthening analytical skill and techniques.

Technological Development and Forms of Distance Education

Distance Education can be classified into three stages of development or generations, each reflecting major technological innovations.

(1) First generation is characterized by the prominent use of a single technology (initially correspondence by mail, subsequently radio, and then television) and lack as direct student interaction with teacher originating the instruction.

(2) Second generation distance education is characterized by a deliberately integrated multimedia approach, with learning materials specifically designed for study at a

distance, but with two way communication still mediated by a third person.

(3) Third generation education is based on "Two way communication media" which allow for direct interaction between the teacher who originates the instruction and the remote students either individually or as groups and third generation as a progressive increase (from first to third generation) in learner control opportunities for dialogue and emphasis on thinking skills rather than mere comprehension.

Expansion of Technologies for Distance Education

There has been a rapid expansion in the range and types of technologies available to distance education, The more traditional technologies of broadcasting through television and radio, audio and video cassettes and Print production are being utilized but have still have to be fully exploited, either because of the high operating costs, problems of adaptation to local conditions, want of skilled personnel and want of effectiveness.

In addition to these older technologies there are new technologies that are available to distance educators such as electronic publishing, teletext, satellites, cable T.V, teleconferencing, video text, video discs, electronic media, cell phones, etc.

Resources of Online Learning

The electronic journals are trough (computer mediated communication) network. They are increasingly important resources for information and learning.

Learning Methods

Online Teaching: The methods of choice are instructor centered such as On-line lectures or Teacher Oriented dialogue. The teacher has an active role and 1earners are guided and receive precise instruction, as to what they are to learn. During this learning process prepared knowledge and thinking schema are imparted.

Quality Assurance and Enhancement in Open and Distance Learning

Open and Distance Learning (ODL) aims at providing need-based quality education to large and heterogeneous groups of learners at affordable cost. The learners who are in services or doing other jobs can pursue further studies or vocational training in specific field through ODL system. In the ODL system learning outcomes are prescribed as the same for both formal and distance mode learning. ODL system produces self-instructional materials (SIM) for self-learning, arranging personal contact programs, conducting examinations and offering student support services throughout the period of study.

A systematic service-delivery mechanism is essentially followed by the ODL system to cater to the needs of distance learners, student accessible environment, resourcefulness; qualified personnel to guide and online transaction of curriculum are all set for the learners at the institution. Periodical assessment, assignment evaluation, and term-end examinations are done promptly. Incorporation of lCT, adequate training inputs, monitoring, and follow-up activities are taken care of logically. Difficulties of the students, difference in service mode, change in schedule of activities, etc. are addressed immediately for successful learning. Guidance and counseling with regards to successful completion of the program, further study, are given to learners through reachable mode.

The flexibility approach in learning schedule, curricular transaction and examination patterns of these criteria, the quality should also be assured along with the quantity intake in the ODL system.

The ODL institution should satisfy the requirements of the learners by prompt service delivery, apt curriculum flexibility in-approach, cost-effectiveness and career opportunities. In ODL system study materials personal contact programmers learning support system, examination and evaluation system are expected to be systematic. Qualitative measures must be designed in such a way as to learners enrolled. Every ODL providing institution should maintain quality.

Quality in education should extend its reach to the fulfilment of educational objectives. Educational institutions should design quality instruction planning programs to optimize the learning situations.

ODL should aspire for philosophy in inspiration, principle in vision for lifelong learning - strategy for learning skills, technology for easy learning, resources for maximizing facilities, organization for student support service. Internal evaluation for remediation and enhancement to be inbuilt in institutional structure.

The conventional universities have also started offering their programs in both on campus and off-campus modes. India has more open and distance universities and more distance learners than any other country in the world.

Challenges in ODL for Maintaining Quality

(1) Adequate infrastructure
(2) Recruitment of efficient and sincere staff
(3) Quality self-instructional material
(4) Prompt dissemination of course materials
(5) Courses being offered to be redrafted every five years such that only relevant dynamic modules are changed without changing the core-content.
(6) Proper orientation of workforce of ODL.
(7) Prompt communication gadgets and repliers.

Updating the curriculum from time to time and maintaining international standards of evaluation mechanism to meet the essential changes taking place in the global scenario. To meet these challenges, all ODL providers should undergo the national/international assessment and accreditation mechanism.

A new policy has been developed that requires every Distance Education program to be certified by the Distance Education Council (DEC) by IGNOU.

A system for sharing teaching materials and knowledge should be developed that incorporates quality control. Organizations such as IGNOU have a major role to play in assuring quality through a team of experts. IGNOU has the same role to play for distance education as the University Grants Commission (UGC) in India plays for conventional education and is responsible for ensuring quality in distance education.

IGNOU, the premier distance learning institute in India has been in the forefront in collaborating and offering quality education. In the recent past, IGNOU had signed a Memorandum of understanding (MoU) with various organizations for example the collaboration of MANUU with IGNOU. In preparing SIM's for ODL through Urdu under the supervision of translation division. Presently MANUU has its vast ODL system through which it is offering various courses as given:

(1) M. A. Urdu
(2) M. A. History
(3) M. A. English
(4) Bachelor of Education
(5) Bachelor of Arts
(6) Bachelor of Commerce
(7) Bachelor of Science (MPC and BZC)
(8) Diploma in Teaching English
(9) Diploma in Primary Education
(10) Diploma in Journalism and Mass Communication
(11) Certificate in Food and Nutrition
(12) Certificate in Proficiency in Urdu through English
(13) Certificate in Proficiency in Urdu through Hindi
(14) Certificate in Functional English

MANUU and IGNOU had in 2009 signed an MoU for sharing electronic resource material. MANUU is telecasting video lessons for its students through Doordarshan Urdu channel since January 2008.

The Directorate of Distance Education has mainly targeted to serve Uneducated Youth, Dropouts, Women, Housewives and Uneducated Adults. Most of the students are from middle and lower income socio-economic strata and the proportion of the females in the enrolled students is highly appreciative. Different courses are being introduced on need basis from time to time. The courses are being augmented with various types of student support facilities like Toll Free telephone lines, audio-video programs, dynamic website etc.

MANUU offers education through formal mode as well. B.Ed. distance mode classes are also conducted by subject experts to teach their concerned subjects.

Open Distance Learning in Andhra Pradesh

A.P. with an area of 2,75,069 sq. km is the fifth largest state in the Indian Republic, starting with the School of Correspondence Courses of Andhra University, Vishakhapatnam and the Institute of Correspondence Courses in Sri Venkateswara University in 1972.

The government of A.P. established in 1982 to serve the cause of open distance learning. This university was renamed as Dr. B.R. Ambedkar Open University in 1991.

National Open University

1. Indira Gandhi National Open University, New Delhi

State Open Universities

1. Dr. B.R. Ambedkar Open University, Hyderabad
2. Dr. Babasaheb Ambedkar Open University, Ahmedabad, Gujarat
3. Kamataka State Open University, Mysore, Karnataka
4. Krishanakant Handique State Open University, Guwahati, Assam
5. M. P. Bhoj (Open) University, Bhopal, MP
6. Nalanda Open University, Patna, Bihar
7. Netaji Subhas Open University, Kolkata, WB
8. Pt. Sunderlal Shanna (Open) University, Bilaspur, Chattisgarh

9. Tamil Nadu Open University, Chennai, Tamil Nadu
10. U.P. Rajarshi Tandon Open University, Allahabad, UP
11. Uttarakhand Open University, Haldwani, Uttarakhand
12. Vardhaman Mahaveer Open University, Kota, Rajasthan
13. Yashwantrao Chavan Maharashtra Open University, Nasik.

Dual Mode Universities Andhra Pradesh

1. Andhra University, Vishakhapatnam
2. University of English and Foreign Languages, Hyderabad
3. Jawaharlal Nehru Technological University, Hyderabad
4. Kakatiya University, Warangal
5. Maulana Azad National Urdu University, Hyderabad
6. Acharya Nagarjuna University, Guntur
7. National Academy of Legal Studies and Research University (NALSAR), Hyderabad
8. Osmania University, Hyderabad
9. Potti Sreeramulu Telugu University, Hyderabad
10. Sri Krishnadevaraya University, Anantapur
11. Sri Venkateswara University, Tirupati
12. Sri. Padmavathi Mahila Visvavidyalayam, Tirupati
13. University of Hyderabad, Hyderabad
14. Dravidian University, Kuppam
15. GITAM University, Vishakhapatnam
16. Rashtriya Sanskrit Vidyapeetha, Tirupati

CONCLUSION

The institutional models of open universities are designed to effectively respond to the growth and development of ODL particularly to meet the educational requirements of the regions, for which they have the mandate.

ODL systems contribute to human capital formation and pave the way for higher education and for making the economy globally competitive.

REFERENCES

1. Open Distance Learning – Journal.
2. Educators – monthly Journal.
3. A Host of Books on ODL.
4. Self-Experience and Observation.
5. www.manuu.ac.in.

30

Quality Parameters of ODL Teacher Education Programmes

A. Lakshmi Devi
Lecturer, Annamacharya College of Education, Rajampet, Kadapa Dt (A.P.)
Dr. K. C. Shankaraiah
Principal, Sreedevi College of Education, Borampalli (V), Anantapur.

ABSTRACT

Teachers do not enter the class room as finished products. Most teachers who remain in the profession grow overtime and become better. Though there is evidence over the qualifications of those who enter the profession and their potential foryality, curriculum of preservice teacher education programs and in-service teacher education programs could raise the standards of those who enter the profession and support the teachers through their careers. The article describes what quality in a teacher education is and examines various aspects from the context of teacher's progression along with the continuum of teaching from teacher preparation through ongoing professional development and performance evaluation.

Introduction

According to the Delor's Commission (1996) education must be organized four fundamental types of learning (a) Learning to know (b) Learning to do (c) Learning to live together (d) Learning to be.

Teacher education is involved in the process of preparing teachers and supports them throughout their careers.

According to No Child Left Behind Act (NCLBA, 2004) to be highly qualified the teacher should have a bachelor's degree or certified by the State and demonstrate subject-matter competence in each academic subject they teach.

- Good teachers produce good students
- Both subject knowledge and content-based Pedagogy are important
- Good teaching techniques basic academic skills, through content knowledge of each subject taught, knowledge of both generic and content specific pedagogy, and hand on teaching skills
- According to Dave (1998), there are five performance areas for teachers
- Performance in the class room
- School level performance· Performance in out of school activities
- Performance related to community contact and cooperation
- Dave (1998) has also given ten competency areas
- Contextual competencies
- Conceptual competencies
- Curricular and content competencies
- Competencies in other educational activities
- Competency related to teaching learning material
- Evaluation competencies
- Management competencies
- Competencies related to community contact and cooperation
- Competencies related to parent contact and cooperation

Quality Parameters of ODL Teacher Education Programmes

Quality has been described as a degree of excellence and superiority in kind. Depending upon the view point of the state holders in ODL teacher education quality is viewed :

- In terms of highest standard

- In terms of consistency
- As fitness for purpose
- As value of money
- For effective quality parameters of ODL teacher education, the following aspects need to be monitored and assessed:
  - Infrastructure development
  - Curriculum design
  - Human resources and research development
  - Teaching and learning methodology
  - Evaluation and monitoring
  - Linkages with community

University leadership programmes for college teachers and seminars, workshops and summer schools in various subjects in the states are necessary to help the teachers upgrade their knowledge and skills.

Areas of ODL Teacher Education Programmes

- Community health education
- Injury prevention and rehabilitation
- Nutrition, health and human performance
- Personnel development
- Family and consumer sciences
- Student support services
- Technical and career education

The teachers need to be equipped to handle:

- Different types of schools
- Different types of boards
- Text books
- Accountability and rights
- Discipline from within
- Availability of teacher educators in the institutions for a minimum of five hours if not eight hours for five days a week
- Satisfaction in the profession
- Visionary outlook

Strategies

- Group discussions
- Demonstrations
- Seminars
- Symposia
- Field trips
- Debates
- Essay competitions
- Peer view exchanges
- Role-plays
- Activities

Practicals

- The practical training in guidance and counseling need to be included in the teacher education curriculum.
- Peer tutoring.
- Case studies.
- Computer literacy.
- Teaching assistance~ships.
- Use of school bus.
- Boarding and lodging facilities for in-terms who need it.
- Socio-cultural foundations of educations in a multi-cultural environment.
- Educational psychology - a focus on teaching and learning in the school setting.
- Envisioning, exploring and creating a social world.
- Curriculum studies and its critical analysis.
- Value education - competencies to be develop.

CONCLUSION

The quality parameters of ODL teacher education is directly linked to the Nation's development. Therefore care should be taken in providing quality education to future teachers and also in the teacher support services. Teacher evaluation should be a regular feature to sensitize the teachers regarding development in their subjects.

REFERENCES

1. Abraham. J. (2003), Guidance and counseling for teacher education, Delhi: Sarp and Sons.
2. Ausbel, D. (1968), Educational Psychology, Winston.
3. Harnett, A.M. (1990-91), Preparation of middle school teachers, search results.

Theme–VII

ODL Teacher Education Programmes and Other ODL Programmes

31

Using Social Media to Create a Personal Learning Network for Continual Learning

Ghazala Ansari
Alak HSC, B-1/0-1, Sector 19-A, Nerul (East), Navi Mumbai-400706

ABSTRACT

In a student's journey through formal education, teachers play one of the most important roles. As such, a teacher's preparedness in teaching students has a direct impact on the quality of student education. While formal teacher education forms an important component in this preparedness, by nature, such education is structured and event-based. There is a need for effective and continual preparedness through informal self-learning. One way of doing this is by leveraging the capabilities offered through social media. Today, social media provides varied opportunities in helping teachers constantly prepare and update themselves on strategies and tools to tackle the challenges of effective teaching. With such opportunities, teachers are equally responsible to shoulder the onus of getting themselves trained. Social media can help teachers organise and develop their own Personal Learning Network (PLN) to work towards continual preparedness.

This paper deals with the benefit of using social media for continual teacher training. Key activities of a PLN have been identified as 'learn', 'collaborate', 'share', 'organise' and 'network'. How each of these activities can be leveraged in a PLN ecosystem has been elucidated by considering popularly used or representative tools. Through an understanding of this framework, new teachers can independently establish an individualised and cost-effective

PLN for themselves in their goal towards continually bettering their teaching and facilitating skills.

Keywords: PLN, social media, informal learning, training, tools.

Background

Fast-paced, Information-rich World

We live in an information-rich world. With so much information changing so rapidly, 'information overload' has become a common byword in our lives. As professionals, deciphering and managing such a quantum of information is quite a challenge. However, precisely because of the quantum, it is also a necessity to be accomplished. To develop oneself as an informed and progressive teacher, this challenge needs to be addressed. Some immediate consequences of living in a fact-changing, information-rich world for a teacher would be:

1. Necessity of immediate updates on key perspectives and practices prevailing in the education domain.
2. A framework to be able to sift through enormous information and quickly reach relevant information.
3. Inability of structured teaching to instantly address the change of pace.

In this age of fast-paced, information heavy environment, individuals can no longer afford to wait to be taught in a structured manner.

Informal Learning

Jay Cross in his book 'Informal Learning: Rediscovering the Pathways that Inspire Innovation and Performance' (2007) makes a case that around 80 per cent of what people learn is through informal learning. "Workers learn more in the coffee room than in the classroom. They discover how to do their jobs through informal learning: talking, observing others, trial and error, and simply working with people in the know. Formal learning—classes and workshops—is the source of only 10 to 20 per cent of what people learn at work. ... In short, informal learning is generally more effective and less expensive than its formal counterpart."

The 80:20 (informal:formal) model indicates that for effective learning to occur in adult professionals, the informal zone needs to be better harnessed. Effective learning leads to contextual retention and the ability to translate that learning into real-life practices.

Social Media

The technological environment today has made online networking and collaboration through social media interesting, varied and interactive. The nature of tools available through social media makes informal learning through observation, discussion and collaboration a real-time, contextual, effective, and personal activity.

By using the right combination of tools, individual teachers can set their own personal learning network which will ensure a framework for continual learning and expertise building.

Benefits of Informal Learning

By focussing on informal learning, teachers will experience several benefits. They will be able to:

- Set their own objectives.
- Organise information to the logic of how they learn and work.
- Set their preferences.
- Be in touch with practitioners rather than structured learning courseware.
- Pull the information they need rather than have a bundled programme pushed towards them that may not be of immediate benefit.
- Get access to what they need, when they need it.
- Have room for trial and error methods that require observation, discussion, questions to experts, pilot solutions, and reflection.
- No certificate awarded; however, there will be an observable capability improvement.

Why Social Media?

The 2000s have brought in a revolution in the way people meet, communicate and collaborate. Building acquaintances and friendships merely on the basis of online interaction has become a regular phenomenon. From shopping, buying books or the weekly groceries, booking movies, following news and journals, to financial planning and banking, most activities can be done online.

For instance, one may envision the following scenario:

1. You start your day by checking your RSS feed reader for specific updates and reading material. Over a period of time you have spent time is personalising the feed reader so that you get only the information you want.
2. You find out about an online workshop and decide to enrol. You tweet about it to your friends using a micro-blogging site like Twitter. You come to know that several from the network of people you follow on Twitter have enrolled for it.
3. Using Elluminate, a web conferencing tool, you listen to the speakers through audio transmission and slide presentations and then participate in the extended discussion using the tool's instant messenger.
4. At the same time you upload links to resources being shared during the workshop on your school's closed social networking platform, Ning.
5. One of your colleagues posts a query to you that you immediately relay back at the workshop.
6. After the workshop, you write a note on your learning and experiences and post it on your blog.
7. Someone in another country picks up your post and links it to a new forum.
8. Because of the trackback feature on your blog, you get notified of this linking. People start posting messages to you on this new forum.
9. With all the queries that you get, you decide to create a quick presentation using Microsoft PowerPoint and upload it on a file sharing site like Slideshare.

Before you know it, you have new connections and peers to interact with. Thus, the hallmark of social media is:

- Flexibility
- Non-linear interactions
- Range of tools with different purpose and features to choose from
- Free access
- Intuitive and easy-to-use tools
- Free training/help modules on tools easily available on the Internet

How will a PLN Help ?

A PLN allows teachers to create their own unique and personalised network. A PLN is not technologically dependent. Even a network of school colleagues would be considered a PLN if there is sufficient sharing, connecting, collaboration and reflection occurring within the group. However, with the variety of social and online tools available, creating and following a PLN has become an immediate, personal, effective, and creative activity.

Learning is a multi-dimensional activity. A PLN will only be successful if it acts as a reciprocal learning system. While it allows a teacher to find what they like and the opinions that they value, in turn they have to add their experience back to the conversations.

The PLN Environment

Listed below are some of the key benefits of establishing a social media based PLN for teachers:

Experience

- Updates on new developments (practices, methods, programmes, tools, industry news/trends)
- Answers to questions from peers and experts
- Tuning into the ideas, developments and concerns that are engaging the larger audience nationally and internationally
- Sourcing of collaborators to work with them on their projects/ideas
- Establishing multiple sources of getting information

Contribute

- Creating/participating in a network of like-minded people for exchange of ideas
- Collaborating on projects that they find interesting
- Being able to reach a large audience
- Receiving inputs from peers and experts to improve their ideas/work.

Personalise

- Learn at your own time and pace
- Filter information - learn what you find relevant
- Make sense of the chaos that is the Internet in ways that is relevant to you
- Engage in contextual (hence effective) learning
- Engage in just-in-time learning
- Inexpensive and personalised framework.

Core Focus

Very broadly, we can place the popularly used social media tools under 5 categories.

The tools associated with the focus areas are for illustrative purpose. Due to its largely open source nature, several tools

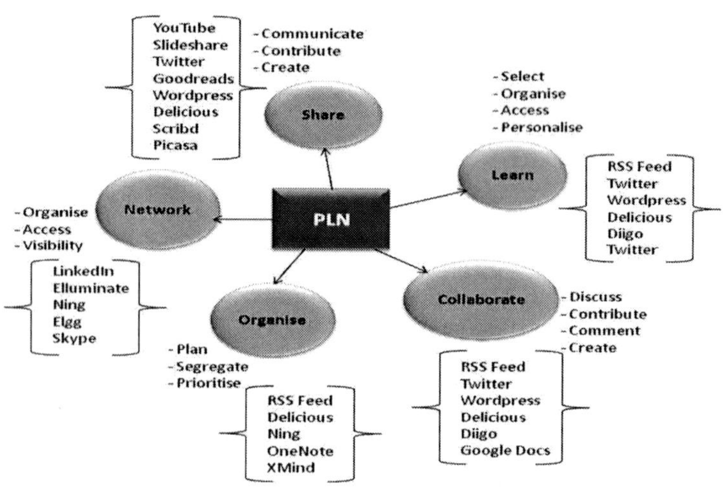

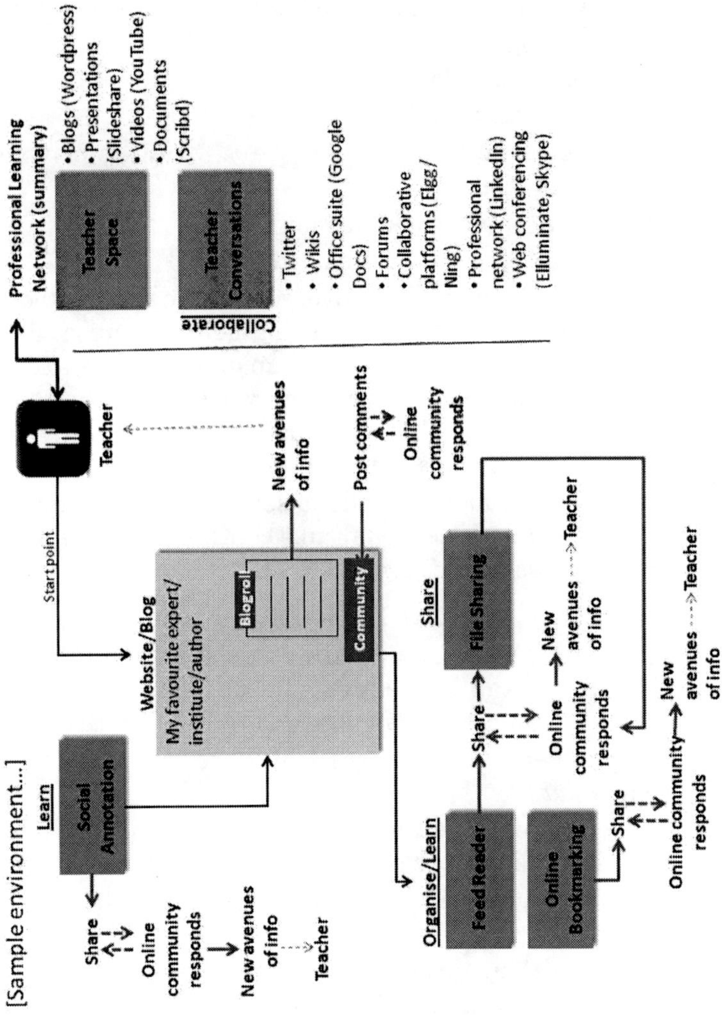
[Sample environment...]
Learn
Social Annotation
Share
Online community responds
New avenues of info
Teacher
Start point
Teacher
Website/Blog
My favourite expert/ institute/author
Blogroll
Community
New avenues of info
Post comments
Online community responds
Professional Learning Network (summary)
Teacher Space
• Blogs (Wordpress)
• Presentations (Slideshare)
• Videos (YouTube)
• Documents (Scribd)
Collaborate
Teacher Conversations
• Twitter
• Wikis
• Office suite (Google Docs)
• Forums
• Collaborative platforms (Elgg/ Ning)
• Professional network (LinkedIn)
• Web conferencing (Elluminate, Skype)
Organise/Learn
Feed Reader
Online Bookmarking
Share
File Sharing
Share
Online community responds
New avenues of info
Teacher
Share
Online community responds
New avenues of info
Teacher

will be available for the same purpose. For instance, both Wordpress and Blogspot may be used for blogging. The choice of tool is largely an individual decision.

So far this year (2010), the top 5 tools that are emerging are:

1. Twitter (micro-blogging)
2. YouTube (video sharing)
3. Google Docs (office suite – collaborative documentation)
4. Delicious (online bookmarking)
5. Slideshare (presentation sharing)

As is evident from the list above, several file sharing tools are quite popular. Online bookmarking helps organise sites using tags and tag bundles in the same manner that the folder structure allows on the desktop. However the tool that has currently caught everyone's imagination is the micro-blogging site that limits all conversations to 140-characters.

The illustration above provides a sense of the interactive, immediate, non-linear, personal and continual nature of a PLN structured using social media tools.

CONCLUSION

The 90-9-1 principle in online social communities, referred to by usability expert Jakob Nielsen as the 'Participation Inequality', is an accepted fact. As per the rule.

- 90 per cent of users read or observe, but don't contribute.
- 9 per cent of users contribute from time to time, and are largely limited to comments.
- 1 per cent of users account for most of the active contributions.

If a PLN based on social media is to be successful, teachers have to aim to be a part of the 1 per cent of the active community. By making the PLN a reciprocal activity, teachers can truly experience the power of collaborative learning. The more they contribute, the stronger will be their skill enhancement as innovative and inspiring educators and facilitators.

With existing technological capabilities, the onus is equally on the teacher to take initiative in self-training and development. Teachers can take control of their own learning to make it a continual process.

REFERENCES

1. Cross, Jay. Informal Learning: Rediscovering the Pathways that Inspire Innovation and Performance. San Francisco: Pfeiffer, 2007. Print.
2. Hart, Jane. "Introduction to Social Media for Learning and Working." Centre for Learning and Performing Technologies. <http://c4lpt.co.uk/academy/ism/index.html>
3. Hart, Jane. "The Top 100 Tools for Learning 2010 list is emerging." Jane's Pick of the Day. 24 Jul. 2010 <http://janeknight.typepad.com/pick/2010/07/the-top-100-tools-for-learning-2010-list-is-emerging-.html>90-9-1 principle. "90-9-1 Principle." The 90-9-1 Principle, How Users Participate in Social Communities. <http://www.90-9-1.com/>
4. Nielsen, Jakob. "Participation Inequality: Encouraging More Users to Contribute." Jakob Nielsen's Alertbox. 9 Oct. 2006 <http://www.useit.com/alertbox/participation_inequality.html>

32

Quality Aspects in ODL System : A Study of Dr. BRAOU

Dr. G. Laxma Reddy
Joint Director (SS), Dr. B.R. Ambedkar Open University, Hyderabad.

ABSTRACT

The ODL (Open Distance Learning) system has gained in India and at present nearly about 25% of enrolment in the higher education is in the ODL system. Today there ate nearly about Fourteen State Open Universities and one hundred and thirty dual mode institutions apart from one National Open University. Various private stakeholders are also entered into distance education and started offering different programmes. The foreign universities are also in the fray to enter into the education market. In order to survive in the market the ODL institutions have to offer quality product to the learners. Keeping in view of the situation, the present study on Quality Aspects of BRAOU System was taken up. The understanding of quality concerns of particular institution would have wider implications on sustainable development of an ODL system. Quality in ODL system is frequently judged in terms of its teaching-learning systems, its nature of programmes, support services, and Governance. In order to get an understanding on various issues, the present study has covered quality concerns pertaining to – Programmes, enrolment, course development and delivery, support services and governance. Based on the study certain suggestions were also offered.

Programmes

One of the important objectives of the university is to "provide programmes to complement the existing ones of the universities in the state and to maintain highest standards on par with the best universities in the country". To fulfil the objective the university has started variety of programmes at different levels.

The academic programmes of BRAOU consists of:

(i) Undergraduate programmes
(ii) Post graduate programmes
(iii) Research programmes
(iv) P.G. Diploma programmes
(v) Certificate programmes

The University is offers 56 programmes in total. The programmes fall under Arts, Commerce and Sciences and these are offered in Telugu, English and Urdu medium. The undergraduate programmes of the university are very popular with an enrolment of 1.67 lakh out of total 1.76 lakh enrolment. Except UG, all other programmes require formal qualification to get an entry into the programme. For UG, the students from formal and non-formal streams are admitted. But the non-formal students are admitted on the basis of an Eligibility Test. Total twenty two optional are offered at undergraduate level leading to B.A., B.Com. and B.Sc. degrees. Student has to take three subjects from the listed optional from four faculties i.e. Arts, Social Sciences, Commerce and Sciences.

The most significant feature of university UG programme is the flexibility in the choice of subjects and flexible designs in learning. Of the three optional subjects which a students is required to study in this UG programme, the student should take two optional from the faculty in which he/she seeks to acquire his/her degree. The third optional can be from any of the other faculty. For example, a student of B.Com, can opt two subjects from commerce and one subject from any other faculty i.e. science or arts or social science. The BRAOU takes credit for the introduction of job oriented courses in UG programmes. For instance, the B.Sc. programme provides specialization in Fishery science, Sericulture, Crop production etc.

In consonance with the concept of Open Education System, the BRAOU has adopted an admission policy which has no restriction based on sex age, area and educational qualifications as seen in conventional system with regard to B.A./B.Com. degrees, with regard to B.Sc. programme the admission is open only to those who have relevant intermediate qualification (10+2 level) or to those who have one year experience in science and technology related organisations. The minimum duration of the UG programme is three years. But the students are allowed to complete the programme in nine years from the year of admission.

With regard to other programmes the BRAOU offers fifteen PG programmes, seven professional programmes and nine diploma programmes. The BRAOU also offers M.Phil. and Ph.D. programmes in ten disciplines which includes – Arts, Social Science, Commerce and Business Management faculties. In order to promote system based research (Prof. G. Ramreddy Research Academy of Distance Education GRADE offers Ph.D. programmes in Distance Education.

The BRAOU plays a partial an important role in imparting higher education to diversified groups of learners including socially disadvantaged sections.

In order to provide educational opportunities to the down trodden section of society, students belongs to SC, ST communities are exempted from tuition fee. As a result nearly 15% of SC's and 7% of ST's got enrolled in the university's UG programme.

Enrolment

Since its inception, BRAOU has been enrolling a large number of students from all over the state. Flexible and innovative nature of course offering is the main cause of increase in student enrolment. The non-formal students enrol in large numbers in undergraduate programmes. In the first year the enrolment was around 6000 (1982-83). Now it has reached to 1,72,000. The enrolment is high in UG programmes and constitutes about 97%. The enrolment of PG, PG Diploma and Research programmes constitute 3% only.

The progress if students are very slow in UG programme. Out of 59,000 enrolled in 1 year in 2000-03 only 33,000 students have taken admission into II year. Out of these 33,000 only 23,000 paid tuition fee and got admission into III year on the whole of 59,000 who have taken admission into UG I year only 23,000 students have joined UG III year. In this process, 26,000 students have list as drop-outs in II year and 10,000 students have dropped in III year.

Some of the quality concerns pertaining to the Dr. BRAOU pragrammes and their admissions and emrolment are:

- There is no transfer of credit system. Though the programmes are divided into course and units, the modular structure required for credit transfer is not seen.
- Most of the BRAOU programmes are Conventional in nature and there are very few vocational and professional courses.
- The enrolment in PG, Diploma and Certificate programmes are very less when compared to UG programmes.
- The students, dropout ratio at successive stages (i.e. from I to II year and II to III years) is very high.

Course Development and Delivery

Three authorities of the university which are entrusted with the responsibilities of programme planning and development are:

(i) The Academic Senate

(ii) The Planning and Monitoring Board

(iii) The Board of Studies.

The development of a programme consists of four stages:

- Identification of programme
- Prescribing the curriculum and syllabus
- Laying down procedures for evaluation
- Development of self instructional material.

The university appoints a committee to indentify the syllabus, the courses, course writers and editor. After identification of new programmes, the academic staff starts preparation of course materials in self instructional formats. The course materials are developed by the course team consisting of a subject editor, a few course writers, language editor and course coordinator. After the course material has been prepared and edited, the printing and distribution follow. The BRAOU enjoys a good reputation for its quality course materials. This course material is widely used by the students of conventional universities and colleges in the state.

The following are some of the quality related problems observed in the case of course development and delivery: Systematic need survey mechanism is not in place. The programmes are designed more by a general understanding rather than going by systematic study of market demand and social needs. Though the board of studies has to decide the programmes to be offered and recommend to the Academic Senate, the representatives from different sectors who could guide the faculty were not included in the board. In practice the initiative for new programmes usually originate from the faculty and the Vice-Chancellor. There is enormous delay in conduction of board meetings. All these lapses raises the question of quality criteria of programme planning.

The problems pertaining to print and audio-visual material are:

With regard to the self instructional print materials.

- The structured format was not appreciated by the conventional faculty;
- The SIM material failed to address diverse needs of learners. The study material is not revised regularly. The quality of the paper is poor. There is delay in the delivery of course material.
- The quality aspects are not effectively applied in the production of audio-visual materials.
- The learners are not in a position to acquire adequate support from audio-visual materials due to inconvenient schedules and lack of information.
- The print materials are not effectively supplemented with audio-visual materials.

Student Support Services

The university has started 219 Study Centres and 23 Regonal Coordination Centres (RCC's) for the delivery of the programmes and to provide quality support services to learners. The university also has special centres for women, prisoners and learners of remote area. The important support services delivered through Study Centres include – information support, guidance support, Contact-cum-Counselling support, library support and audio–visual support. The student support services branch at headquarters takes up the responsibility of the planning and monitoring of delivery of services through study centres/RCC's.

The Study Centres are located in the premises of host colleges and they are largely managed by part time staff. Operational effectiveness and efficiency largely depend on the knowledge levels, attitudes and abilities of the personnel and availability of infrastructure at the Study Centres. RCC's will act as representative unit of the university at district level and offer all the programmes. Whereas the Study Centres offer limited programmes. BA programme is offered through all the Study Centres and other programmes like B.Com./ B.Sc., PG and Diploma programmes are offered through limited Study Centres.

The quality concerns observed in the area of support services include :

- Most of the support services offered to the learners are group based and not individual based.
- The support services are mainly related to subject based tutorial services. The system based Counselling and guidance services are very limited.
- The services are more structured and less flexible.
- The Study Centres depends on host colleges for its infrastructure. As a result most of the Study Centres do not have adequate office space which effect quality of support services.
- Most of the Study Centres are managed by part time staff who are drawn from the host college. As they are

busy with host college work they may not able to spare enough time for Study Centre activities.

- The students attendance at Counselling classes is poor due to disturbance of Counselling classes, Counsellors absentism and sometimes due to poor quality of Counselling.
- The learners are not making optimum use of Study Centre based services.
- Lack of proper coordination at head office, effecting quality of services at the Study Centres.
- As the scale of operations is very large the inadequate use of technology is affecting quality of support services.
- Though the university has established RCC's at District centres as middle level tier, adequate administrative and financial powers are not provided and as a result the RCC's are functioning as any other Study Centres in the state.
- The BRAOU is confined to Study Centres and RCC's for the delivery of support services. There is no multi-channel delivery system like work centres, Multi-media centres and distance education facilitators.

Governance

Governance, organization structures, and administrative arrangements for undertaking the activities of the institution is an important factor in the effective functioning of an institution. The organizational structure of BRAOU is designed to perform all the essential functions of an ODL (Open Distance Learning) institution. For BRAOU, the Governor of A.P. is the Chancellor. The Vice-Chancellor, Rector, Directors, Deans' Registrar, COE and Finance Officer are the main functionaries of the university. Divisions and faculties are the main components of the university. The Executive Council, Academic Senate and Monitoring Board and Finance Committee are the important authorities of the university.

Organisational Structure of Dr. Braou

The university has initiated several quality measures for the improvement of the system. The vision and mission clearly states the long-terms goals of the university and sets the direction for effective implementation of the goals. The university has established Quality Assurance Cell to Promote, design, develop and monitor quality assurance activities of the university. The university document on "Administration with a Difference" advocates a Simple, Measurable, Accountable, Responsive and Transparent (SMART) administrative system. Coordination committee was constituted with all heads of branches to ensure proper cooperation and coordination among different division. Several training programmes, workshops were organized by the training division to improve the skills of the staff. Manuals were developed for the purpose of staff development. Infrastructure was developed at head-quarters and RCC's for efficient functioning. Since inception, the university adopted multimedia technologies for instructional purposes. Computer technologies are used for data management.

The quality aspects related to the Governance includes:

- Rigidity in the structure conventional thinking and lack of system based understanding is effecting is effecting the progress as desired by the vision and mission statement goals of the university.
- The academic authorities i.e. Academic Senate and Planning and Monitoring Board meetings are not conducted periodically and as a result the decision to start new programmes does not seem to go through a rigorous scrutiny.
- The present level of delegation of administrative and financial powers to senior officers are inadequate to the best of their potential.
- The Open University with its large and complex system and the number of components, dependence of one on the other demands for effective computerization. The computer services of the university are grossly inadequate and do not have software's required for all the departments. There is no integrated software to connect all the departments. The computer centre lacks

adequate staff. There is no Wide Area Network (WAN) for connecting RCC's and Study Centres.

Quality concerns in the areas pertaining programmes, admission, enrolment, course development and delivery, student support services and Governance, would bring complete quality picture of ODL system. The complete assement of the Dr. BRAOU system has identified certain shortcomings. The suggestions in those areas would have impact on long run sustainability of the system.

Suggestions

Most of the Dr. BRAOU's programmes are conventional in nature and there is a need to introduce continuing education and vocational education on massive scale. The university should develop a method for assessing the existing and emerging demands of manpower in various sectors. The Dr. BRAOU will have to enter agreement with major employers, industrial organizations, training institutions, professional associations and institutions, which offer continuing education programmes.

- The university should develop a procedure for assessing the costs of different programmes. Well defined criteria has to be evolved to decide whether a programme is economically viable or not. If university wants to subsidize the programme it should have clear-cut policy to decide to what extent subsidy has to be allowed for a programme. The policy should clearly identify the subsidized programmes and self supporing programmes. All the programmes should be subjected to economic viability each year.
- Two separate bridge courses are to be planned to reduce the dropout ratio. A bridge course of at least six months duration must be introduced for the non-formal students before starting of UG 1st year programme. The objective of introducing the bridge course is to bring the student knowledge level to that of intermediate level. Another bridge course is to be designed to the formal students who have long study

gap (i.e. for the students who have studied intermediate long back) in order to bridge their knowledge gaps.

- The university should initiate steps to see that transfer of credits becomes a reality.
- The Academic Senate and planning and monitoring bodies must be activated. These bodies must met regularly and should identify new programmes and prescribe required curriculum and syllabus. For offering new programmes, a programme proposal with details of description of programme, survey of target groups, anticipated enrolment, programme expenditure and revenue should be prepared. These proposals must be reviewed by expert body.
- In order to avoid delay, the course materials have to be delivered through multiple channels – through Study Centres, postal services and courier services.
- Difficult topics in the syllabus should be indentified and audio-visual materials for these topics are to be prepared and effectively supplemented with print materials.
- The adequate office space and class rooms at the study centres is to be ensured, so that they can deliver the services effectively.
- Diversified delivery channels for the effective delivery of the services are to be used. The delivery channels should include – work centres, distance learning facilitators, multimedia learning centres and mobile centres.
- The functioning of the study centres are to be reviewed for its infradstructure, services extended and their utility.
- The university should strengthen its computer centre with adequate software and hardware in order to facilitate data sharing and for extension of LAN, WAN facilities.

CONCLUSION

Quality is an all embracing concept and should be a key feature in all the areas of ODL system. The quality concerns has a developmental potential and serves as a corrective measure for policy formulation and system and system development. In order to understand the ODL system, the present study has covered the quality aspects pertaining to BRAOU's programmes, enrolment, course development and delivery, support services and governance. The understanding quality concerns of particular institution would have a wider implications on sustainable development it an ODL system.

REFERENCES

1. Kulandai Swamy, V.C. (1997), Dr. BRAOU: The Next Decade– A Vision, Vancouver: The Commonwealth of Learning.
2. Laxma Reddy G. (2006), Organization and Management of Student Support Services in ODL System, Kakatiya Journal of Distance Education, Vol. 10, No.1, pp. 46-68.
3. Prasad V.S. and Venkaiah, V. (2005), India's First Open University – Experience of Two Decades, Hyderabad: GRADE, Dr. BRAOU, pp. 73-86.
4. Prasad V.S. (2006), Quality Assurance of Distance Education, in Suresh Garg. Estal (Ed.), Four Decades of Destance Education in India – Reflections on Policy and Practice, New Delhi: Viva Books Pvt. Ltd.
5. Shesharatnam (2002), India's First Open University: Two Decades of Journey, Hyderabad: Book Links Corporation, pp. 77-167.

33

Quality Concerns in Distance Teacher Education Programmes

Dr. K. Sumalatha
Asst. Prof., Dept. of Education, S.V. University, Tirupati-517502
A. Nagamani
Asst. Prof., Dept. of Physical Education, S.V. University, Tirupati

ABSTRACT

Distance education is now internationally recognised and accepted as an alternative channel for providing broader access to education in a cost-effective manner; wider and diversified curricula and a means for continuing life-long education. However distance education, like every new technology, has both a light and a dark side. The potential advantages of distance education are many. The disadvantages of distance education are not as readily apparent. One of the most serious of these problems is a lack of attention to educational quality control issues. Courses, certification programs, and degrees are being offered in nearly every imaginable field including, incredibly, the helping professions such as education and counselling. Distance teacher education too carries benefits and drawbacks, just as traditional instruction does. Quality concerns in institutions of teacher education are quality of educational product, quality of learning, and quality of technology. High quality multimedia learning materials; dedicated academic support; sleek logistics; and a strong research base are the factors which help in assuring quality of the programmes.

Introduction

Distance education is the single most promising educational innovation of our lifetime. However distance education, like every new technology, has both a light and a dark side. The potential advantages of distance education are many. These include, among others, the ability to reach learners in geographically remote locations or those in circumstances that mitigate against attendance at regular and traditional hours; the potential to reach many types of non traditional students; and most importantly, the opportunity for students to work and learn at a style and pace most consistent with their own mental and physical constitutions.

The disadvantages of distance education are not as readily apparent, although they are becoming much more evident as implementation spreads across the country and across the world. One of the most serious of these problems is a lack of attention to educational quality control issues. This problem is so pervasive that a mushrooming system of shoddy, online diploma mills have sprung up, complete with individual courses, complete certification programs in various fields, and bachelor's, master's, and even doctoral degrees available today online. Courses, certification programs, and degrees are being offered in nearly every imaginable field including, incredibly, the helping professions such as education and counselling.

Open and Distance Learning Teacher Education Programmes

Distance education is a new means of training teachers, but there's a limited amount of research on this practice, and most of it is performed in developed countries (Edwards, 2005). However, it has been stated that the use of distance education in teacher training has yielded positive outcomes [Usun, 2003; Perraton, Creed, and Robinson, 2001; Moon, 1997; Anderson and Simpson (2005), Nielsen and Tatto, 1991]. There is good evidence that the distance education programmes in the field of knowledge, general culture, educational theories, and practical dimensions of teacher training have been successful (Perreaton, Creed, and Robinson, 2001). Studies concerning teacher training practices performed in such countries as Tanzania, Guyana, Zimbabwe, Sri Lanka and Indonesia also indicate that the teachers trained through distance education might be as good as and, in some cases, better than the teachers trained through the traditional method (Yates, 2000). In addition, it has been argued that the teachers who participate in teacher training via distance education consider distance education programmes to be equal to face-to-face programmes (Jackson, 2006; Miller, 2000); teacher training by means of distance education programmes in comparison with traditional programmes is more effective in increasing teachers' knowledge and skills (Shrestha, 1997); and teachers participating in distance education are able to teach more effectively than those participating in traditional programmes (Brophy and Dudley, 1983; Nielsen and Tatto, 1991).

Distance education is viewed by those teachers who are willing to improve themselves and manage their time as an accessible and inexpensive approach to teacher training (Martinez, 2002). Therefore, distance education programmes are implemented today in many countries for both pre-service and in-service training of teachers (Sherestha, 1997). In their analysis, Perraton, Creed and Robinson (2001) state that countries adopt the distance education approach for teacher training in order to achieve various aims. These aims are outlined below:

Initial Qualification

Some countries utilize distance education so that a large number of teachers can gain basic qualifications. This practice might occur as a way of enhancing the qualifications of beginner level or low-qualified teachers.

(a) Continuing Professional Development

Since face-to-face teacher training is not considered efficient in terms of scheduling, distance education is used in order to improve skills, maintain cognitive depth, and expand knowledge. Some programmes might focus on special groups.

(b) Re-orientation for Teachers for Curriculum Reform and Change

Distance education plays a significant role in programme reforms aimed at changing educational content and activities.

For instance, the programmes intended to contribute to the use of educational technologies at schools are carried out with this aim.

(c) Teachers' Career Development

Distance education is utilized in order to support teachers' career development. When teachers study for the purpose of professional development, they aim to improve their qualifications so that they can advance to higher level positions, such as head teacher or educational inspector; in short when they need new skills, they derive benefit from distance education.

Quality Concerns of Distance Teacher Education Programmes

Distance teacher education carries benefits and drawbacks, just as traditional instruction does. Nevertheless, professionals, especially educators in higher education, are much more concerned about quality of the former than the latter. There are many reasons for this.

The main reason is the inferiority of distant communication as compared to face-to-face communication. In a traditional classroom, instructors and students can afford to take a more individual approach to quality; instructors can see when students are struggling, exchange non-verbal feedback, and have more latitude for improvisation. In contrast, such communication is limited in the distance learning environment.

The second reason is that distance learners have additional characteristics and needs from traditional learners. Compared with the students in traditional classrooms, distance education students tend be older, have more professional experience, and often have families and careers to juggle. Many of them are not merely interested in obtaining a degree, but in gaining the competence and knowledge necessary to rise within their professions.

The third reason is that distance education has something to prove – its effectiveness. Teacher education needs to prove that course credits obtained at a distance are as valuable as the ones obtained in traditional formats.

Distance education is combined with face-to-face education for teacher training. The undergraduate programme is designed to equip student teachers with the knowledge, skills, and attitudes they need. It is a two year programme consisting of theory courses in professional knowledge on teaching, field knowledge, and methodology of school subjects. In addition to the theoretical courses, there are practical courses in the distance teacher education programme. Teaching Practice is a course aimed at allowing teacher candidates to test and improve the knowledge and skills they acquire through theoretical courses in a school environment and to gain the required professional skills.

One of the fundamental problems with the use of distance education in teacher training is how to combine theory with practice (Robinson and Latchem, 2003). As most of the learning in distance education takes place independently of teachers and is based on the instructional tools prepared beforehand (Evans, 1994), practical activities have strategic significance in teacher training programmes. It is important for teacher candidates to achieve their teacher qualifications, transform theoretical knowledge into practice, and gain positive attitudes regarding the teaching profession.

Teaching-learning Processes of the Programme

The programme consists of printed materials, television programmes, and academic assistance services. Printed materials (books and manuals) are written by field experts under the supervision of an editor. Printed materials are written based on the principles of distance education and in a way that makes self-learning possible.

The problem with the quality of learning is that distance teacher education curricula have been driven more by the technology than by pedagogy; that is, educators have focussed more on the educational materials and formats made possible by the technology than on student learning. Moreover, both students and faculty are not adequately prepared for effectively using distance technologies.

Therefore quality concerns in institutions of teacher education are quality of educational product, quality of learning, and quality of technology.

How to Control Quality?

John Daniel (1997) highlights four main areas of distance education. High quality multimedia learning materials; dedicated academic support; sleek logistics; and a strong research base. The same holds good for distance teacher education programmes as well.

High quality learning materials prepared by professionally competent teams of distance educators assure the learner of a positive learning experience.

Dedicated support services help the learners through counseling, tutoring, assignment marking and the final evaluation.

Efficient logistics assure the learners the receipt of study materials, evaluated assignment responses and other required information in time.

A strong research base helps the academics in updating the course materials, and alerts the policy makers and administrators about what is required to respond meaningfully to the new developments and changing needs.

The difficulty is not so much in recognizing the importance of the above ingredients in assuring quality as in acquiring the necessary competence to develop these ingredients and put them in place. Even if competence is available, the environmental and political factors may not use it in time or may treat the quality aspects rather superficially and casually. Such non-serious approach is common with institutions which do not declare quality assurance as their basic concern (Koul, 1997).

REFERENCES

1. Anderson, B. and Simpsson, M. (2005). *From distance teacher education to beginning teaching: What impacts on practices.* Retrieved June 16, 2004, from http://www.unisa.edu.au/odlaaconference/PDFs/70%20ODLAA%202005%20-%20Anderson% 0&%20Simpson. pdf

2. Brophy, M. and Dudley, B. (1983). Training teachers in the world, *Teaching at a Distance, 23*, 40-45.
3. Daniel, John S. (1997). *Mega Universities, Virtual Universities and Knowledge Media: Can we have Quality with Quantity?* Conference Proceedings, 11th AAOU Conference, Kuala Lumpur, Malaysia, 11-14, Nov. 1997, Vol. 1, 3-13.
4. Edwards, F. (2005). The neglected heart of educational development: primary teacher education strategy in Malawi. *Journal Education for Teaching, 31*(1), 25-36.
5. Evans, T. (1994). *Understanding learners in open and distance education.* London: Kogan Page.
6. Jackson, B. G. (2006). *Distance technology teaching: A view from the trenches.* http://www.techknowlogia.org/TKL_active_pages2/CurrentArticles/main.asp?IssueNumber=18&FileType=HTML&ArticleID=447, Retrieved January 20, 2006.
7. Koul, B.N. (1997), Quality assurance practices and principles: The case of Indian distance education, *Perspectives on Distance Education: Quality Assurance in Higher Education: Selected Case Studies (Ed.),* The Commonwealth of Learning, Canada.
8. Martinez, A. (2002). Distance learning and teacher education. *Karen's Linguistics Issues.* Retrieved June 25, 2006, from http://www3.telus.net/linguisticsissues/longdistance.html
9. Miller, E.(2000). Models in distance teaching in teacher education in Jamaica. *Proceedings of Distance Education in Small States Conference.* The University of the West Indies Distance Education Centre (UWIDEC), Ocho Rios, Jamaica. http://www.col.org/resources/publications/monographs/Pages/2000-SmallStates.aspx
10. Moon, B. (1997). Open learning and new technologies in teacher education: New paradigms for development. *European Journal of Teacher Education, 20*(1), 193-217.
11. Nielsen, H. and Tatto, M. T. (1991). *The cost effectiveness of distance education for teacher training.* BRIDGES Research Report Series, No. 9, Cambridge, MA: Harvard University.
12. Özer, B. (1993). *Acquisition of teacher behaviour through distance education.* Eskisehir: Education Faculty, Anadolu University Press.

13. Perraton, H., Creed, C., and Robinson, B. (2001). *Teacher education through distance learning: Technology-curriculum-cost-evaluation.* Paris: UNESCO. Higher Education Division, Teacher Education Section.
14. Robinson, B. and Latchem, C. (2003). Teacher education: challenge and change. In B. Robinson and C. Latchem (Eds.), *Teacher education through open and distance education.* London: Routledge.
15. Sherestha, G. (1997). *A review of case studies related to distance education in developing countries.* Retrieved June 10, 2004, from http://www.undp.org/info21/public/review/pb-rev.html
16. U'sun, S. (2003). The applications and problems on the distance teacher training in Turkey. *Turkish Online Journal of Distance Education-TOJDE. 4*(4).

34

A Module of Inclusive Education Through ODL System in Teacher Education Programmes—Scope and Challenges

B. N. Ch. Shekhar
RTA, IGNOU Regional Centre, Hyderabad
K. Anitha Raj
RTA, IGNOU Regional Centre, Hyderabad
Kiran Singh
RTA, IGNOU Regional Centre, Hyderabad

The Backdrop of the Issue

Education has witnessed many deviations and changes in its modes and approaches. Many factors like religion, caste, creed, social and economic status, political will have exerted their influence on education confining its reach to a limited section of society. Many sections such as differently abled, Scheduled castes and Scheduled tribes are deprived from the access of educational facilities inspite of the provisions of the constitution for equal opportunity and access of the educational facilities for all irrespective of the above mentioned factors. Among the 102.9 millions of the Indian population, SCs constitute around 16.7 millions, STs took their place with 8.4 millions and the differently abled constitute more than 2.1 millions (2001 census), The literacy rates of the children between 7 to 15 age group of SCs and STs is 54.7% and 47.1%, although remarkable steps have been taken for broadening the scope and reach of education. Special efforts have been done to take care of the special educational needs of the marginalized and deprived sections of the society. Consequently many forms of education have emerged besides the mainstream education like special education and tribal education etc. The Government also focused by constituting many committees and enacting many policies. NPE1986 contributed much for the disadvantaged groups stressing on the education of the disabled as far as possible in general school and educating the tribal children with special attention etc, POA 1992 also supported this measures. RCI Act 1992, PWD Act, 1995 etc. are the mile stones in the development of educational facilities for the differently abled. Balwanthrai Committee (1958-59), Dhebar Commission (1961), Thakkar Committee (1947) recommend for the education of tribes with special attention and imparted in their own language or dialect. Central advisory board of education and many committees like Renuka Ray Committee stressed on a single stream of education but with special attention to each and every group caused the emergence of parallel streams in education remarkably different from each other in quality and relevance and thus limiting the capacities of the diverse group of people in availing he opportunities offered by life. In the course of this context many changes took place in thinking and actions with a paradigm shift from single stream catering to a limited scope of learners to splitted streams for the diverse groups and again a shift to a broader scope of a single structure considering the educational needs of every learner. Inclusive Education is emerged as an effective instrument in the context to handle it effectively. The potential of the proposed system of inclusive education becomes limited in scope due to limitation in the present system of teacher preparation in India in terms of both - producing adequate number of teachers and producing teachers to work effectively in inclusive set up of education. All the efforts by the educational organizations and apex bodies focusing on the improvement and enhancement of the quality and quantity of educational facilities to the maximum and raising the standards of the system but the teacher who is an important element of the system for the successful accomplishment of the objectives of education was given very little focus. The scope of the system is increasing but accordingly the role and the up gradation of the professional skills of the teacher was not given much emphasis. The teacher education curriculum prepared by the NCTE (2010) has acknowledged the needs of the inclusive educational setup for the future but no particular component in the present curriculum was suggested neither any duration change for the training of the teacher was recommended.

The present paper is an attempt to find answers to the questions like - to what extent Open and Distance Education system can help in producing adequate numbers of teachers possessing requisite knowledge, understanding and skills to work effectively in inclusive set-up, what are the issues and challenges in developing, designing and executing a Teacher Education Programme for preparing Teachers for Inclusive Set-up?

Methodology

- A review of the teacher education curriculum frameworks 1998, 2005 and 2010 was done.
- An interview schedule was developed and administered for gathering the point of views of experts and professionals in the field of education regarding the issues under focus.

Major Findings

Review of Teacher Education Curriculums

National Curriculum for Teacher Education, 1998, National Curriculum for Teacher Education Draft, 2005, and National Curriculum for Teacher Education Draft, 2010 have given emphasis on inclusion at early childhood stage and elementary stage particularly because of the fact that inclusion at other stages of education follows automatically and smoothly once the child with special needs is included and thus become accepted and oriented by the mainstream system of education, but explicit direction is missing in all the three curriculum frameworks. Therefore, they maintain the status-quo.

Present Education System

Present education system when contemplated by the experts whether it is really catering every need and development of every learner, then they are mixed reactions. A thought from a group of experts the scope is confined to only few sections of the society and only to a certain extents it is primarily meant for catering to the needs of average ability student and they express that lot more have to be done by the Government and NGO intervention is also significant. Another stream was positive towards our system but they even feel unsatisfactory regarding of commitment and spirit. Some opine that there should be a revamp and restructuring of the whole system with a new approach, changing even the role of teacher from a mere instructor to a facilitator, they even express concern though many acts and policies are enacted by the parliament, their realization is not witnessed.

Teacher Education Curriculum

When a thought was given on whether the present teacher education program is capable to produce a well equipped teacher to tackle every learner few experts expressed that though the spirit and objectives of the curriculum are encouraging towards the production of such teacher, the system is not well tuned and the scope is limited. Not fully, teachers are prepared to cater the needs of a homogenous group mainly. Orientation to the diversity existing in the classrooms in real life situation is missing in all most all the existing programmes of teacher education. They felt that the present mechanisms are also not supportive. Few felt that curriculum and its structure have to be given are thought. Some of them strongly criticized the structure of the programs and courses and the duration pattern. Altogether it is the common thought of the group that there should be a restructuring and revamp of the curriculum by the transformation of the concept from specific to different groups or sections with a concept of inclusion. Even the structure of the program and training should be designed with a new approach and with broader perspective to achieve the expected levels.

Education-single Stream

The views of the experts when the issue of the union of all streams of education into a single stream catering the needs of all learners was discussed are supportive towards the creation of such stream. It can be made possible, by making structural changes in the existing system would become necessary first. They felt that union is needed as the inclusion is best for the holistic development of the learner by the inculcation of moral and human values in his/her character. They even realized that the present system and its elements are lagging back with spirit and commitment and techno-savvy nature. So they opined that before the creation of such stream there should be thought of the present situations and restructuring is needed at every levels. Equipping the teachers both materialistically and attitudinally and making quality infrastructure and advanced technologies available should be initialized first then if such a stream was created, it will yield good fruits. A learner should be provided with basic living and other necessary skills before entering the system.

Inclusive Teacher Educational Programes—Scope in ODL

The inbuilt characteristics of flexibility and reachability to the learners at large are making the ODL system distinct from that of conventional system. Regarding the issue of intervention of ODL system in preparing teacher education programs all the experts are with the supportive stand. According to them if the scope of direct interaction such as contact classes in number and the practical component if increased it would certainly succeed in providing quality teacher education serving the purpose as teacher education is a powerful and significant professional program.

As the system is more flexible, if it opens the intervention of the technological advancement, making even the elements of the system techno friendly supporting the every need of the student teachers, equipping him/her to tackle any type of learner. ODL system with the intervention of ICT can do by some courses initially with diploma and certificate courses on inclusive education and certainly by raising the level of awareness of ICT among learners as opined by a group of experts. There should be a proper and strategic planning and structure and even care for its effective implementation, another view focus on the incorporation of inclusive concept in the present bachelors' teacher education program. Consequently training needs can be fulfiled extensively and the aspired continuity can be maintained in teacher education for professional growth and development of teachers.

Conceptualising Teacher Education with Inclusion

When the issue of conceptualizing the teacher education with that of inclusive education came infront, there are different opinions. Few said that it should be incorporated as a separate course optional. Some other felt that it can be introduced as a compulsory core course and adding to this another view came into focus that along with introducing it as a core course the thought and concept of inclusion can also be injected generally in the foundations of education leading to the concept formation among the student teachers. Inter-disciplinary approach should be adopted and diversity element should be incorporated in each and every element of teacher education programme. Another group felt that it depends upon the structure and design of the course and it is a big exercise which involves intensive planning and care. The role of the apex bodies is more significant in this regard.

Presumed Duration

Experts felt that the duration pattern of the teacher education program should undergo a revision keeping in view the present conditions and societal needs. It depends on the design and structure of the course and according to the present conditions and societal demands it should be more than one year. Teaching being a significant profession, it should be at par with other professional programs like engineering etc., so definitely it should be more than one year for bachelors program and many diploma and certificate courses along with refreshment crash courses can be even made the duration of which can be determined according to its syllabus and design. A few who supported the integrated teacher education program felt that it should be of three to four years duration. In which one full year should be devoted to practice of diversity.

Preparation of Self Learning Material

Two thoughts came front broadly on the availability of expertise for tackling the issue of preparing self learning material and other practical component material in inclusive education teacher education program. Lack of adequately trained teacher educators to give requisite exposure to the prospective teachers and also the lack of requisite infrastructural facilities for supporting practical component. Another thought projects that though shortage of resources is there is a plenty of expertise available from other streams which can be reoriented with the concept of inclusion and can be utilized. Many special organizations like NIMH, NIVH etc., from disabled services and ITDA and TCR and TI etc., for tribal services and many more from different sectors can be taken into consideration. Proper planning and utilization of expertise in the right way should be given priority.

Proportion of Theory and Practical Components

The views of the experts pertaining to the ratio of theory and practical component in the Inclusive teacher education program reveal that as it is an integrated approach they are wrapped together and go hand in hand throughout the duration making it as 50%-50%. Another opinion says that it should be atleast 40% practical component.

Practical Component—Resource Availability

The assistance of the present school system is enough and relevant to deal with the practical component for inclusive teacher education program but the role and assistance of the special organizations can only be welcomed if it as catalyst otherwise it can be an obstacle as opined by a group. Another thought say that the resource available in the form of present school system and special organizations are relevant and enough but they are to be properly channelized and utilized.

Nationalwide Regional Need Based

As it is based on paradigm shift and role change and concept transformation, it should be Nationwide initially with the integration of the regional needs accordingly. The curriculum should be on National standards but 10 to 15% of the structure should be given for state and regional needs as the right place should be given for the local culture and needs. It should be on National standards but with minimum preferences for the regional priorities like language, culture etc. These are the views expressed by the experts when posed a question on the designing the program whether at the National level or at the state or regional level for catering to the needs of the particular region

CONCLUSIONS

- Revamping and restructuring of the present teacher education program is needed to meet the expected marks as inclusion will be the future perspective.
- Spirit of inclusion and commitment from gross root level is needed for the achievement of the aims of education and inclusion will be the right approach.
- Inclusion is the indispensible instrument for equipping the teacher for tackling every learner making the objective of all round development successful.
- Indianization is the must, practicing our culture should be given priority and that Indianism or Nationalism should invite unversalization for the positive and developmental aspects from other cultures and streams.
- There is a need of inclusive education accordingly teacher education program should be so designed empowered to tackle every learner and being award of every individual differences and equip him/herself to serve the humanity at large. Inclusive education should come into reality rather remained in discussions in papers and conferences etc.

- Lack of commitment both at the structural, organizational level and on the part of the student teacher is a big draw-back which can be resolved by the commitment of the experienced faculty by inculcating moral and ethical values at every level.
- Opportunities and facilities are good unlike olden days but their proper utilization and channelization in the right direction is needed for making inclusion a reality broadening the scope of present education system.
- ODL is having strengths to cater and fulfil the training needs of the masses. But it requires an appropriate direction and a good intention. This direction and intention is missing.
- A strong commitment along with the support at legal and policy level is required.

35

Print Material of UG Chemistry Programme of Dr. B.R. Ambedkar Open University (Dr. BRAOU) : A Study of it's Self-instructional Characteristics

Dr. D. Ugandhar Raju
Deputy Commissioner of Prohibition and Excise, Kurnool
Prof. G. Ramachandraiah
Head, Dept. of Chemistry, Dr. BRAOU, Hyderabad

ABSTRACT

Independent learning in Open Distance Learning (ODL) system is mostly dependent on the self-instructional quality of the print material. Even in this age of e-learning, print material is still a dominant medium of instructional system in ODL in India. Hence, the evaluation of the print material of UG science programmes of Dr. BRAOU is undertaken with reference to the characteristics of self-instructional material (SIM.) The perceptions of both learners and counsellors on print material of science, with particular reference to chemistry, are obtained. And the print material is found mostly self-instructional.

Keywords: Self-instructional characteristics, correspondence analysis.

Introduction

It is generally accepted that the print material is still a dominant medium of instructional system in ODL in India. This applies to conventional correspondence study as well as to highly sophisticate multimedia presentation like courses of the open university. The distance learner in the initial stage looks for the print material for motivation. Dr. BRAOU since its inception in 1983 has the distinction of offering science education through distance mode. The University has designed the course material in such a way that it meets the higher content and institutional standards and has parity with similar courses from other educational institutions and adheres to rigorous internal and external academic norms. It is learners oriented and meets appropriate merit exit standards. With its sound academic practices and innovative teaching-learning methodologies, the University has recorded a state of distinction in imparting science programmes through ODL. After such a long journey, it is high time to make an analysis of the strengths and weaknesses of the system in order to improvise the existing practices, if need be. The instructional characteristics of the print material being the most important component of ODL a detailed study of it is taken up.

Indicators were framed to understand learner's and counsellor's agreements on five point scale from 'strongly agree' to 'strongly disagree' to know their perception on the self-instructional characteristics of print material of chemistry of Dr. BRAOU. Open-ended questions are also given to the counselors to know their opinion on various aspects of Chemistry material. The responses were collected from both Learners and Counsellors by administering separate questionnaire on both the groups.

Demographic Charactersitics Learners

The details of demographic characteristics of Learners are given in Table 1.

Table – 1
Demographic Characteristics of Learners

Variable	*Group*	*Number*	*Percentage*
1	2	3	4
Centre	Hyderabad	94	12.4
	Rajahmundry and Guntur	142	18.8
	Karimnagar and Adilabad	317	41.9

1	2	3	4
	Tirupathi & Kurnool	203	26.9
Gender	Male	366	48.4
	Female	390	51.6
Location	Rural	440	58.2
	Urban	316	41.8
Age (in years)	18-24	528	69.8
	25-30	173	22.9
	31-40	49	6.5
	41-50	6	0.8
Optional Subject in Inter/ITI level	Science	728	96.3
	Arts	11	1.5
	Commerce	2	0.3
	Others	15	2.0
Year of study	II year	357	47.2
	III year	399	52.8
Mode of entry	Eligibility Test	57	7.5
	Inter/ITI	675	89.3
	Based on experience in Science and Technology related organizations	14	1.9
	Others	10	1.3
Optional subjects	MPC	356	47.1
	BZC	292	38.6
	MC and other	22	2.9
	C and other	86	11.4
Medium	English	160	21.2
	Telugu	566	74.9
	Urdu	30	4.0
Employment status	Employed	284	37.6
	Unemployed	448	59.3
	Self- Business	24	3.2
Ration Card		484	64.0
White Pink		272	36.0

Characteristics of Counsellors

It is also of interest to analyze the characteristics of the counsellors. The opinions of the counsellors of chemistry of BRAOU of the state of Andhra Pradesh were collected through mail. For analytical convenience, Counsellors with 5 years and less experience are grouped as 'Juniors' and those with more than 5 years experience are termed as 'Seniors' in the analysis and discussion. Of the Counsellors 27 are with only M.Sc, 6 are with M.Sc, M.Phil., 13 with M.Sc, Ph.D., 6 with M.Sc., B.Ed./M.Ed. and 3 with M.Sc., Ph.D., B.Ed./M.Ed.

Hypotheses

The following null hypotheses have been formulated on the self-institutional characteristics of print material.

1. The print material of Chemistry of UG programme is not satisfying all the characteristics of self-instructional material.
2. There is no significant difference in perception between the male and female learners.
3. There is no significant difference in perception between rural and urban based learners.
4. There is no significant difference in the perception of learners of Chemistry with Mathematics combination and those without Mathematics combination.
5. There is no significant difference in perception between white ration card holders and pink ration card holders on the self-instructional characteristics of print material.
6. There is no significant difference in perception between the learners who took admission into UG programme of BRAOU through entrance test and those with other eligibility criteria.
7. There is no significant difference in perception between the learners of II year and III year.
8. There is no significant difference in perception among the learners of Telugu, English and Urdu medium.
9. There is no significant difference in perception among various centers viz. Hyderabad, Karimnagar and Adilabad, Rajahmundry and Guntur, Kurnool and Tirupathi.

Statistical Analysis of Data

In the analysis the percentage of responses is mostly reported by combining the two outside categories: "strongly agree" and "agree", "disagree" and "strongly disagree".

The agreeability mean for most of the indicators on print material, calculated based on the response of learners, were high above (3) indicating that almost all respondents had common thought in term of the indicators as given in Table 2.

Table 2

Self-instructional Print Material MEAN Values of Learner's and Counsellor's Agreement for the Items of SIM of UG Programmes of BRAOU

S.No.	*Item*	*Learner's response*		*Counsellor's response*	
		Mean	*S.D*	*Mean*	*S.D*
1	2	3	4	5	6
1.	In the reading material of chemistry the instructional objectives are clearly stated.	3.50	1.30	4.22	0.87
2.	I have understood the format of the units of chemistry.	3.42	1.36	4.29	0.75
3.	It is possible to read and understand the course material of chemistry without attending counseling session.	2.66	1.31	2.98	1.21
4.	The language presentation in chemistry course material is simple.	3.43	1.23	3.96	0.70
5.	The concepts are adequately supported by figures and graphs in the course material of Chemistry.	3.67	1.05	3.96	0.70
6.	There are sufficient number of model problems in the reading material of chemistry.	3.67	1.05	3.75	0.86
7.	There are sufficient number of examples to explain a concept in the course material of chemistry.	3.38	1.11	4.07	0.628
8.	The course material of chemistry stimulates interest in the subject.	3.67	1.13	3.84	0.84
9.	The learners are able to understand the mathematical and chemical equations on their own.	3.14	1.30	3.24	1.06

1	2	3	4	5	6
10.	The course material of chemistry is well organized.	3.33	1.30	4.2	0.88
11.	The course material of chemistry is well integrated.	3.45	1.30	4.22	0.88
12.	There is too much material in chemistry course.	2.32	1.04	2.38	1.02
13.	The check your progress exercises in the course material of chemistry can be answered by the learners on their own.	3.5	1.13	3.67	0.739
14.	The check your progress exercises help in understanding the Units.	3.93	0.91	4.09	0.287
15.	The number of check your progress exercises are sufficient in the course material of chemistry.	3.53	1.38	4.04	0.503

But the response of learners is not favorable on the print material with regard to the statement that it is possible to read and understand the course material of chemistry without attending counselling session. They responded positively on the statements that there is too much material in chemistry course and the course material of chemistry takes more time compared to other science subjects.

The figures in Table 2 also give an overview of the relative importance of these indicators based on the responses of the counsellors.

But the response of counsellors is not favourable on the print material with regard to the statement that it is possible to read and understand the course material of chemistry without attending counselling session. They responded positively on the statements that there is too much material in chemistry course and there are print mistakes in the reading material of chemistry

A graph drawn (Fig. 3) comparing the perception of the learners (Fig. 1) and the counsellors (Fig. 2) on common statements that the counsellors perception is more positive that of the learners on the course materials of chemistry.

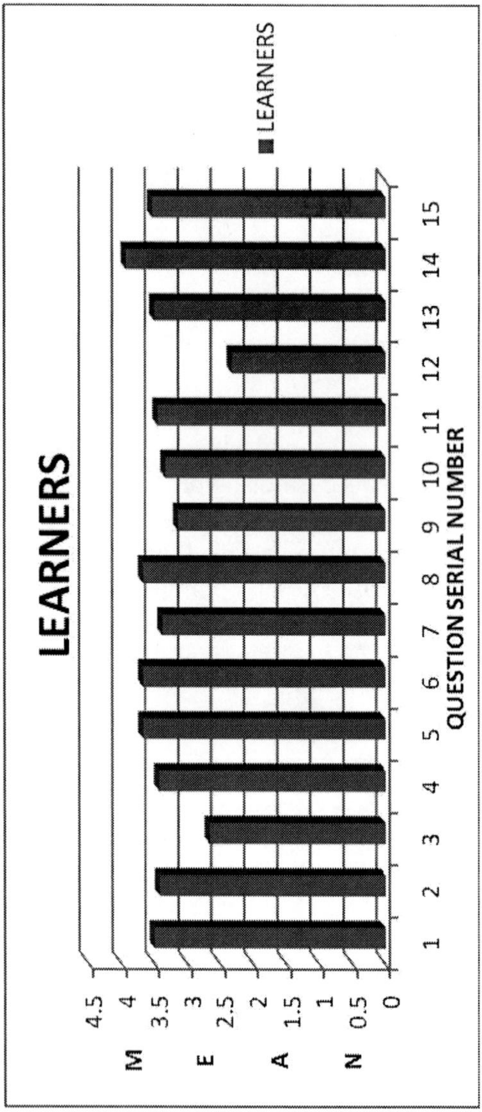

Fig 1. Mean score of learner's perception of assessment components of print material.

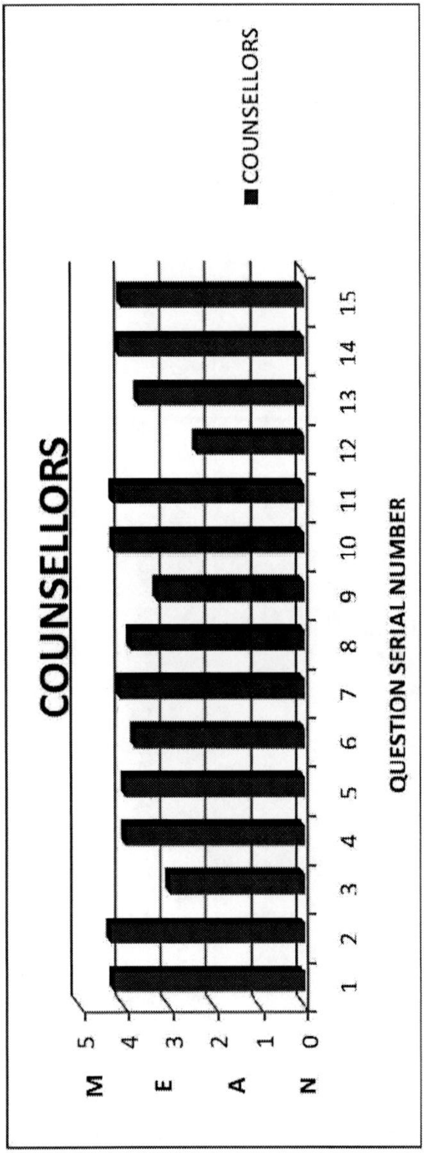

Fig 2. Mean score of Counsellor's perception of assessment components of print material.

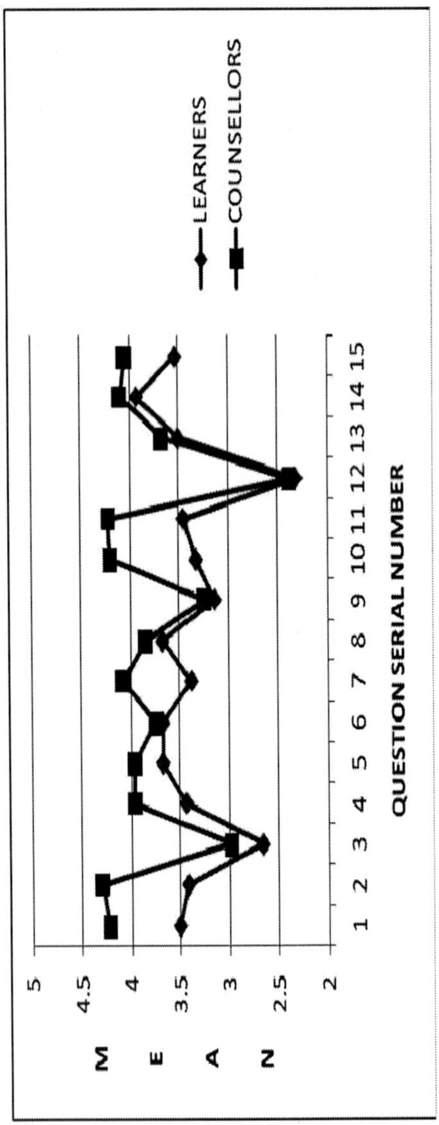

Fig 3. Graph showing comparative perceptions of Learners and Counsellors on print material.

Inferential Analysis

Student's 't' values and 'F' values were calculated to accept or reject the hypothesis proposed. The numerical results obtained were interpreted meaningfully.

Table 3 shows the Mean, Standard Deviation and 't' Values of learners on the self-instructional characteristics of print material.

Table 3

The Mean, Standard Deviation and 't' Values of Learners on the Self-instructional Characteristics of Print Material

	Sub-sample	*N*	*Mean*	*S.D*	*'t' value*
Gender	Male	366	3.34	1.31	0.79 [NS]
	Female	390	3.32	1.23	
Location	Rural	440	3.31	1.25	2.69*
	Urban	316	3.37	1.23	
Combination	Chemistry with maths	378	3.36	1.21	1.57 [NS]
	Chemistry without maths	378	3.32	1.26	
RationCard	White	272	3.37	1.23	5.09 0*
	Pink	487	3.25	1.27	
Mode of entry	Entrance test	57	3.53	1.20	2.53*
	Inter, ITI etc.	699	3.42	1.25	
Year of study	II yr	316	3.45	1.22	3.32*
	III yr	357	3.37	1.24	

Note: * Significant at 0.05 level, *NS*: Not Significant at 0.05 level.

It can be observed from the Table that calculated value of 't' ratio is less than Table value at 0.05 level significance with regard to gender and learners of Chemistry with and without Mathematics combination. Thus null hypothesis is accepted. It indicates that there is no significant difference between male and female learners and between learners of Chemistry with and without Mathematics combination in their perception on the self-instructional characteristics of print material of Chemistry of UG programme.

With regard to other groups viz. learners of rural and urban background, learners with white and pink ration cards, learners who are admitted through eligibility test and those with other eligibility criteria and learners of II year and III year, the calculated value of 't' ratio is greater than the Table value. Thus null hypothesis can be rejected. This indicates that there is significant difference between these groups on the self-instructional characteristics of print material of Chemistry of UG programme.

The data for the analysis of variance of independent variables such as medium of study and center were tabulated in the following Tables 4 & 5.

Table 4
Result on ANOVA on Print Material-Medium-wise

Groups	*Count*	*Sum*	*Average*	*Variance*	
Telugu	5	9056	1811.2	1604027	
English	5	2739	547.8	288294.7	
Urdu	5	480	96	3832	
Source of Variation	*SS*	*df*	*MS*	*F*	*F crit*
Between Groups	7903690	2	3951845	6.252413	3.885294
Within Groups	7584614	12	632051.1		
Total	15488303	14			

The calculated value of 'F,' on the self-instructional characteristics of print material of Chemistry of UG programme of learners of different media, is greater than the Table value at 0.05 level of significance. Thus the null hypothesis is rejected. It indicates that then is significant difference among the learners of different medium on the self-instructional characteristics of print material.

Table 5
Result on ANOVA on Print Material-Centre-wise

Groups	*Count*	*Sum*	*Average*	*Variance*	
Hyderabad	5	1504	300.8	52672.7	
Karimnagar and Adilabad	5	5068	1013.6	476923.8	
Rajahmundry and Guntur	5	2622	524.4	133224.3	
Tirupathi and Kurnool	5	3248	649.6	310701.8	
Source of Variation	SS	df	MS	F	F *crit*
Between Groups	1334037	3	444679.1	1.827093	3.238872
Within Groups	3894090	16	243380.7		
Total	5228128	19			

The calculated value of 'F,' on the self-instructional characteristics of print material of Chemistry of UG programme of learners of different centers, is less than the Table value at 0.05 level of significance. Thus the null hypothesis is accepted.

It shows that there is no significant deference among the learners of different centers on the self-instructional of print material.

Observations

The learners have fully supported that the print material of Chemistry of UG programme is satisfying all the characteristics of self-instructional material.

- There is no significant difference in perception between the male and female learners.
- There is significant difference in perception between rural and urban based learners.
- There is no significant difference in the perception of learners of Chemistry with Mathematics combination and those without Mathematics combination.
- There is significant difference in perception between white ration card holders and pink ration card holders.
- There is significant difference in perception between the learners who took admission into UG programme of BRAOU through entrance test and those with other eligibility criteria.
- There is significant difference in perception between the learners of II year and III year.
- There is significant difference in perception among the learners of Telugu, English and Urdu media.
- There is no significant difference in perception among various centers viz Hyderabad, Karimnagar and Adilabad, Rajahmundry and Guntur, Kurnool and Tirupathi.

Correspondence Analysis

The advanced statistical technique of correspondence analysis is used in case of certain selected questions, to

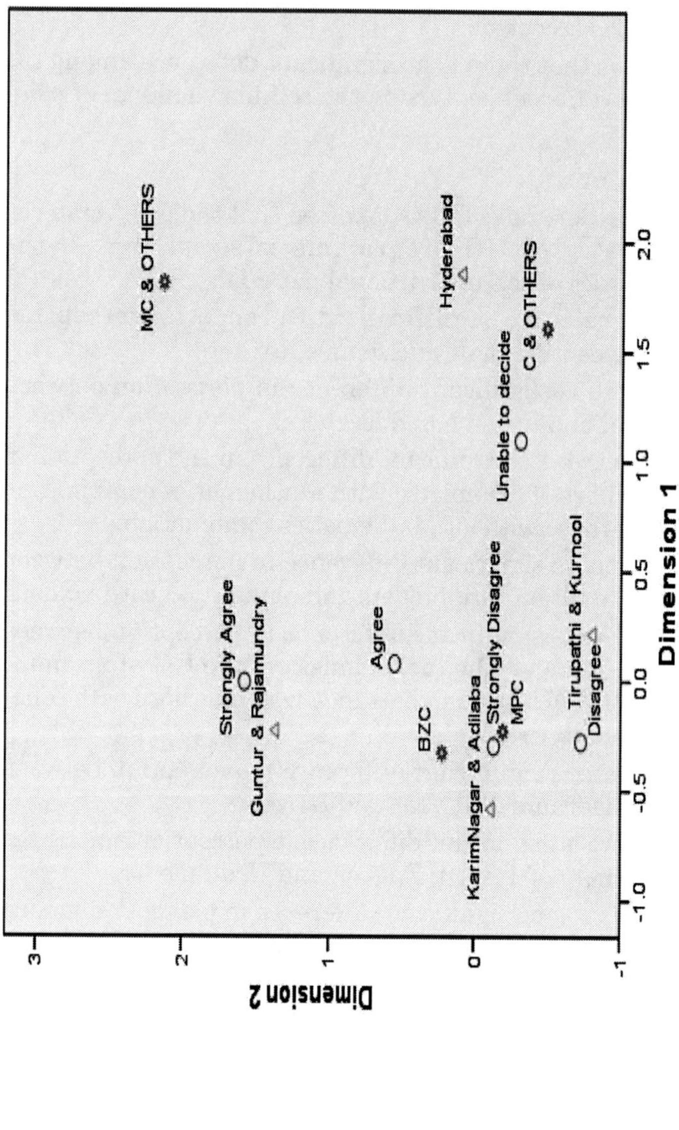

Fig 4. Joint plot of category points on reading and understanding course material.

graphically display the relationship between the categories of variables as well as the relationship between the variables. The variables selected for the study of correspondence analysis are the centers, gender, location, subject combination, ration card and responses to the selected questions and statements.

The joint plots of category points are drawn (Fig 4) in the case of responses from learners for same of the statements and the plot drawn for the statement, 'it is possible to read and understand the course material of Chemistry without attending the counselling session' Is presented as an example.

- Responses to the statement that it is possible to read and understand the course material of Chemistry without attending counselling session.
- Selected study centers.
- Subject combinations in UG programme.

Table 6
Model Summary Category Points on Reading and Understanding Course Material of Chemistry

Dimension	*Cronbach's Alpha*	*Variance Accounted for*		
		Total (Eigen value)	*Inertia*	*% of variance*
1	0.283	1.232	0.411	41.072
2	0.193	1.148	0.383	38.253
Total		2.380	0.793	
Mean	0.239[a]	1.190	0.397	39.663

a . Mean Cronbach's Alpha is based on the mean Eigen value.

The joint plot of category points on the statement that it is possible to read and understand the course material of chemistry without attending counseling session shows that—

- The learners of Guntur and Rajahmundry centers are close to 'strongly agree' option.
- MPC students of Karimnagar and Adilabad centers are closely associated with 'strongly disagree' category.
- The BZC students are at equal distance from 'agree' as well as 'strongly disagree' options.
- The learners of Tirupathi and Kurnool centers 'disagreed' the statement.

- The learners 'C and other' combination and those of Hyderabad centres are 'unable to decide' anything on the statement.
- The perception of learners of 'MC and other' combination is not significant.
- The plot explains 79.3% of variance (Table 6).

Suggestions

1. Reading material of Chemistry may be revised for improving readability characteristics of it. Readability is dependent on sentence structure, vocabulary and style. Hence simple lucid and direct sentences may be used. Use of difficult words may be avoided. Conversational and friendly style may be adopted for making the material self-instructional in true terms.
2. The bulkiness of reading material may be reduced by avoiding lengthy discussions. '*Simplicity' and 'Brevity'* may be kept in mind while revising the print material. The material should be so self-instructional that there should not be any necessity for the learners to go for the purchase of guides, notes etc.
3. Some of the concepts of atomic structure, periodic table and chemical bonding may be transferred to either foundation course or bridge course. The principles of qualitative and quantitative analysis may be taught in the Introductory session of the practical programme.
4. "*Key technical words, important conclusions and definitions"* may be given in different print to draw more attention towards them and keep their imprint on the minds of the learners. The differentiations features of a concept may be highlighted in print for clarity in understanding them.
5. Clarity and symmetry in the structures of compounds, and proper alignment of them with their labels is necessary to avoid confusion in the minds of learners.
6. Three dimensional diagrams may be given wherever necessary. Care may be taken to select simple, thought provoking and informative diagrams.

7. Chemistry has its own language. Print mistakes in symbols, equations and structures side-track the independent learners from proper understanding of them. Hence they are to be corrected.
8. Mathematical and chemical equations are to be derived stepwise and whenever any rule/theorm/formula is applied, it may be given in brackets for easy understanding of its applications.
9. An APPENDIX giving the important mathematical principles used in the chapters may be given at the end of the volume.
10. Sufficient number of model problems of various varieties may be given for clarity and easy understanding of concepts.
11. In order to stimulate interest of students the experiences of the inventors, their photographs, thought provoking diagrams, examples of daily life situations etc. may be given wherever possible.
12. Answers of check-your-progress exercises may be given at the end of unit.
13. To explain the concepts simple examples may be given for understanding.
14. *"Notation"* used for mathematical equations should be simple. Coordination among the authors should be ensured while writing common topics so that the same notation can be adopted uniformly.
15. Transliterations of technical terms may be preferred to translation of them, in case of 'translations', English version of them may be given within brackets by the side of them.
16. Giving a glossary of technical terms at the end of each unit may be useful.
17. At the end of each unit 'summary' of that unit is being given. Summary may be written to reflect the thought content of the unit in concise.

REFERENCES

1. Mouli, C. Raja and Rama Krishna, C. Pushpa (1991). Readability of Distance Education Course Material; Research in Distance Education, Vol. 3(4).
2. Prasuna, K. Gnana (1994). Teaching Physics through Distance Education –Distance Education an Interphace, Dr. BRAOU, Hyderabad, pp. 160-168
3. Ramachandraiah, G. (1994). Teaching Science through Distance Education - Distance Education an interface, Dr. BRAOU, Hyderabad, pp. 153-159.

Index

Q

R

S

T

U